Journal of the Society of

Christian
Ethics

VOLUME 38, NUMBER 1 • SPRING/SUMMER 2018

Copyright © 2018 by the Society of Christian Ethics. All rights reserved.

Contents

Preface

The essays in this issue were presented at the Society of Christian Ethics Annual Meeting in New Orleans, Louisiana, in January 2017. The annual meeting theme was "Structural Evil, Individual Harm, Personal Responsibility." Articles in the previous issue (*JSCE* 37, no. 2) closely matched this theme. Several of the articles in this issue also match the theme, but others that were selected address wider themes.

The first three articles deal with the ongoing challenges of race and social justice in the United States as well as the larger question of the proper means of resistance to entrenched conditions of injustice. Luke Bretherton's article, "Exorcising Democracy: The Theopolitical Challenge of Black Power," examines the Black Power movement as a theopolitical response to poverty and white supremacy and looks within the movement for resources for transformation and healing, while Sarah MacDonald and Nicole Symmonds's "Rioting as Flourishing? Reconsidering Virtue Ethics in Times of Civil Unrest" challenges the assumption that civil unrest is at odds with the virtues inherent in establishing justice within society. On the contrary, they argue, public expressions of anger are important prerequisites to the possibility of human flourishing. David Henreckson's article, "Resisting the Devil's Instruments: Early Modern Resistance Theory for Late Modern Times," takes a different approach, reaching back to the work of Johannes Althusius to retrieve resources for the development of a modern approach to rooting the struggle for justice in the covenantal theological tradition.

The next three articles deal with specific issues of Christian ethics in contemporary society. Vic McCracken's "Can Love Walk the Battlefield? A Reply to Nigel Biggar" critiques a central claim of Biggar's recent book *In Defense of War*. McCracken calls into question Biggar's assumption that killing in warfare is compatible with love of one's enemy, arguing that recent research reveals a much more ambiguous connection between the violence of war and the love of enemy.

Angela Carpenter's "Exploitative Labor, Victimized Families, and the Promise of the Sabbath" uses the theology of Karl Barth to shed light on the way in which the idea of Sabbath rest can provide respite from employment practices that exploit families on the economic margins by providing an opportunity for joyful fellowship free from the demands of wage labor.

Kathryn Getek Soltis examines the question of family victimization from another perspective, looking at the role that mass incarceration plays in the negative consequences experienced by children in the absence of a parent. Criticizing the cultural attitude that sees children as pets, she argues that child-rearing needs to be understood as a form of contributive justice that contributes to the overall common good, and that the needs of children of incarcerated parents need to be taken into account in the administration of justice.

The next three essays deal with questions at the intersection of Christian ethics, philosophy, and moral theory. Ki Joo Choi's article, "The Priority of the Affections over the Emotions: Gustafson, Aquinas, and an Edwardsean Critique," uses the theology of Jonathan Edwards to argue that the affections and the emotions are two separate concepts for understanding the nature of moral deliberation, and that recognizing the distinction between the two opens up new possibilities for ethical reflection.

Kate Ward's "Toward a Christian Virtue Account of Moral Luck" considers the category of moral luck with respect to the conference theme of structural evil, developing a Christian virtue account of moral luck in order to distinguish the role that different life circumstances play in moral action.

Emily Dumler-Winckler's article, "Personal Responsibility in the Face of Social Evils: Transcendentalist Debates Revisited," examines the way in which American transcendentalists addressed the problems of structural evil through an analysis of the way in which debates about the proper means of combatting evil and addressing injustice in the nineteenth century took place among leading figures in the movement, and she illuminates the way in which these debates can inform contemporary discussions.

Finally, Karen Guth's article, "Moral Injury, Feminist and Womanist Debates, and Tainted Legacies," examines the question of moral injury and the problem of tainted legacies through a feminist analysis of the continuing damage done by revelations of sexual abuse by John Howard Yoder and the legacy of slavery at Georgetown University. She argues that feminist and womanist ethical strategies for addressing these tainted legacies provide resources for overcoming the moral harm that those legacies continue to cause.

In 2017 we began using a new set of demographic categories to explore who is submitting and presenting at the annual SCE meeting, and who is submitting and getting published in the JSCE. (For a summary of historical data prior to this, see volume 37, no. 2.) The data in the associated graph use ethnic-racial groupings and gender categories that have been altered from what we have used in the past. The graph also includes new data on the professional status of contributors. This will help to track the impact of contingent faculty contributions to the society. While we are still collecting data distinguishing those on their first, second, and third submissions to the conference, in order to streamline the information that we publish here, we are no longer publishing those data in this form.

The transition to our new system is not without kinks. We are still working on the best way to gather and process data on professional status for the layers of data not taken directly from the demographic survey. We also need to update the demographic categories that are used when collecting membership data to match with the categories we are now using in the demographic survey. We are hopeful that, when revised, these multiple streams of data can be coordinated in a way that presents a broader picture of how the demographics of our society are related to the demographics of the wider academy, and how our submission and publication processes influence the demographics of those who present and are published through the work of the Society.

Demographic Distribution Results
Proposals Submitted for the 2017 Annual Meeting of the Society of Christian Ethics through Papers Published in the Journal of the Society of Christian Ethics, 37.2 and 38.1.

	Gender					Ethnic-Racial Group									Professional Status							Membership			Authors	Papers
	M	F	T	I	O	Ar	As	Af	AA	HL	NA	P	W	O	I	Asst	Assoc	F	Adj	S	O	S	F	L		
Proposals Submitted for SCE	73	32	0	0	1	0	9	1	4	2	1	0	90	3	14	18	20	16	6	16	16	22	84	0	106*	138
Proposals Accepted for SCE	49	25	0	0	0	0	6	1	3	1	0	0	47	0	NA	NA	NA	NA	NA	NA	NA	13	54	1	74	71
Paper Submitted to JSCE	36	21	0	0	0	0	5	1	1	0	0	0	44	0	NA	NA	NA	NA	NA	NA	NA	11	40	1	57	54
Papers Published in JSCE	11	12	0	0	0	0	2	1	0	0	0	0	20	0	0	7	5	2	1	6	2	6	17	0	23	20

Gender: M = Male, F = Female, T = Transgender, I = Intersex, O = Other

Ethnic-Racial Group: Ar = Arabic, As = Asian, Af = African, AA = African American, HL = Hispanic/Latino/a, NA = Native American/Alaskan, P = Native Hawaiian/Pacific Islander, W = White, O = Other

Professional Status: I = Instructor, Asst = Assistant Professor, Assoc = Associate Professor, F = Full Professor, Adj = Adjunct, S = Student, O = Other

Membership: S = Student, F = Full, L = Lifetime

*Demographic data for proposals submitted were gathered from a demographic survey. Only 106 authors responded to the demographic survey. Other demographic data were gathered by correlating author names and demographic data held by the SCE or were publicly available. NA indicates that the data were not available in an accessible form.

Selected Essays

Exorcising Democracy: The Theopolitical Challenge of Black Power

Luke Bretherton

The first part of this article analyzes the Black Power movement within the context of wider debates about how black nationalism conceptualized the need to form a people as a response to white supremacy. The second part examines how white supremacy conditions the nature and form of democratic citizenship in the United States and how the formation of a "nation within a nation" is a vital adjunct to dismantling white supremacy as a political system. Part three situates Black Power within a theological conception of poverty understood as powerlessness. Building on James Cone and Cheryl Kirk-Duggan, it closes by suggesting that forming a people as a response to powerlessness constitutes a double movement of healing and exorcism.

BLACK RADICAL THOUGHT HAS CONSISTENTLY GENERATED penetrating critiques of democracy in America. Yet these critiques are almost wholly ignored by dominant strands of political theory—most notably, political liberalism.[1] In response, Charles Mills calls for an end to the segregation of black political thought from "mainstream" political theory.[2] He argues that there is an important set of shared concerns. However, these shared concerns cannot be recognized let alone articulated if racism in North America, which has been judicially backed, morally and theoretically rationalized, and structurally institutionalized, is treated as an anomaly rather than as basic to the construction of the American body politic. When treated as a deviation from an otherwise healthy system, then the remedy that presents itself is to keep doing more of the very things that have historically been part of the problem: the further application of "colorblind" liberal principles and redistributive policies.[3] Mills's critique also applies to political theology generally and to discussions of the relationship between Christianity and democracy in particular.

Luke Bretherton is a professor of theological ethics at Duke Divinity School, Duke University, 407 Chapel Dr., Duke Box #90968, Durham, NC 27708; luke.bretherton @duke.edu.

Journal of the Society of Christian Ethics, 38, 1 (2018): 3–24

Beyond Mills's critique is the contention that democracy itself is a "creolized" phenomenon born out of the violent entanglements of Europe, Africa, and the Americas.[4] Modern conceptualizations of terms such as "democracy," "sovereignty," and "citizenship" do not emerge pristine from the European context to be exported elsewhere. There is no single or innocent point of origin. Rather, as C.L.R. James, Édouard Glissant, Cedric Robinson, Stuart Hall, Paul Gilroy, and others have argued, a crucible of modern political concepts is what Gilroy called the "Black Atlantic" and the configurations and disruptions of the relationship between metropole and colony that circulated within it. Moreover, the condition and possibility for the formation of liberal democratic nation-states were colonial political economies. Again, Eurocentric political theology and discussions of the relationship between Christianity and democracy, in particular, have largely ignored or concealed the creolized nature of modern political terms and their colonial and racialized formation.

This essay is an attempt to abide with and learn from the stringent challenge that Mills, Glissant, and others pose.[5] It is not an attempt to "do" black liberation theology. Rather, it listens to the questions the black radical tradition brings to the fore that should be addressed by any form of political theology and, in particular, attempts to reflect on the relationship between Christianity and democracy. In my own work, I have contended that particular kinds of democratic practices are a means through which radically different visions of the good, conflicts of interest, and asymmetries of power can be contested and negotiated in such a way that antagonistic and sometimes violent friend–enemy relations can be converted into a world of shared meaning and action.[6] But what if the basis and accepted performances of democratic politics constitutively excluded certain kinds of persons or groups? What happens when "we, the people" are defined over and against those who are not considered a people or even persons (e.g., nonwhites)? How, then, should the body politic be reconstituted? Is a common life politics possible when state and market processes are shaped by a structure of power (white supremacy) that inherently advantages one group (whites) in relation to another (blacks) while at the same time actively ensuring the domination, disaggregation, and devaluation of the latter? And is a world of shared meaning and action possible when reactions to instances of civil unrest such as those in Ferguson, Missouri, and Baltimore in 2014–15 generate incommensurable interpretations—when one person's riot is another's uprising?

The questions outlined above are ones that the Black Power movement of the 1960s and 1970s, and the Black Atlantic diasporic traditions that the movement drew on and reiterated, have discussed with an existential urgency and perspicuity. This essay seeks to learn from the critiques of democracy they generated.[7] It examines how debates within and about Black Power help us understand the conditions and possibilities of democratic citizenship as a means of challenging white supremacy as an oppressive political system, when white supremacy is at the same time constitutive of how democratic citizenship is constructed in North America.

Reflecting on the Black Power movement within the fields of political theology and Christian ethics is particularly salient. Alongside the experience of the black churches, Black Power was the catalyst for the work of James Cone and the emergence of black liberation theology.[8] In tandem with Latin American liberation theology, black liberation theology heralded a seismic shift in Protestant social ethics and the use of Christian realism as a dominant framework for thinking about political and social questions.[9] From Cone's work onward, liberationist paradigms of one sort or another became increasingly normative in North American liberal Protestant circles and determinative points of reference and critique in others. Despite its impact, however, Black Power as a social movement has received less attention in the fields of Christian ethics and political theology than the civil rights movement. There are numerous reasons for this; one is that the civil rights movement can be read as a validation and exemplification of core Christian claims. By contrast, Black Power, as Cone discerned, represents a profound challenge to the morality and legitimacy of Christianity and the role of churches in resisting and deconstructing racism. This challenge has been extensively explored in work that examines the interrelationship between Western European strands of theology and white supremacy and the complicity of Western churches in racialized structures of oppression.[10] But while much of this work highlights how racism is a cultural and theological problem, it does not probe in detail how racism conditions the nature and form of democracy. To address this lacuna, this essay investigates how Black Power unveils the link between democracy and white supremacy. Part of the rationale for this focus is that it enables clarity about why black and white nationalism in the United States are *not* morally equivalent, as many today still assume, and helps debunk the spurious claim that Black Power and, latterly, Black Lives Matter are forms of "reverse racism."

Like its antecedents, Black Power was complexly religious and nonreligious. James Noel argues that within the emergent Atlantic world, from the fifteenth century onward and under the brutalizing and atomizing impact of slavery, the need to be a people and the expression of being a people through the creation of new religious forms and practices was contiguous.[11] Black political activism has continuously drawn on and been sustained by religious symbols, rituals, institutional formations and discourses.[12] Denmark Vesey, Nat Turner, Pauli Murray, Martin Luther King Jr., and Malcolm X are just a few prominent examples of how politics and religion are interwoven in black-led struggles for liberation. More specifically, certain strands of black nationalism, as exemplified in the work of Marcus Garvey and Albert Cleage Jr., are forms of political theology.[13] The Black Power movement echoed the intersection of religion and politics, even when Christianity was not a primary point of reference.[14] While much of this essay is not explicitly theological in focus, this should not be read as setting up a false dichotomy between black political thought and black theology. As already noted, political theory and theology are intertwined in the black radical tradition. Rather, for the sake of clarity of exposition, the focus here is on the explicitly political problems black nationalism and Black Power addressed. Shifting key and tempo, the essay closes by bringing the theological resonances of these problems to the fore.

Black Nationalisms and the Formation of a Demos

The following quotation from Stokely Carmichael and Charles Hamilton's early articulation of what was meant by the term "Black Power" illustrates the tensions within the movement and the issues it sought to address: "The goal of the racists is to keep black people on the bottom, arbitrarily and dictatorially, as they have done in this country for more than three hundred years. The goal of black self-determination and black self-identity—Black power—is full participation in the decision making processes affecting the lives of black people, and recognition of the virtues in themselves as black people."[15] For Carmichael and Hamilton "black self-identity" and "black self-determination" were intrinsic goods as well as means through which to dismantle racist structures. And combining these goods with the goal of ending racial oppression constituted a means of pursuing another intrinsic good: democratic politics, a definitional feature of which is that people should have a say in decisions that affect their way of life (i.e., have a measure of self-determination). The relative weight to accord these goods and means were points of vehement and sometimes violent contention among Black Power activists: To what extent should self-determination be pursued as an end in itself? Could self-determination be coordinated and consonant with realizing democracy in America? And what was the nature and basis of racism, and thus what was the best strategy for liberation from its effects? For example, if racial oppression was a symptom of class relations and capitalism, then broader coalitions with revolutionary proletarian movements were the answer.[16] However, if white supremacy was the primary problem, then coalitions with white-led groups such as the Students for a Democratic Society would exacerbate the problem and the need was for total autonomy. This was exactly the point of contention between the Pan-Africanism of Stokely Carmichael / Kwame Turé, and the Marxist-Leninism of an early Black Panther Party leader, Eldridge Cleaver. But for both Turé and Cleaver, democratic citizenship as constituted within American liberal democracy was not merely an ineffectual means of pursing black self-determination, generating democratic freedoms, and ending racial oppression; it was part of the problem that needed overcoming.[17]

The primary discursive framework within which these issues were debated was black nationalism. Like other modern ideologies that inform aligned social movements—for example, socialism, feminism, and environmentalism—black nationalism is a multivalent discourse with local, national, and cosmopolitan variants that intersect and riff off each other. And like all modern social movements, it generated its own internal and external critiques: of note in this regard are black feminist and womanist critiques that challenge the role of gender and sexuality in black nationalist discourse. Central to debates within all the various strands of black nationalism was the question of how to form a people[18]—for that is the necessary implication of a commitment to self-determination constituted around the axis of "blackness" (whether blackness is conceived in "essentialist" or "pluralist" terms).[19] Michael Dawson distinguishes between three overlapping ways of conceptualizing what it means to be "the" black nation:

> The first is built on state power and land. The second defines African-Americans as more than "just another American ethnic group" but as a separate, oppressed people, a nation-within-a-nation, with the right to self-determination. A third, usually less political, conception of "the" black nation defines it as a community with a defined and unique spiritual and cultural identity. All three definitions of the black nation presume that people of African descent within the borders of the United States have at least some common interests based on their race or their common history of racial subjugation.[20]

Black nationalists answered variously the question, how can an oppressed group constitute itself so as to constructively address both the subjective and objective conditions of domination? Cultural nationalists tended to focus more on the subjective conditions of domination whereas revolutionary nationalists mainly focused on the objective, structural conditions of domination. Different modes of analysis gave rise to different orientations. Within the different strands of black nationalism there is a division between the common life and noncommon life forms. Rather than "integration," cultural and community forms of black nationalism seek to radically reconfigure the polity so that African Americans can be at home where they live while at the same time forging non-white-supremacist forms of common or intercommunal life with others.[21] As Maulana Karenga puts it, "We can live with whites interdependently once we have Black power."[22] Separatist forms do not seek a common life; rather, they seek a wholly separate and independent form of existence (which may or may not involve territorial separation).[23]

Even though the analyses drawn on and the form nationalism took varied, the basic goal was the same. The aim was to form a demos/people capable of, in the first instance, surviving; in the second instance, resisting; and, finally, thriving within an oppressive system that refuses to see, hear, or talk about the dehumanizing impact it is having on others and on its white beneficiaries. Realizing these goals entails wrestling with two paradoxes central to radical democratic politics in modernity. The first is that democratic citizenship is seen as an expression of individual liberty, but its performance and defense is in great measure dependent on participation in a group. Without being embedded in some form of association, the individual is naked before the power of either the market or the state and lacks a vital means for his or her own self-cultivation. The questions are then what kinds of associations are needed and how are they to be generated? The civil rights movement largely relied on churches for its institutional and associational basis.[24] But spearheaded by the development of the Lowndes County Freedom Organization by the Student Nonviolent Coordinating Committee, the Black Power movement experimented with a huge array of often contradictory methods in an attempt to form the kinds of associations and institutions that were needed to defend and cultivate the individual liberty and dignity of black people. These included third-party platforms, rifle clubs, guerrilla cells, community organizing initiatives, schools, clinics, single-issue campaign groups, cooperatives, entrepreneurial businesses, reading circles, newspapers, and arts organizations.[25] These efforts represented an attempt to create the kinds of associations, institutional forms, and political practices that are the necessary condition for democratic freedoms to be possible but which democratic politics by itself cannot produce.

The second paradox is that democracy presumes the existence of and depends on people and institutions committed to respecting the dignity and agency of each individual, talking and acting together as a means of resolving conflicts, and believing that people should have a say in decisions that affect their way of life; yet democratic politics is forged out of immoral people and hierarchal and often authoritarian institutions, and is plagued by the despotism of either the one, the few, or the many. As Grace Lee Boggs puts it, "To make a revolution, people must not only struggle against existing institutions. They must make a philosophical/spiritual leap and become more *human* human beings. In order to change/transform the world they must change/transform themselves."[26] Again, the Black Power movement tried to address this paradox in various ways.[27]

Understanding black nationalism in general and Black Power in particular as ways of addressing these two key democratic paradoxes not only renders absurd accusations of it being a form of "reverse racism" but also, per Mills, helps delineate some points of shared concern with other strands of political theory and political theology. Moreover, it points to a parallel but not equivalent theological question: how are a virtuous and holy people to be formed out of a disaggregated and demoralized crowd shaped by oppressive institutions and structures? This concern is the central drama of Exodus, a vital scriptural reference point in liberation theologies. I return to this question in the final section.

An aligned problem for black nationalists, one arising directly out of white supremacy as a political system, complicated their ability to navigate these two paradoxes. It is what W.E.B. Du Bois famously called "double consciousness" and relates to the paradoxically insider–outsider status of being African American. Black lives matter in the United States insofar as they are commodities or sources of cheap labor and, latterly, consumers and debtors. This way of valuing black life is a historic and ongoing basis of North American economic and political development. Black labor and ways of life are constitutive of the United States as a nation-state; however, as Du Bois puts it, "I have been in the world, but not of it."[28] While black bodies are a vital means of life for the system, they are simultaneously and consistently being constituted as among those who are paradigmatic outsiders (as are Native Americans), through and against whom the political, cultural, and economic structures come to be defined.

Whiteness is a constitutive part of how normalcy is constructed in North America. However, whiteness is neither an ethnic identity nor a clearly demarcated subject. Rather, as George Yancy puts it, whiteness is "a historical process that continues to express its hegemony and privilege through various cultural, political, interpersonal, and institutional practices, and that forces bodies of color to the margins and politically and ontologically positions them as sub-persons."[29] The practices converge over time to create white supremacy, which is here taken to mean "a political, economic and cultural system in which whites overwhelmingly control power and material resources, conscious and unconscious ideas of white superiority and entitlement are widespread, and relations of white dominance and nonwhite subordination are daily reenacted across a broad array of institutions and social settings."[30] On this account, white supremacy becomes a self-perpetuating part of the political system that is veiled behind a desire to benefit from existing, supposedly neutral structures of privilege and "rational" forms of self- and group-interest.[31] Thus, white nationalists, rather than, as they claim, seeking to defend an embattled minority, are seeking to perpetuate a system of injustice that directly benefits them.

The trope of being a nation (however conceived) is a way to develop an alternative, positive construction of identity to that determined by being the opposite of what is white and therefore abnormal. But as Paul Gilroy argues, the use of the term "nation" is problematic as it takes up a trope central to modern European political discourse and often falls prey to an "ethnic absolutism."[32] There is, however, another dimension to the use of the term "nation" that Gilroy does not acknowledge: it was a ready-to-hand discursive framework through which to challenge the insider–outsider status of being a racialized other in America. As Dawson notes, this challenge operated on two fronts simultaneously: the claim to be a nation was a way of demanding entry to and recognition within white channels of public discourse (whether mainstream, such as universities, or subaltern, such as the labor and women's movement) and a way of developing an alternative counterpublic, providing a space for critical reflection and self-cultivation, a form of life within which to live and move more freely.[33] The claim to be a nation, even a nation within a nation, is a claim to be all that being a nation invokes as a social imaginary: belonging, sense of place, a history, a future, self-determination, citizenship, and a distinctive culture. It is a claim to possess a way of being in the world that lives an alternative to and refuses racialized constructions of blackness as a form of nonbeing and an antitype of the good citizen. By contrast, white nationalism, in the name of self-defense, intentionally seeks to subvert and destroy attempts to move toward shared ways of imagining citizenship and forming a genuinely common life. As argued here, black nationalism can contribute to the intensification of a democratic common life whereas white nationalism, even though it shares many of the discursive tropes of black nationalism because of the structural location of its participants, is inherently antidemocratic.

Black nationalism has addressed the insider–outsider problem in numerous ways. For example, some separatist strands resolve it by seeking a territorially defined sovereign polity whereas community-orientated, cultural, and some revolutionary and separatist forms sought to create enclaves of self-determination within the existing structures where blacks constituted either a majority or a large, concentrated minority.[34] One example of this latter strategy was the 1968–71 mayoralty of Carl Stokes in Cleveland.[35] Stokes's campaign heralded a turn to the Democratic Party as a means of gaining power. Another example is Rev. Albert Cleage Jr., who represents a very different modus operandi to achieve similar ends. Cleage argued there was a need for full citizenship (which he viewed as using "enemy institutions" to serve black people) and a need to struggle for self-determination via separate "counterinstitutions," as blacks needed an independent economic base and should never be reliant on the government for protection or the provision of welfare.[36] This was marked in his own practice: for example, he ran for governor of Michigan in 1964 as part of the Freedom Now Party and founded the Black Christian National Movement in 1967 along with a wide range of independent institutions. What is at stake in these different forms of praxis is the problem of how to form a people: Is peoplehood based on some prepolitical basis, often imagined in familial terms (brother and sister)? Or on the basis of economic agency, whether capitalist or socialist in form?[37] Or as necessitating a sovereign, bounded territory? Black Power was a response to the need to honor existing yet demeaned forms of life and construct a basis of power in a context where democratic citizenship is indexed to whiteness yet its primary discursive framework, liberalism, proclaims itself colorblind.[38] Proclamation of nationhood is a way to make the blind see, a way of rendering the invisible visible.

Herrenvolk Democracy and Citizenship as the Performance of White Supremacy

Let me substantiate the assertion that democratic citizenship in the United States is structured by white supremacy, understood as a political system. Citizenship, and the benefits and protections that came with it, were historically limited to "white" immigrants.[39] The most obvious instantiation of this was the denial of civic and political status to kidnapped and enslaved Africans. Even after the emancipation of slaves in the 1860s, the racialization of citizenship continued. For example, immigrants from Asia were excluded from being full citizens through legislation in 1882 aimed at those from China; in 1917, from India; in 1924, from Japan; and in 1934, from the Philippines.[40] Processes of racialization also deeply shaped who received social rights from the New Deal era onward. For example, in 1935 the National Labor Relations (Wagner) Act, which guaranteed the right of employees to organize or join a union, and the Social Security Act excluded farm and domestic workers from coverage, thus denying these disproportionately minority sectors of the workforce the protections and benefits now legally afforded other, predominantly white workers. At the same time, the Federal Housing Act of 1934 was implemented through overtly racist categories in the Federal Housing Agency's city surveys and appraisers' manuals that directed the overwhelming majority of loan money toward whites and away from communities of color.

All these social policies, and many more besides, widened the gap between the resources available to those judged white and those available to nonwhite, predominantly black communities.[41] The cumulative social, economic, and political impact of these policies in disadvantaging nonwhites is immeasurable. This is a process that has continued apace with the contemporary reinscription of systemic disadvantage through the "New Jim Crow."[42] Yet most whites are entirely oblivious of this history and the ways in which white privilege is baked into the social, economic, and political structures of North America. Long-standing policies of affirmative action for whites are ignored, while black poverty is blamed on a dearth of collective virtue and a lack of individual vigor in pursuing the American Dream.

It is on the basis of this history and contemporary practices of systemic exclusion that some argue that the United States is a *Herrenvolk* democracy.[43] What is meant by this term is that the *demos* is constituted on the basis of white supremacy. Citizenship is not indexed to a singular ethnos or *Volk* as in German legal conceptions of *jus sanguinas*. There never was a singular *Volk* or ethnicity in the United States, white Anglo-Saxon Protestant or otherwise. Rather, citizenship was indexed to whiteness politically constructed and theoretically rationalized as a caste; that is, whiteness entails stratification not just by class and race but also on a scale of purity and moral worth. As David Roediger contends, "blackness" became identified with dependency and servility, which were antithetical to the virtues that republican citizenship demanded.[44] Mills argues that underlying this prejudice were the ways whiteness functioned as an ontological category as much as a racial and class-based one.[45] Alongside other registers, most notably Protestantism, property ownership, militarism, and masculinity, democratic citizenship was imagined and idealized as white. This is articulated in the following quote from a white Alabaman in 1860: "Your fathers and my fathers built this government on two ideas; the first is that the white race is the citizen and the master race, and the white man is the equal of every other white man. The second idea is that the Negro is the inferior race."[46] As Mills points out, this view was not idiosyncratic. Rather, it was enshrined in law through the 1857 *Dred Scott* decision.

In the light of this history, the shrill and vindictive reaction that Black Power provoked can be understood. The converse of trying to form a black people/nation in a context where "we, the people" is structured in part by white supremacy is that any attempt to do so will inevitably be seen as an attempt to undermine the existing system: black self-determination and self-affirmation become by definition acts of sedition. Members of the Black Power movement constantly confronted the vindictive reaction that their apostasy from faith in the American Dream generated. For example, while the Black Panther Party in Oakland, California, set up educational initiatives and a free breakfast program, the FBI publicly labeled the Panthers a threat to national security and secretly licensed a series of counterintelligence operations against them.[47]

The civil rights movement addressed the formal exclusion of blacks from citizenship. However, its apogee—the Voting Rights Act of 1965—addressed only two dimensions of citizenship. The primary use of the term "citizenship" is to denote a legal status with certain civil, political, and social rights as granted and distributed by the institutions of a national government whose sovereignty is derived from the citizens themselves. The second usage of the term "citizenship" refers to participation in a system for representing, communicating, and legitimating the relationship between governed and government. In large-scale nation-states, this process of authorizing cannot be done by popular assembly and so involves a system of representation. To be a citizen is to be designated as someone who can participate in these kinds of mechanisms, whether as a voter or a representative or both. Democratic citizenship demarcates who is authorized to govern and the processes by which their authority is legitimized. The civil rights movement powerfully addressed these two dimensions of citizenship, which up to that point had largely excluded blacks. The 1965 Voting Rights Act was in effect the end of the *Herrenvolk* democracy as a formal, de jure system. However, as a de facto system, it has continued to undergird three other dimensions of citizenship.

The third dimension of citizenship is identity. To be a citizen of a polity is to identify or be identified with an "imagined community."[48] As a political identity that coinheres with an imagined community, citizenship is not just a legal term; it has an affective and subjective dimension that is the result of cultural processes. Key questions to be asked about this aspect of citizenship are what does a citizen look like, and who counts as included in or as a "normal" member of the body politic? In relation to these questions, issues of belief, race, gender, class, physical ability, and sexuality come to the fore. In a *Herrenvolk* democracy, a central way in which the community is imagined is as normatively white. Blacks by definition cannot be full citizens except by passing as white.[49]

The fourth dimension is how citizenship necessarily includes the performance of a vision of politics. In this guise, citizenship involves doing certain things. However, the performance of citizenship is not reducible to formal mechanisms of representation or involvement with the apparatus of the state. Rather, it entails a much broader assemblage of beliefs, narratives, practices, bodily proprieties, habits, and rituals reiterated and enacted in contexts as diverse as the workplace, social media, the football stadium, and the mall, which together constitute a social imaginary of what good and bad politics entails and, thus, what the good citizen should do. Again, in America's *Herrenvolk* democracy, whiteness constitutes a key regulative performance of good citizenship. To perform well as a citizen—that is, to be considered respectable—is to perform as or in a way analogous to being white.[50] Failure to do so provokes suspicion of being anti-American.

Finally, citizenship names a political and moral rationality through which a "common sense" is forged and reproduced; that is, it constitutes a way of discerning and deliberating about goods in common and a vision of the good life through which "we, the people" come to decide how we shall live. In relation to this denotation of citizenship, the question is how should citizens talk and deliberate together and on what basis can they make shared judgments about what to do and how to do it? The construction of citizenship involves an ongoing debate about what constitutes the requisite kinds of moral and political rationality that make one capable of talking and acting with others in ways that build up the common life of a polity. As Dawson notes, within liberal conceptions of citizenship, "rational dialogue among reasonable citizens is problematic when those with power determine both who is reasonable and with what weight their dialogue is accepted."[51] When nonwhites are deemed irrational, their voices are not just excluded but demeaned.

Black Power's political, cultural, spiritual, and economic interventions can be read as addressing how white supremacy is a key way in which the third, fourth, and fifth dimensions of citizenship are structured. What Black Power activists discerned was that "integration" on terms set by the existing forms of citizenship was self-negating. The terms and conditions of citizenship needed to be fundamentally recalibrated and resignified. The aim could not be recognition in the existing *Herrenvolk* system. Rather, the need was and still is to change the means and criteria by which the identity, performance, and rationality of citizenship are produced and evaluated.

Arguably, black feminist and womanist authors such as Audre Lorde, bell hooks, Angela Davis, the Third World Women's Alliance, and the Combahee River Collective catalyzed a revision of black nationalism from the 1970s onward by drawing attention to the often conflicting sources of identity that race, class, gender, and sexuality generate.[52] Some called for a more intersectional and coalitional approach to addressing injustice that could encompass multiple loyalties and avoid illusions of innocence.[53] An echo of this call for a revision in approach to confronting white supremacy is heard in the following statement from James Cone: "The ideals of integration and nationalism are insufficient for the problems we now face and for the issues with which we will have to deal in the future. We need to do more than try to be assimilated into white American society or to separate ourselves from it. Neither alternative is possible or even desirable. We need a broader perspective, one that includes the creative values of both but also moves beyond them to an entirely new vision of the future."[54]

Revisionist conceptions of black nationalism take the view that black solidarity does not require territorial separation, a homogenous identity, or even a shared consciousness. For example, Tommie Shelby questions whether these are morally justifiable, politically fruitful, or even empirically possible. In their stead, he argues for a "pragmatic" vision of black nationalism as an alternative way to conceptualize the need for black political solidarity.[55] Shelby contends that "Blacks can and should agree, in the present, to collectively resist racial injustice, not only because it is the morally responsible thing to do but also because it negatively affects them all, albeit to varying degrees and in different ways. Mobilizing and coordinating this effort will be difficult enough without adding the unnecessary and divisive requirement that blacks embrace and preserve a distinctive ethnocultural identity."[56]

Shelby goes on to argue that rather than being measured in terms of the "thickness" of someone's identity, a "political mode of blackness" entails "loyalty to the collective struggle" and particular kinds of civic engagement.[57] His argument echoes that of Angela Davis and Cornel West. Davis calls for a consciousness that is "politically rather than racially grounded and at the same time anchored in a more complex antiracist consciousness."[58] Or, as she puts it elsewhere, "basing the identity on politics rather than the politics on identity."[59]

Likewise, West contends that "any serious form of black resistance" must build alliances and coalitions with Latino/a, Asian, Native American, and white people committed to transforming capitalist, patriarchal, and racist America.[60] Parallel arguments are found in the work of bell hooks, Grace Lee Boggs, and Lani

Guinier. Their arguments point to how antiracist political solidarity, whether black nationalist or multiracial in form, requires a commitment and contribution to shared democratic practices that generate non-white-supremacist forms of civic identity, performance, and rationality and which reckon with the realities of mutual dependence. Any such form of democratic politics will operate within a different framework to either political liberalism (which emphasizes equality but leaves untouched asymmetries of power) or multiculturalism (which emphasizes recognition by the prevailing structure of power rather than the need to change the power structure as such).[61]

Rome Dethroned Is Not Israel Empowered

It is here that I want to pick up a theological trail hinted at earlier. When James Cone says Jesus is black and "Christianity is not alien to Black power; it is Black power," these are theological statements about how the revelation of who God is cannot be understood apart from Jesus's identification with the poor and oppressed.[62] For Cone, Black Power was a contingent but concrete manifestation of divine action in the history of North America. What follows is an attempt to locate theologically the Black Power movement and its various forms of praxis through which it sought to generate a sense of peoplehood and address constructively poverty understood as powerlessness.

Within scripture, the predominant way in which poverty is understood is as powerlessness, which denotes a lack of agency and vulnerability to the actions of others. The most common word for poverty in the Old Testament (*'ānî* and *'ānāw*) implies vulnerability to oppression more than material destitution. The biblical sense of poverty as powerlessness dovetails with Greek conceptions of the *demos* and Roman notions of the *pauperi*, the *plebs*, and the *populis*. They are not destitute, but they are politically and therefore economically and socially vulnerable. The analogy in the contemporary context is with terms such as "the working class," "the proletariat," and, I suggest, "the black nation." Rather than philanthropy or social welfare programs, poverty as powerlessness demands the formation of a people. Part of how God addresses poverty as powerlessness is by forming a people. However, it matters how the *demos*/people is constituted.

The narrative paradigm of God addressing powerlessness by forming a people is Exodus. Exodus opens with Pharaoh making a claim to control the bodies and discipline the biological processes of the Israelites. As Zora Neale Hurston parses it, "The Hebrew womb had fallen under the heel of Pharaoh."[63] Fleeing after killing an Egyptian overseer, Moses eventually returns as a thaumaturge who performs miraculous "biopolitical" wonders in contrast to the counterfeit magic of Pharaoh's priests. The contrast here is between Moses's attempt to address the plight of the Israelites by merely taking life, which is shown to reproduce the problem, and his subsequent ability to draw on new sources of power outside of and undetermined by the prevailing system, through which the people are liberated. The conflict depicted between Moses and Pharaoh is over who has the power to fructify creation or render it desolate. The flourishing of creation is intertwined with and represented by whether the one who claims to rule sees the Israelites as humans capable of being a people or a mere population to be exploited for the good of those with a monopoly of power.

The movement from release from captivity to the formation of a people who inhabit creation in shalom-like ways is the central drama of Exodus, and it is a drama that runs through the course of scripture. Following Moses, the messianic figure, the ultimate measure of righteous political agency, is to bring not mere justice but healing and a new form of common life in which human and nonhuman life flourish together. The primary achievement of healing is not simply the restoration of sight or the ability to walk but the restoration of the ability of those currently excluded to be involved in the formation of a common world, walking and seeing, symbolizing active participation in the people of God. Echoing Moses's actions, what Christ's miracles of healing and exorcism are doing is, on the one hand, enabling the oppressed to discover new forms of agency so they can act for themselves and, on the other hand, showing up the impotent nature of Roman and Temple power. Christ brings wine out of water, healed bodies out of diseased ones, calm out of storms, and life out of death; when challenged, the established authorities can only whip, imprison, and crucify.

As enactments of new forms of power that reestablish the agency of the oppressed, exorcism and healing generate conflict. Exorcism involves convulsion and struggle and is sometimes achieved against the conscious desire of the one being exorcised. The story of the Gerasene demoniac (Mk 5:1–20) is paradigmatic in this respect. In this episode, the one in need of exorcism does not realize he is possessed, despite being driven to extreme, unrestrainable violence that harms himself and others. The nameless demoniac sees the prospect of release as a form of torment (v. 7). This is despite the fact that he is possessed by a militaristic, colonial, and death-dealing power, as indicated by the demon's name, Legion, and the location of the episode, a graveyard. Indeed, with the demonic spirits standing metonymically for Roman military might, this incident can be read as a symbolic and thaumaturgic battle with the Roman colonial political economy wherein Jesus shows Roman power as an out-of-control, demonic, shameful, and self-destructive force at once alien and oppressive.[64] The location of the battle reveals the impotence of Roman rule: the possessing spirits have made their *oikos*—that is, their household and place of economic production—in the land of the dead, a dwelling place that is at once absurd because it is lifeless and yet also produces fear and shame. Jesus challenges this system from the inside out, liberating the demoniac from physical and psychic enslavement and purifying the land from imperial forms of mass production that exploit and defile it and the people who live there: a herd of pigs is not only an abomination but is a near industrial level of agricultural production. Yet exorcism, as a form of liberation from an individually and collectively traumatizing power, involves dispossession and so is encountered by those invested in the status quo as a source of terror. Those who see the formerly demon-possessed man standing clothed and in his right mind are not grateful but afraid, and they demand that Jesus leave them alone (v. 15–17). In short, exorcism horrifies those who benefit from the status quo. Rightly so, as exorcism is a public promulgation of God's apocalyptic judgment against the principalities and powers that feed off the oppression and torment of the powerless and the self-destructive collusion of those with power.[65] Thus, those whose way of life depends on the operations of the principalities and powers cannot but hear this judgment as condemnation and threat.

This act of exorcism points beyond itself to how merely changing the structures of power is never enough: Rome disempowered does not of itself generate the empowerment of Israel.[66] The people of God need reconstituting, and the broader body politic needs a new animating spirit. To accomplish this, Jesus embodies and introduces a new source of power—the power of the Spirit—unavailable to those who oppress. Jesus's acts of power serve to reconstitute an atomized people so that they may be capable of acting together in pursuit of life-giving, eschatological ends. But this covenantal community is unassimilable by the existing religious and political structures, and its formation is at the same time an act of exorcism of the wider body politic that generates attempts to banish or suppress it.

Echoing scripture, Cone and Cheryl Kirk-Duggan use exorcism as a way of framing divine action within history. In Cone's early statement of black liberation theology, racism is identified as a demonic force and Black Power a form of exorcism.[67] On Cone's account, as well as a means of survival, black nationalist and Black Power efforts to form a nation within a nation can be understood as theopolitical gestures of exorcism within the wider body politic. He states:

> First, the work of Christ is essentially a liberating work, directed toward and by the oppressed. Black power embraces that very task. Second, Christ in liberating the wretched of the earth also liberates those responsible for the wretchedness. The oppressor is also freed of his peculiar demons. Black power in shouting Yes to black humanness and No to white oppression is exorcizing demons on both sides of the conflict. Third, mature freedom is burdensome and risky, producing anxiety and conflict for free men and for the brittle structures they challenge. The call for Black power is precisely the call to shoulder the burden of liberty in Christ, risking everything to live not as slaves but as free men.[68]

Like Cone, Kirk-Duggan uses exorcism as a way of framing a theopolitical vision of liberation. She identifies racism and slavery as forms of "collective possession," stating: "The treatment for collective possession is a collective exorcism."[69] She identifies the nineteenth-century abolitionist movement and the civil rights movement as forms of collective exorcism that seek to expel structural evil. More so than Cone but in keeping with other womanist theologians, Kirk-Duggan emphasizes the self-loving, solidaristic, and mutually up-building dimensions of the ongoing work of liberation and the need for new forms of agency undetermined by white supremacy.[70] A leitmotif through which this process of formation is explored in womanist theology is that of individual and communal healing.[71] In the light of Kirk-Duggan's work and the analysis given above, Black Power can be framed not only as a means of exorcism, addressing the objective conditions of domination, but also as a source of healing that helps form a people, thereby addressing the intersubjective conditions of domination.[72]

Drawing on Cone, Kirk-Duggan, and others, the Black Power movement can be understood as a way of forming a people as a response to pervasive conditions of powerlessness.[73] It sought to address the objective and subjective conditions of powerlessness through drawing on and recalibrating existing forms of community and patterns of belief and practice. My contention is that different forms of democratic politics were a vital means through which to accomplish this. That said, forming a sense of peoplehood through democratic politics is an inherently ambiguous task since the identity of the people is itself ambiguous. On the one hand, there is the aspirational sense of the term "people" as denoting the whole; on the other, there is its factionalist use as a term for one section of the whole, the "have-nots." Black nationalism, as a response to how blacks are situated within the wider American polity, tends to emphasize the latter while multiracial forms of community organizing as a form of praxis tends to emphasize the former.

One way to coordinate these divergent emphases is by understanding how the aspirational use of the term "the people" can denote heterogeneity rather than homogeneity. The people as a whole are not monolithic and should not necessarily be equated with a nation-state. Rather, the people can be an intricate, differentiated, intercommunal, or "consociational" body.[74] An emphasis on wholeness understood as either a form of intercommunalism or consociationalism rather than oneness or integration encourages a vision of peoplehood as about mutual exchanges between different parts of the whole.[75] This point is clarified by Marcia Riggs in relation to the church understood as the people of God: "People of different racial-ethnic groups organizing themselves into separate movements and structures within and outside of the church are not in and of themselves signs of failure in the quest for unity in the body of Christ. Such separation is, however, a sign of moral failure when its sole purpose is exclusion, and differences are used to set us over and against one another. Exclusionary separation is divisive; functional separation recognizes differences as meaningful for interrelationship between groups."[76]

Politically, a whole body politic is not one where everyone is the same but one where all may be recognized as having gifts to bring. But for wholeness to stand, there is a need to identify and pursue goods in common, and democratic politics (that is, a politics that aims at forming a people as a whole through distributing political agency and power as widely as possible) is one ongoing way by which to do this. Yet, at the same time, the witness of Black Power points to how any such project of intercommunalism or consociationalism in the United States has to take as a sine qua non the dispossession/exorcism of white supremacy and the formation of independent and self-organized forms of black political, social, economic, and spiritual agency.

Conclusion

I have tried to suggest that, against the atomizing impact of white supremacy, the affirmation of personhood through the formation of a people is best achieved not via recognition of individual rights (as liberalism supposes), nor via changes in the means of production (as scientific Marxism suggests), nor via the redistribution of resources via the state (as in social democratic visions), nor through recognition as a mode of incorporation into a wider system (as multicultural accounts envisage). Each of these approaches tends to ignore the specific history and experience of African Americans. In doing so, they fail to reckon with how integration into the political economy as currently structured reinscribes white normativity within the third, fourth, and fifth dimensions of citizenship. These approaches thereby treat white supremacy as an accidental rather than a formal feature of political order in the United States. What the Black Power movement points to, even in its failures, is how a prerequisite for reconstituting the polity and democratic citizenship to address the subjective and objective dimensions of racial injustice as a formal feature of the political system entails some way of being a "nation within a nation" (i.e., independent and self-organized forms of communal political, social, economic, and spiritual agency).

The need to enable dominated people to form a "nation within a nation" is a vital insight that political theology can learn from in conceptualizing the relationship between Christianity and democracy. And it connects to a central thematic of modern theological anthropology: namely, that humans are not isolated, autonomous, self-reflexive subjects but persons constituted through relations with others, and ultimately through communion with God. Consequently, personhood involves being embedded in some form of life, culture, or people. The formation of a people, whether ecclesial or civic, involves questions of love, politics, and power. In Augustinian terms, the common object of its loves defines a people. The pursuit of these loves necessitates action in time (power) and making judgments about when, where, and with whom to act, and what to do and how to do it in order to forge and sustain some kind of shared life (politics). The Black Power movement represents but one iteration of attempts to form a people through the pursuit of power via politics. The formation of this people inherently shows up the self-negating ways in which the United States is "under the dominion of its very lust for domination." Indeed, what Augustine said of Rome can be said of the United States: "That republic never actually existed, because there was no true justice in it."[77] Rather, Black Power unveils how the peace and order of the United States is what the twelfth-century prelate Rufinus of Sorrento called "the sleep of Behemoth," which, when disturbed, reveals its beastly nature by turning on those with the temerity to challenge its disordered and unjust tranquility.[78] However, the formation of even a modestly just earthly peace requires agitating the monster rather than leaving undisturbed a subjugated quiescence that dresses up compliance as harmony. The formation of a nation within a nation can be one means of agitation through which the body politic is shrived and purged, purgation taking the form of healing for some and exorcism for others, depending on one's structural location within the system as a whole.

Notes

1. On this, see Michael C. Dawson, *Black Visions: The Roots of Contemporary African-American Political Ideologies* (Chicago: University of Chicago Press, 2001), 29–43; Tommie Shelby, *We Who Are Dark: The Philosophical Foundations of Black Solidarity* (Cambridge, MA: Belknap Press, 2005), 6–13; and Joel Olson, *The Abolition of White Democracy* (Minneapolis: University of Minnesota Press, 2004).

2. Charles W. Mills, *Blackness Visible: Essays on Philosophy and Race* (Ithaca, NY: Cornell University Press, 1998), 119–37.

3. For a critique of redistributive mechanisms as a means of addressing racism, see Olson, *Abolition of White Democracy*, 114–18.

4. Édouard Glissant, *Caribbean Discourses: Selected Essays*, trans. J. Michael Dash (Charlottesville: University Press of Virginia, 1989).

5. For a historical account of the emergence of black nationalism prior to the beginning of the Great Migration, see Steven Hahn, *A Nation under Our Feet: Black Political Struggles in the Rural South, from Slavery to the Great Migration* (Cambridge, MA: Belknap Press, 2003).

6. See Luke Bretherton, *Resurrecting Democracy: Faith, Citizenship, and the Politics of a Common Life* (Cambridge: Cambridge University Press, 2015). While *Resurrecting Democracy* provides an analysis of how economic globalization, religious plurality, and secularity shape the conditions of democratic politics in Europe and North America, this essay is an attempt to add to that analysis by addressing how white supremacy is a further condition within which democratic politics is situated and with which it must contend in this context.

7. Joseph Peniel argues that, while Black Power activists such as the Black Panther Party rejected any identification with the United States, they embraced its democratic principles and played an important role in shaping, contesting, and transforming the meaning of American democracy. Joseph Peniel, "The Black Power Movement: A State of the Field," *Journal of American History* 96, no. 3 (2009): 751–76.

8. James H. Cone, *Black Theology and Black Power* (1969; repr., Maryknoll, NY: Orbis, 1997).

9. Gary J. Dorrien, *Social Ethics in the Making: Interpreting an American Tradition* (Chichester, UK: Wiley-Blackwell, 2008), 390–532.

10. See, for example, Willie James Jennings, *The Christian Imagination: Theology and the Origins of Race* (New Haven, CT: Yale University Press, 2010).

11. James A. Noel, *Black Religion and the Imagination of Matter in the Atlantic World* (New York: Palgrave Macmillan, 2009).

12. Gayraud Wilmore, *Black Religion and Black Radicalism: An Interpretation of the Religious History of African Americans* (Maryknoll, NY: Orbis, 1998).

13. Cardinal Aswad Walker, "Princes Shall Come out of Egypt: A Theological Comparison of Marcus Garvey and Reverend Albert B. Cleage Jr.," *Journal of Black Studies* 39, no. 2 (2008): 194–251.

14. For an early reflection on the inherently religious nature of the Black Power movement, see Vincent Harding, *The Religion of Black Power* (Boston: Beacon Press, 1968). For a detailed, placed-based historical study, see Kerry Pimblott, *Faith in Black Power: Religion, Race, and Resistance in Cairo, Illinois* (Lexington: University Press of Kentucky, 2017).

15. Stokely Carmichael and Charles Hamilton, *Black Power: The Politics of Liberation in America* (New York: Random House, 1967), 47.

16. This was the analysis of the Black Panther Party, which formed alliances with numerous other radical organizations regardless of ethnic background. These included the Young Lords, the Young Patriots, and the Red Guard. It also actively supported the boycotts organized by the United Farm Workers. See Lauren Araiza, "'In Common Struggle against a Common Oppression': The United Farm Workers and the Black Panther Party, 1968–1973," *Journal of African American History* 94, no. 2 (2009): 200–223.

17. Joseph E. Peniel, *Stokely: A Life* (New York: Basic Civitas Books, 2014).

18. Dawson, *Black Visions*, 85–134.

19. Paul Gilroy, *Black Atlantic: Modernity and Double Consciousness* (Cambridge, MA: Harvard University Press, 1993), 32.

20. Dawson, *Black Visions*, 91. Marcus Garvey is an example of the first; Martin Delany, the second; and LeRoi Jones (before he became Amiri Baraka), the third. For an alternative typology to Dawson's, see John T. McCartney, *Black Power Ideologies: An Essay in African-American Political Thought* (Philadelphia: Temple University Press, 1992), 111–32.

21. The term "intercommunal" draws on Huey Newton's work. For an account of the development of his thought, see Judson Jeffries, *Huey P. Newton: The Radical Theorist* (Jackson: University Press of Mississippi, 2002).

22. Clyde Halisi and James Mtume, eds., *The Quotable Karenga* (Los Angeles: US Organization, 1967), 3.

23. For a nonterritorial, separatist vision of black nationalism, see Albert Cleage, *Black Christian Nationalism: New Directions for the Black Church* (New York: William Morrow, 1972).

24. On this, see Aldon D. Morris, *The Origins of the Civil Rights Movement: Black Communities Organizing for Change* (New York: Free Press, 1984); and Kevin Anderson, *Agitations:*

Ideologies and Strategies in African American Politics (Fayetteville: University of Arkansas Press, 2010).

25. Joseph Peniel, ed., *Neighborhood Rebels: Black Power at the Local Level* (New York: Palgrave Macmillan, 2010); and Rhonda Williams, *Concrete Demands: The Search for Black Power in the 20th Century* (London: Routledge, 2015).

26. Grace Lee Boggs, *Living for Change: An Autobiography* (Minneapolis: University of Minnesota Press, 1998), 153; and bell hooks, *Salvation: Black People and Love* (New York: HarperCollins, 2001), 4–17.

27. Although it has also been criticized for its failure to do so. See, for example, Boggs, *Living for Change*, 151–89.

28. W.E.B. Du Bois, *Darkwater: Voices from within the Veil* (New York: Harcourt, Brace and Howe, 1920), vii.

29. George Yancy, Introduction to *Christology and Whiteness: What Would Jesus Do?* (London: Routledge, 2012), 5.

30. Frances Lee Ansley, "Stirring the Ashes: Race, Class and the Future of Civil Rights Scholarship," *Cornell Law Review* 74, no. 6 (1989): 993–1077, n129.

31. Mills, *Blackness Visible*, 139–66.

32. Gilroy, *Black Atlantic*, 3–5. See also Dawson, *Black Visions*, 91.

33. Dawson, *Black Visions*, 27–28.

34. An important early statement articulating this position was James Boggs and Grace Lee Boggs, "The City Is the Black Man's Land," *Monthly Review* 17, no. 11 (1966).

35. Leonard Moore, *Carl B. Stokes and the Rise of Black Political Power* (Urbana: University of Illinois Press, 2003).

36. Cleage, *Black Christian Nationalism*, especially 123–70.

37. For example, despite their ideological differences, the Black Panthers, the Congress of Afrikan Peoples, and the League of Revolutionary Black Workers all rejected a separate, bounded territory and instead posited socialist forms of economic production and ownership as a key basis for achieving black liberation. Dawson, *Black Visions*, 217. In contrast, Floyd McKissick's failed venture, "Soul City" in North Carolina, envisaged an enclave of self-determination based on capitalist enterprise. Williams, *Concrete Demands*, 167.

38. For a critique of how colorblind policies reinforce racism, see Olson, *Abolition of White Democracy*, 100–105. For a classic statement on the supposed neutrality of liberalism, see John Rawls's treatment of the "veil of ignorance" in *A Theory of Justice*, rev. ed. (Boston: Harvard University Press, 1999), 118–21.

39. George Lipsitz, *The Possessive Investment in Whiteness: How White People Profit from Identity Politics* (Philadelphia: Temple University Press, 2009), 2.

40. Ibid. For an account of the political and ideological backdrop to these policies, see Gary Gerstle, *American Crucible: Race and Nation in the Twentieth Century* (Princeton, NJ: Princeton University Press, 2001), 44–127.

41. For a detailed account of the ways in which, from the New Deal through to the GI Bill, social policy privileged whites, see Ira Katznelson, *When Affirmative Action Was White: An Untold History of Racial Inequality in Twentieth-Century America* (New York: W. W. Norton, 2005).

42. Michelle Alexander, *The New Jim Crow: Mass Incarceration in the Age of Colorblindness* (New York: New Press, 2010).

43. David R. Roediger, *The Wages of Whiteness: Race and the Making of the American Working Class*, rev. ed. (New York: Verso, 1999); Mills, *Blackness Visible*; Olson, *Abolition of White Democracy*; and Gerstle, *American Crucible*.

44. Roediger, *Wages of Whiteness*, 172. An example of this attitude is the figure of Theodore Roosevelt; see Gerstle, *American Crucible*, 14–43.

45. Mills, *Blackness Visible*, 67–118.

46. Quoted in ibid., 109.

47. Joseph Peniel, *Waiting 'til the Midnight Hour: A Narrative History of Black Power in America* (New York: Henry Holt, 2006), 229.

48. On the term "imagined community" and its relationship to identification with a nation-state, see Benedict Anderson, *Imagined Communities: Reflections on the Origin and Spread of Nationalism*, rev. ed. (London: Verso, 2006).

49. A recent articulation of such a view is given in Samuel P. Huntington's *Who Are We? The Challenges to America's National Identity* (New York: Simon & Schuster, 2004). For Huntington, American identity is normatively English (i.e., white) and Protestant.

50. On this, see Theodore Allen, *The Invention of the White Race* (New York: Verso, 1994); Noel Ignatiev, *How the Irish Became White* (New York: Routledge, 1995); and David R. Roediger, *Working Toward Whiteness: How America's Immigrants Became White* (New York: Basic Books, 2005).

51. Dawson, *Black Visions*, 246.

52. "Combahee River Statement," in *Home Girls: A Black Feminist Anthology*, ed. Barbara Smith, 264–74 (New Brunswick, NJ: Rutgers University Press, 2000); and Angela Davis and Lisa Lowe, "Reflections on Race, Class and Gender in the USA," in *The Angela Y. Davis Reader*, ed. Joy James (Malden, MA: Blackwell, 1998), 313.

53. Bernice Johnson Reagon, "Coalition Politics: Turning the Century," in *Home Girls: A Black Feminist Anthology*, ed. Barbara Smith, 343–55 (New Brunswick, NJ: Rutgers University Press, 2000); and Audre Lorde, *Sister/Outsider: Essays and Speeches* (Trumansburg, NY: Crossing Press, 1984), 138.

54. James Cone, *For My People: Black Theology and the Black Church* (Maryknoll, NY: Orbis, 1984), 193. The thesis of this statement by Cone is explored at length in James Cone, *Martin and Malcom and America: A Dream or a Nightmare?* (Maryknoll, NY: Orbis, 1991). It should also be noted that Cone himself revised his own position in the light of criticism he received from black feminist and womanist theologians.

55. Shelby, *We Who Are Dark*.

56. Ibid., 229.

57. Ibid., 246–47. Shelby does not propose the deconstruction of loyalty to the black nation but a redefinition of the object of loyalty.

58. Angela Y. Davis, *The Angela Y. Davis Reader*, ed. Joy James (Malden, MA: Blackwell, 1998), 323.

59. Ibid., 320.

60. Cornel West, "The Paradox of the African American Rebellion," in *Is It Nation Time? Contemporary Essays on Black Power and Black Nationalism*, ed. Eddie S. Glaude Jr. (Chicago: University of Chicago Press, 2002), 38.

61. Bretherton, *Resurrecting Democracy*, 179–218.

62. Cone, *Black Theology and Black Power*, 38; and James H. Cone, *God of the Oppressed*, rev. ed. (Maryknoll, NY: Orbis, 1997), 122–26.

63. Zora Neale Hurston, *Moses, Man of the Mountain: A Novel* (1939; repr., New York: Harper Collins, 2009), 1.

64. For a reading of Mark 5 that draws out the theopolitical dimensions of the episode, see Ched Myers, *Binding the Strong Man: A Political Reading of Mark's Story of Jesus* (Maryknoll, NY: Orbis, 1988), 190–94.

65. Or, as Cone puts it, "In Jesus' exorcisms . . . he was pointing to the new age that was breaking into the present, disrupting the order of injustice" (*God of the Oppressed*, 205).

66. Oliver O'Donovan, *The Desire of the Nations: Rediscovering the Roots of Political Theory* (Cambridge: Cambridge University Press, 1996), 95.

67. Cone, *Black Theology and Black Power*, 41–42. See also James W. Perkinson, *White Theology: Outing Supremacy in Modernity* (New York, Palgrave Macmillan, 2006), 237–39.

68. Ibid., 42–43.

69. Cheryl Kirk-Duggan, *Exorcising Evil: A Womanist Perspective on the Spirituals* (Maryknoll, NY: Orbis, 1997), 132.

70. See also Katie Cannon, *Black Womanist Ethics* (Atlanta: Scholars Press, 1988); Marcia Y. Riggs, *Awake, Arise and Act: A Womanist Call for Black Liberation* (Cleveland, OH: Pilgrim Press, 1994); and Melanie Harris, *Gifts of Virtue: Alice Walker and Womanist Ethics* (New York: Palgrave Macmillan, 2010).

71. See, for example, Emilie Townes, *Breaking the Fine Rain of Death: African American Health Issues and a Womanist Ethic of Care* (New York: Continuum, 2001); Stephanie Mitchem, "Healing Hearts and Broken Bodies: An African American Women's Spirituality of Healing," in *Faith, Health and Healing in African American Life*, ed. Stephanie Mitchem and Emilie Townes, 181–91 (Westport, CT: Praeger, 2008); and Shawn M. Copeland, *Enfleshing Freedom: Body, Race, and Being* (Minneapolis, MN: Fortress, 2010).

72. Kirk-Duggan, *Exorcising Evil*, 160–68. It should be noted that Cone, like Kirk-Duggan, also sees the spirituals as a paradigmatic instance of community formation and transformation.

73. This was also a theme developed by Albert Cleage in *Black Christian Nationalism*.

74. For a definition of consociationalism, see Bretherton, *Resurrecting Democracy*, 219–42.

75. Danielle Allen notes: "The metaphor of wholeness can guide us into a conversation about how to develop habits of citizenship that can help a democracy bring trustful coherence out of division without erasing or suppressing difference." Danielle Allen, *Talking to Strangers: Anxieties of Citizenship since Brown v. Board of Education* (Chicago: University of Chicago Press, 2004), 20.

76. Riggs, *Awake, Arise and Act*, 95–96.

77. Augustine, *The City of God*, trans. William Babcock (New York: New City Press, 2012), 59.

78. Rufinus von Sorrent *De Bono Pacis* (Hannover, Ger.: Hahn, 1997).

Rioting as Flourishing? Reconsidering Virtue Ethics in Times of Civil Unrest

Sarah MacDonald and Nicole Symmonds

From Black Power to Black Lives Matter, political resisters protesting systemic racism have used riots and other manifestations of outrage as a way to grasp at flourishing. Yet such a tactic seems antithetical to the core concept of flourishing as recognized within virtue ethics. Building on the work of womanist and feminist ethicists and moral philosophers who have defended anger as a morally apt, even virtuous response to injustice, we reconsider the relationship between a community's flourishing and public manifestations of anger and rage. We argue for expanding the moral response to rioting as a tactic of political resistance, and we suggest that more culturally particular understandings of both virtue and flourishing can open space to better see the role anger may play in a community's flourishing.

THE AUGUST 2014 POLICE SHOOTING OF MICHAEL BROWN, AN unarmed black teenager, triggered weeks of street protests in Ferguson, Missouri. Law enforcement personnel confronted the demonstrators with riot gear, tear gas, and rubber bullets. Three months later, when a grand jury decided not to indict the police officer who had shot Brown, even fiercer protests erupted. Rioting protesters looted businesses and set buildings and vehicles on fire.[1] Public commentary on the rioting was mixed, with some voices condemning the civil unrest while others called attention to the despair and structural inequalities provoking the riots.[2] In a *Democracy Now* interview taped the day after the announcement of the grand jury decision, Rev. Osagyefo Sekou described the rioters as outraged, alienated young people who "have been betrayed by every level of government." When interviewer Amy Goodman referenced Martin Luther King Jr.'s famous declaration that "a riot is the language of the unheard," Reverend Sekou agreed that King's words reflected the Ferguson rioters, who

Sarah MacDonald is a PhD candidate in the Graduate Division of Religion at Emory University, 201 Dowman Dr., Atlanta, GA 30322; semacdo@emory.edu.

Nicole Symmonds is a PhD student in the Graduate Division of Religion at Emory University, 201 Dowman Dr., Atlanta, GA 30322; nicole.sarita.symmonds@emory.edu.

Journal of the Society of Christian Ethics, 38, 1 (2018): 25–42

felt they had no other recourse to vent their anger and oppose the systemic racism they had been enduring for years.[3]

In a challenge to social scientists at the American Psychological Association in 1967, King explained how riots enable "the most enraged and deprived Negro to take hold of consumer goods with the ease the white man does by using his purse."[4] Although he critiqued the rioters, King more heavily critiqued white society and policymakers for the deprivations giving rise to the riots. Further, he recognized how rioting represents a needed emotional catharsis for oppressed people.

King's careful assessment of rioting—holding in tension the violence of the act with the greater violence of the conditions that provoke it—reveals the complications of morally evaluating such actions of social outrage. In the face of sustained systemic oppressions, which responses are appropriate? Which are ethical? And which, ultimately, are life-giving? Wrestling with questions like these, womanist and feminist moral philosophers and ethicists have defended anger as an apt, even virtuous response to injustice. Lisa Tessman describes the sustained anger that drives militant political resistance as a "burdened virtue." She presents this anger as politically and morally necessary yet crippling to bear, in tension with the enraged resister's own flourishing.

While such arguments helpfully reframe what—and who—may count as "virtuous," in this essay we push these questions further by reconsidering the relationship between a community's flourishing and public manifestations of anger and rage, such as rioting. This reconsideration unfolds in three steps. First, we examine conceptualizations of virtue and of anger, with attention to how these conceptualizations participate in contexts of oppression and efforts of liberation. Second, we argue that rioting may be not simply destructive civic disorder but an intentional tactic of political resistance that allows the rioters to reclaim agency and seize power in the teeth of disempowering systems. Third, we assert the importance of attending to the cultural particularity of flourishing and challenging the ways flourishing may function as a privilege, accessible only to some. Throughout this three-point argument, our underlying question is whether it may be possible to conceive of rioting *as* an expression of human flourishing. Or at least, might one think of rioting as a means of moving *toward* flourishing, as a way for an oppressed people to more fully express their personhood and potentially force positive social change?

Evaluating the relationship between rioting and flourishing is an urgent discussion for our times. Since Michael Brown's death in 2014, many more incidents of fatal police violence directed toward black Americans have seized local and national attention. Protests over racism and other systemic injustices continue to manifest through social media campaigns, political advocacy, demonstrations—and sometimes riots. Rioting remains a prominent topic in our news and a source of ongoing public debate. This issue matters socially and morally since our theorizing about flourishing *and* about rioting will impact our civic engagement, our policymaking, and the ways we as individuals and as a community choose—or not—to confront and resist oppression.

As coauthors, we acknowledge how our own identities and backgrounds shape our approach to this topic. Nicole Symmonds is a black woman and a Black Lives Matter ally, with more than a decade of experience as a professional journalist. Sarah MacDonald is a white woman and former full-time nonviolent activist who has worked in Palestine and in Colombia, supporting community-based nonviolent resistance. We are influenced by our work on the ground with the marginalized and the oppressed as well as by the work of being responsible for interpreting and telling their stories fairly and accurately. This essay reflects not only our current studies in philosophical and Christian ethics but also, more deeply, our commitments to justice and liberation and to critically analyzing and practicing public discourse in ways that further these aims.

Constructing Virtue, Reframing Anger: Their Contested Roles in Oppression and Liberation

Virtue and liberation are relatively rare bedfellows. Adopting a virtue ethics framework is not often the preferred methodology of those with liberationist convictions and goals. In part, this may be due to associations that commonly adhere to the rhetoric of virtue, associations at odds with liberationists' concerns for empowerment, resistance to oppression, and radical social change. Because virtue ethics foregrounds individual selfhood and character formation within the context of communal traditions, this field often seems removed from liberationist approaches that focus on analyzing and confronting structural oppressions.

The tensions between these two approaches arise from more than different focal points of attention and analysis. Theorists concerned with oppression and liberation are often wary of how paradigms of virtue get wielded as a tool to further marginalize or stigmatize certain groups of people. Nancy Snow argues that "most Western approaches to virtue" have contributed to the oppression of women.[5] She examines selected texts from Aristotle, Judeo-Christian Scriptures, and early modern European philosophers to make her case that Western traditions of virtue theory, with few exceptions, have essentialized gender differences and limited women's moral development and agency. Snow does not consider virtue theory necessarily oppressive; on the contrary, she suggests an alternative, non-oppressive approach. Nonetheless, her essay is telling in how it portrays Western religious and philosophical discussions of virtue as typically participating in the subordination of women.

In the field of Christian social ethics, tensions between a virtue ethics paradigm and a liberationist orientation are equally visible. Such tensions play out clearly in the book *Christian Faith and Social Justice: Five Views*.[6] Here Miguel De La Torre represents liberation theology as a methodology that takes as its starting point the experiences of the oppressed. He implies that the tradition of virtue ethics assumes a very different—and fundamentally oppressive—starting point when he writes, "The bourgeois ethics emanating from the Empire, with their concentration on idealized virtues, become problematic for marginalized communities dealing with the 'messiness' of life."[7] Later De La Torre makes his critique explicit when he declares virtue ethics "irreconcilable" with liberative ethics because of how "the language of virtues . . . has historically functioned to marginalize communities of color and continues to do so."[8] Writing as a liberative feminist, Laura Stivers similarly critiques virtue ethics approaches that have, in her reading, "structured virtue and vice in ways that privilege some and exclude others."[9] These criticisms highlight the constructed nature of categories of virtue and illuminate a common liberationist objection to virtue ethics: that dominant understandings of virtue too frequently function to legitimize social and economic inequalities. De La Torre and Stivers, like other ethicists committed to liberation, call instead for ethical approaches that will radically disrupt the status quo.

Liberationist scholars who protest oppressive uses of the *language* of virtue do not necessarily reject virtue per se. But they do point out that what constitutes virtuous behavior for people living under oppressive conditions may look quite different from the ethical ideals and presumptions of a dominant culture. Katie Cannon's interventions in Christian ethics make this argument. Cannon writes, "The real-lived texture of Black life requires moral agency that may run contrary to the ethical boundaries of mainline Protestantism. . . . Racism, gender discrimination, and economic exploitation, as inherited, age-long complexes, require the Black community to create and cultivate values and virtues in their own terms so that they prevail against the odds with moral integrity."[10] As she explains, the virtues valued within "dominant ethics" presume a level of self-determination that most black Americans, especially black women, have not experienced. Consequently, the black community needs other ethical principles more suited to helping them survive their circumstances.

One goal of womanist ethics is to identify and articulate the moral wisdom and virtues that emerge from and support black women's agency. Some of the qualities and practices thus identified as "virtuous" may startle; they may not seem like virtues at all to those who have not needed to develop these kinds of coping mechanisms. For example, inspired by the life of Zora Neale Hurston, Cannon's essay "Unctuousness as Virtue" depicts moral goodness as "that which allows Black people to maintain a feistiness about life that nobody can wipe out, no matter how hard they try." Besides fostering endurance and survival, this virtue of unctuousness encourages resistance through crafty, slippery forms of dissent. As Cannon asserts, "Creatively straining against the external restraints in one's life is virtuous living."[11]

Comparable moves of redefining moral goodness and responsibility appear in Emilie Townes's recent discussions of "colored orneriness," which she glosses as "when folk are difficult to deal with and control" because they are contesting a "fiendish" status quo. Similar to how Cannon depicts virtuous living as creatively straining against imposed restraints, Townes lifts up "faithful colored orneriness" as a way of "learn[ing] to live creatively in the tight circles of choices that are often given to us" and then transforming those circles into "a spiral of possibilities."[12] In the midst of systemic oppressions and violence, virtue must often be reimagined. For those standing on the underside of injustice, traits that trouble or trick the powerful may be not only clever or necessary but ethical, faithful, life-giving.

As Cannon and Townes lift up the moral value of facing injustice with an unctuous manner or an ornery spirit, their paradigm-shifting womanist arguments resonate with the defenses several feminists have made of anger and other so-called negative emotions. Such emotions, Macalester Bell points out, "have distinct and important roles to play in responding to oppression."[13] In her overview of feminist defenses of anger, Bell categorizes at least four ways anger may be a morally and politically fitting response to oppressive conditions: as a form of protesting wrong treatment and retaining self-respect, as a source of knowledge about what is occurring, as a way of bearing witness to injustice, and as a force motivating social change. These defenses, she notes, present anger as instrumentally valuable, functioning to bring about certain desired ends such as personal and social change. She further asserts that the trait of appropriate anger is intrinsically a *"form of excellence"* in character because of how anger expresses opposition to evil.[14]

Lisa Tessman is another feminist moral philosopher who theorizes how, under conditions of oppression, oppositional anger can be a virtue, including anger that is sustained and unmerciful toward oppressors. Tessman develops her discussion of anger within a eudaemonistic virtue ethics. Committed to liberatory resistance struggles, she has made the unusual choice to use neo-Aristotelian virtue ethics as her framework because she believes this approach offers insight into the full extent of the harms and moral damage oppression causes. Two key features of Tessman's theorizing are, first, her attention to how oppression functions as a systematic barrier to flourishing and, second, her consequent insistence that, under such oppressive conditions, virtue must be "unlinked" from flourishing. She departs from the Aristotelian assumption that cultivating virtuous character will normally be conducive to a flourishing life. Instead, she argues, "given adverse external conditions and/or the overwhelming demands of attending well to a very ailing world, the normal pattern will be of exercising virtues and yet still being unable to attain anything that could be called a flourishing life."[15] This unlinking of virtue from flourishing is especially evident in what she names "burdened virtues." These traits may be "practically necessitated for surviving oppression or morally necessitated for opposing it" yet are also "costly to the selves who bear them."[16] In other words, the political resisters who exhibit such burdened virtues are, in Tessman's account, morally praiseworthy—yet unlikely to experience flourishing in their own lives.

This concept of burdened virtues makes Tessman a fruitful interlocutor in this essay. Although she does not explicitly address rioting, her discussion of burdened virtues focuses on radical, militant forms of political struggle such as armed resistance or the refusal to cooperate with existing power structures. Rioting employed as political resistance readily fits among these examples, and even more so if we understand rioting as an enactment of rage against long-term injustices. Notably, the first burdened virtues Tessman explores are the traits of sustained anger and rage in the face of oppression. She believes these traits may rightly be perceived as virtues because they are morally apt responses to injustice and they provide energy, insight, and resolve in resisting that evil. However, she considers them burdened virtues because she finds a "constant or frequently occurring state of anger" psychologically harmful—*not* healthy or flourishing—for the bearer of that anger.[17] It seems likely, then, that Tessman would be receptive to the claim that the rioting political resister can be a virtuous moral agent, and equally likely that she would see this rioter as an example of a burdened virtue-bearer, hampered in achieving a flourishing life. It is this latter point that we propose to question further by examining more closely what constitutes flourishing. But first we turn to the topic of rioting, to explain more fully why we perceive riots not simply as destructive or violent civil unrest but potentially as a tactic of political resistance and a deliberate action of moral agency.

Rioting as a Tactic of Outraged Resistance

As traditionally conceived, a riot is an act of civil disorder characterized by the assembly of a group or individuals who lash out in a violent public disturbance against authority, property, or people. Riots typically involve a mixture of vandalism, destruction of public property, and what is perceived as a general level of chaos and violence.[18] Popular conceptions of rioting range from Super Bowl fans excited about their team's victory—or defeat—to members of a community reacting to a violation enacted by someone in a position of authority. For the purposes of this essay we focus on communities reacting to a violation or what French philosopher Alain Badiou calls the "immediate riot," which he defines as "unrest among a section of the population nearly always in the wake of a violent episode of state coercion."[19]

Badiou provides this orientation to rioting as part of a three-pronged consid-eration of rioting and uprising outlined in *Rebirth of History*. As a philosophical-political response to the Arab Spring uprising, Badiou's *Rebirth* contends that the current political climate is priming society for a historical riot, the uprising that signals a turn in the history of politics. The first of the three categories is the immediate riot, which he describes as a political uprising spearheaded by youth. This riot is located in proximity to it participants and rooted in rebellion and destruction with a semblance of universalizable intention or rage that has seemingly no purpose.[20] Following the immediate riot is the latent riot, which involves the participation of those not directly impacted by injustice or oppres-sion but who see the importance of solidarity and thus employ uprising tactics such as strikes, boycotts, and marches on behalf of the oppressed who can't af-ford to impact their livelihood. Last on Badiou's rioting spectrum is historical rioting, in which the political uprising boundaries move beyond those of the target of anger to a central site where protesters remain until their demands are met, where there is a qualitative extension of those involved in protest that reflects a unified front from diverse constituencies, and, finally, where there is a transition from the "nihilistic din of riotous attacks to the invention of the single slogan that envelops all the disparate voices."[21]

This framing of the riot positions us to analyze it as a tactic of people who have either directly or indirectly experienced systemic oppression or violence and who use rioting to make their voices heard and to grasp at a semblance of justice. Just as Badiou focuses his energy, much of our deliberation about riot-ing holds forth on judgment to "lend an ear to the signal."[22] We work with Ba-diou's immediate riot to frame our discussion of riots as phenomena that erupt in response to police brutality. We will use the conception of the immediate riot, as it presents itself in recent events of political unrest, to work toward a vision of Badiou's historical riot as a virtuous response to systemic oppression that expands the possibility of flourishing. Thus, expanding on the character-istics of the immediate riot, we introduce three characteristics of the function of the immediate riot: the riot as an act of political or economic resistance that is a response to a history of systemic oppression, the riot as a manifestation of anger, and the riot as a tactic employed by the oppressed.

As an act of political or economic resistance, the riot as taken up in response to history connotes it as a response to a system of oppression and injustice at a specific moment in time. Here the immediate riot is in response to political, juridical, and economic systems that have no preference for the least of these, and thus their participants strike back, resisting traditional political and finan-cial support of said systems. In "After the Bombing," a 1965 speech that Mal-colm X delivered in Detroit, Malcolm provides insight into the systematically oppressive conditions that prompt riots by pointing to the inequality between black and white people living in New York. From living conditions where black people in Harlem pay more for run-down dwellings than white people pay for Park Avenue homes, to paying more for "the worst food" than the white man who has to pay for food downtown, Malcolm points out that a history of being exploited is the prerequisite for riots. Of this he says,

> So Black people know that they're being exploited and that their blood is being sucked and they see no way out. When the thing is finally sparked, the white man is not there—he's gone. The merchant is not there, the landlord is not there, the one they consider the enemy isn't there. So they knock at his property. This is what makes them knock down the store windows and set fire to things, and things of that sort. It's not that they're thieves. . . . It's a corrupt, vicious, hypocritical system that has castrated the Black man, and the only way the Black man can get back at it is to strike it in the only way he knows how.[23]

Similarly, one can look at the riots in Ferguson following the fatal shooting of Michael Brown by police officer Darren Wilson. Many speculated about the cause of the unrest, whose immediate cause was certainly a white police officer's shooting of an unarmed black teenager. Yet many also knew that the unrest was in response to a history of systemic racism as enacted by members of the law enforcement community. In "The Ferguson Riots Are Not a Shift Away from Peace, They're a Challenge to Violence," columnist Natasha Lennard suggests that the rage that spawned the riots didn't rise out of a peaceful context but one full of strife: "Sunday night's rally may have begun calmly, but a context in which yet another young, unarmed black teen has been shot dead by police, and riot cops stand stationed to shutdown even a shadow of dissent, is not a context of peace. State violence prevails and sits heavily over Ferguson this week. Mourning residents have limited options: ensure this savage status quo with quiet resignation, or, acknowledging that there is already a state of violence, they can fight back."[24]

Here one can posit that the cause of the riot is manifold, stemming further back than the latest slain black body or economic disenfranchisement to a history of the black body as criminal and inferior, buffeted by racially biased practices and broadcast for the world to see. Given this, the riot is not only a response to history but also an expression of anger.

Interpreting the riot as an expression of anger takes into consideration the emotional root of the practice. In Aristotle's *Rhetoric*, he describes anger as "a longing, accompanied by pain, for a real or apparent revenge for a real or apparent slight, affecting a man himself or one of his friends, when such a slight is undeserved"[25] It is this rupture in one's circle of concern that causes one to respond with anger to the situation. This definition upholds anger as a response to a wrong committed without justification. In his *Nicomachean Ethics*, Aristotle suggests there is praise for the man who is angry at the right things, with the right people, and for the right amount of time. Yet, for Aristotle, although anger can be praised, it may reach its affective limits when it hits the wrong target or is in excess. Tessman takes on these affective limits and sees them as a way that political resisters can go wrong in their expressions of anger by suggesting that political resisters are likely to have trouble aiming their anger toward the appropriate target—those responsible for perpetrating injustice—and misdirected anger cannot be praised.[26] Tessman draws attention to how the Aristotelian account of anger, even with its promises, presents a problem for the political resister who must sustain anger to resist systemic oppression and who may not always appropriately hit the target of those responsible for the oppression.

Regarding the target of the riot, riots can be violent public disturbances that target property and, to a lesser extent, people. But sometimes the violent nature of the riot is overstated when the act of civil disorder is, usually, rooted in the destruction of the inanimate over the animate. University of California, Davis, professor of English Joshua Clover states, "The equivocation of riot and violence has been an essential tool in the political reduction of the riot, its cordoning off from politic proper, the measure of which rests implicitly on a model of self-consciousness or its absence."[27] Here Clover suggests that the conflation of riot with violence is an attempt to depoliticize the riot and house it squarely in the realm of violent criminal activity. Such a move produces the riot as violence and those who participate in riots as criminals, not political resisters striving for justice. In the case of riots that have taken place over the last five years, such a view reproduces the criminality of those perceived to take up rioting as a tactic the most, black people. We uphold the riot as an action of political resistance and the importance of drawing more attention to sustained anger as the emotion that is prerequisite to rioting. We contend there is little to no virtue in resisting sustained anger to maintain virtue, and we acknowledge that this is all the more unavoidable for black people who are constrained by experiences of systemic oppression yet expected to live according to the principles of dominant ethics. The black person in the twenty-first century is bound to anger and its expression because of the violence wrought on them both directly and indirectly. Therefore, when Tamir Rice, Michael Brown, Sandra Bland, Korryn Gaines, and numerous black people are shot and killed by police, this is violence not only wrought on the bodies of the deceased but on those of the black community. It is their immediate circle of concern that is always being ruptured by violence, and it is this constant break that manifests anger and its sometimes subsequent unrest. Here the riot becomes a tactic of the oppressed crying to be heard.

The use of "tactic" is derived from the work of Michel de Certeau who, in the "Making Do: Uses and Tactics" chapter of *The Practice of Everyday Life*, employs the concept of strategies and tactics to discuss how individuals navigate structures. De Certeau sets up a demarcation between strategies used by the powerful and tactics used by the weak when he states that the space of the tactic is the space of the *other* and the art of the weak.[28] He dictates that tactics, particularly of consumption, are "the ingenious ways in which the weak make use of the strong," which "thus lend a political dimension to everyday practices."[29] While rioting is not to be conceived as an everyday practice, it is one in which the weak make use of the strong's power and access, particularly in those instances where the weak are dispossessed of economic power, such as Malcolm X indicates in "After the Fire," or they experience a communal violation such as in Ferguson, Missouri. Therefore, the person who takes up rioting as a tactic is doing so against those in positions of power in order to exert power through an expression of anger.

In "In Defense of the Ferguson Riots," Robert Stephens II states that the riot, like other forms of political action, can build solidarity. Speaking specifically about the unrest in Ferguson he says, "They [riots] can create strong feelings of common identity. The outrage in Ferguson quickly attracted marginalized people through the region. Rather than evidence of illegitimacy, the presence of these 'outsiders' reflected the magnetic power of the political moment."[30] The "outsiders" that Stephens refers to are the marginalized people who mobilized and turned their anger into a political moment, communicating a message to other marginalized people as well as to their oppressors. This political moment connects others and encourages them to express their anger either inside or outside of the moment of the riot. Furthermore, this moment turns the outsider into an insider in a community of people with a common concern for their liberation. This vision of rioting moves the consciousness of the political action from pure violence to political gathering of a concerned community. The riots in Ferguson highlight not only the community's concern for their safety in light of another episode of police brutality but also the history of a community that has been economically disenfranchised. Therefore, participation in oppositional political struggle is participation by and on behalf of the perceived least of these, a cause that one ought to call positive and morally praiseworthy.

Fifty Years Mediating Riots

In the introduction we highlighted Martin Luther King Jr.'s quote "A riot is the language of the unheard," and here we return to it at length to analyze precisely how King can be read as supporting the affective value of rioting as a necessary practice. On September 27, 1966, following a summer of protests and race riots, King appeared on *60 Minutes* for an interview with journalist Mike Wallace. This was the occasion for the often-cited quote, "A riot is the language of the unheard," which has been invoked by those defending riots as a sound political tactic against oppression and injustice as well as those who discourage the tactic because of how they understand King's statement. King, a proponent of nonviolence, opposed rioting and said as much when he declared riots self-defeating and socially destructive. Yet King also recognized the root of riots, and this is what prompted his statement that a riot is the language of the unheard. Of this he said: "Now I contend that the cry of 'black power' is, at bottom, a reaction to the reluctance of white power to make the kind of changes necessary to make justice a reality for the Negro. I think we've got to see that a riot is the language of the unheard. And what is it that America has failed to hear? It has failed to hear that the economic plight of the Negro poor has worsened over the last few years."[31]

Set against the backdrop of a summer of fires that landed him in front of a white reporter to be the mouthpiece for black America, King proclaims that the root cause of the riots is the precarious socioeconomic situation of black people in the 1960s. Here the riot is not only an emotional reaction to oppression but also a form of speech to be heard. Given a charitable hermeneutic, King's words of the riot as a cry of the unheard could be interpreted as suspending understanding of the riot as strictly a violent phenomenon and instead positioning it as a tactical political response to injustice. This permits King to communicate an understanding of why those in the midst of systemic oppression take up rioting but allows him to also hold that in tension with his own principles of nonviolence. Yet, in his closing statements on rioting, he hopes rioting could be avoided, while indicating the necessity of militancy and determination for the summers to come if oppressive circumstances were not resolved. Here it is clear that, although he does not agree with the executed tactic of the riot as taken up by the oppressed, he has regard for its militant and determined quality as a productive characteristic of the oppressed person's action in the world.

Nearly fifty years to the day of King's interview with Wallace, the Reverend Dr. William Barber II, former president of the North Carolina NAACP, wrote an editorial for NBCNews.com in which he responded to the civil unrest that broke out following the shooting of Keith Lamont Scott. Barber writes, "The riots in Charlotte are the predictable response of human beings who are drowning in systemic injustice. We must all pray that no one else gets hurt. But we must understand why this is happening."[32] Similar to King, Barber withdraws from the immediate framing of rioting as violent phenomena in order to draw attention to its root cause. Barber's referring to the riot as a "predictable response" indicates that rioting is among a set of expected responses to systemic injustice. Therefore, Barber's use of "predictable response" is on par with the historical reality of the riot as response to injustice. Also similar to King, Barber is not condoning riots; he is reiterating the conditions under which riots occur. Barber also concludes his statement on the riots by offering hope that alternate means can be used. His alternative means lie in voting and in what he perceives as the productive power of casting a ballot for candidates who have citizens' best interests in mind. In the September 22, 2016, article, he says, "This week our decision is as clear as ever: it's the ballot or the riot. We who believe in the possibility of democracy must mobilize to vote like never before." Barber can be interpreted as implying that rioting is antidemocratic, and, indeed, the riot positions itself as against the democratic process in which people gather in an orderly fashion to reach a consensus about political matters. On the other hand, the riot is increasingly becoming a tactic of the *demos* to gain leverage in a society that consistently refuses to hear their cries and is becoming accustomed to their "predictable response."

Roughly fifty years apart, these two influential black Christian leaders have something to tell us about rioting. At once they hold in tension their view of the problem and the promise of rioting. The problem is that it drives people to act in ways that are perceived as "self-defeating," "socially destructive," and against the democratic process. The promise is that the "acting out" involved in rioting as articulated by King and Barber adds qualification to the political expression of anger as an appropriate response to oppression and injustice by the oppressed. Barber and King provide insight into the riot as not only pure manifestation of frustration and anger but also the cyclical culminating response to perpetual systemic oppression.

King and Barber stand as mediators between those dispossessed of power and those who possess power, and their mediation makes rioting as a tactic of political resistance legible and heard language. This mediated communication helps to acknowledge the riot as a tactic of the weak, but it can also swallow the weak and their anger whole as the riot goes from being "the language of the unheard" to "a predictable response." Thus, where this mediation of rioting by Christian figures and the media falters, we center the political resister whose expression of anger leads to rioting as one who has the potential to be a moral agent for change. We claim this because of the ways in which the political resister's participation in riots and other activities of oppositional political struggle promotes their concern for a broader community, which opens up the possibility for flourishing. This is particularly important as we press against the conception of flourishing as bound to individual welfare over securing the well-being of a community.

Toward a More Inclusive, Attainable Flourishing

Eudaimonia, or human flourishing, is a central concept in the field of virtue ethics. As Tessman explains, virtue ethicists typically answer the question of "how should one live?" by asserting that "one should live so as to flourish in a fully human way, where the human way of flourishing is understood to be constituted, at least partially, by an exercise of the virtues."[33] However, like constructions of virtue or expressions of anger, conceptions of flourishing are culturally and socially particular. Consequently, to assess the relationship between rioting and flourishing requires interrogating how one perceives flourishing. Even more, it requires looking closely at who is able to flourish, who is barred from flourishing, and why.

This essay's examination of flourishing draws on Tessman as a primary interlocutor because her writing illuminates, first, how varying perceptions of flourishing exist and, further, how one's perception of flourishing will shape how one responds to or lives in the midst of oppressive conditions. In particular, as Tessman acknowledges the disconnect between Aristotle's more exclusive, privileged vision of society and her own liberatory aims, she reveals how some conceptions of flourishing allow for and help to sustain systemic oppressions. This is a key concern motivating this essay: To what extent does *eudaimonia* presume conditions of privilege and remain inaccessible to systematically oppressed people? What needs to shift, in both our theorizing and our living, for human flourishing to become more widely attainable?

Tessman's own account of flourishing slides between acknowledging the cultural particularity of flourishing and relying on a more general conception. She tries to avoid both "a universal account of human flourishing" and a "relativist or subjectivist acceptance of just about any version of flourishing that someone might adopt for her/himself."[34] Her argument implies that there should be freedom for members of a democratic, pluralistic society to hold diverging conceptions of the good life.[35] At the same time, she is wary of contemporary ethical approaches that reduce *eudaimonia* to an individualistic, subjective account of one's own happiness or self-interest.[36] This wariness is most apparent when she turns her attention to the privileged members of socially dominant groups, to argue that these people, too—despite their apparent happiness and access to the "good life"—nonetheless fail to flourish if they do not cultivate a moral goodness that benefits others as well as themselves. To construct this argument, Tessman draws on Aristotle's understanding of *eudaimonia*, which not only includes virtue as a necessary component but also is premised on the idea that humans are interdependent, and so practicing other-regarding virtues will generally also benefit oneself, at least in the context of a successful social collectivity.[37]

At this point, however, Tessman critically departs from Aristotle's thinking. For Aristotle, that social collectivity was the polis, which, as Tessman acknowledges, was "notoriously exclusive," omitting women, slaves, most foreigners, and probably landless laborers. Within the polis, the possibility of attaining *eudaimonia* was a privilege limited to leisured adult Greek males. Furthermore, the flourishing of one such privileged member of the polis did not require the flourishing of all people; it required only the flourishing of other privileged members. Tessman paints a damning picture of Aristotelian *eudaimonia* as compatible with sexism, economic exploitation, xenophobia, ethnocentrism, and modern ideologies of racism—in other words, "compatible with an utter lack of concern for the wellbeing of those who have relatively little social, economic and political power."[38] This is similar, she argues, to how contemporary privileged people often pursue our own flourishing: by extending concern for the well-being of those positioned similarly to ourselves, thereby preserving the illusion of our own virtuous character while remaining ignorant of and indifferent toward the ways our privileged position is actively maintained by the exploitation and suffering of others.[39]

This point in Tessman's writing best illuminates the significance of varying interpretations of flourishing. Some theories and practices of *eudaimonia* are explicitly exclusive, functioning as ideology of the powerful. This is hardly the moral goodness Tessman wants to promote. She tries to revise Aristotle's eudaemonism by substituting a broadly inclusive social collectivity for his limited, privileged polis. In her reading, genuine moral goodness (and hence flourishing) requires pursuing the welfare not simply of oneself and a few particular others but also of those most excluded and subordinated by oppression.

Ultimately, rather than rejecting eudaemonism outright as an idealized theory in the service of oppression, Tessman argues for a *non-ideal* eudaemonistic virtue ethics. In this non-ideal eudaemonism, she continues "to posit flourishing in a fully human way (a way that involves an exercise of the virtues) as the central normative value," yet she also assumes such flourishing to be "largely unattainable" under conditions of oppression, due to the barriers oppression creates through moral damage and adverse external circumstances.[40]

For Tessman, the value of this non-ideal theory is that it serves to illuminate "how deeply depriving, damaging, and dehumanizing oppression can be" as well as offer a more realistic portrait of the complications of moral life. But as she also acknowledges, this theory yields a dismal, frustrating, perhaps despair-inducing conclusion: that oppressed people, no matter their striving, will typically be unable to achieve the ideal of flourishing to which they have a legitimate claim.[41] This prompts us to ask: is such an "unattainable" flourishing simply another version of *eudaimonia* as privilege? Tessman's commitment to anti-oppression analysis is clear, yet it is difficult to see how her call to keep practicing an admittedly "absurd" exercise of virtue can offer a potent paradigm for achieving liberation or social change.

At other points in her writing on virtue and flourishing, however, Tessman suggests more nuanced and varying possibilities. This is most apparent when she delineates different categories of "burdened virtues," revealing that, while each of these virtues is costly to the bearer, the burdened virtues are not all equally unlinked from the possibility of flourishing. Most relevant to this essay are the traits Tessman labels as v_3, which are cultivated to enable and sustain struggle and resistance to oppression. In the face of injustice, these traits—such as unrelenting anger or rage—may be judged the most morally apt response and may well be better than their alternatives, such as self-hatred or resigned acceptance of injustice.

Notably, while Tessman declares this trait v_3 as "not conducive to or constitutive of anyone's flourishing at present," she does recognize that such a trait tends "to enable its bearer to perform actions with the aim of eventually making flourishing lives more possible overall (for the bearer of trait v_3 and/ or others)."[42] So here, instead of positing flourishing as simply "unattainable," Tessman leaves open the possibility (though by no means guaranteed) that exercising particular burdened virtues may result in flourishing if that exercise contributes to ending the oppressive conditions currently blocking flourishing. In addition, this point highlights how an individual's flourishing may not always align with communal flourishing or the flourishing of later generations. At times an activist chooses the latter over the former, though arguably this is not as complete an "unlinking" from flourishing as Tessman's non-ideal eudaemonism might imply.

Is it possible that rioting might fit within this category of v_3 burdened virtues? In other words, could rioting represent a form of moral agency and action that is, if not directly constitutive of flourishing, at least linked to the possibility of eventual flourishing? How one answers this question, of course, will depend both on one's conception of flourishing and on how open one is to perceiving rioting as a potentially effective tactic for resisting oppression and demanding change. In this essay, we have laid out a case for framing rioting in these terms. Still, we recognize that, for some readers, this reframing may represent a paradigm shift as marked as reframing anger—or unctuousness, or orneriness—as virtue.

As coauthors, we have wrestled with this question of rioting as flourishing, sometimes disagreeing with each other, sometimes shifting in our own positions over time. We have become increasingly open to the possibility that rioting, when practiced as a tactic of resistance to political and economic oppression, may be a means toward flourishing. Even more, we are convinced that anger is a morally needed response to injustice and that hearing the rage of the rioter is necessary to flourishing. We advocate that more people get uncomfortable and unlink themselves from the virtues that keep them in the individual safe house of flourishing and instead hitch themselves to the wagon of expressed anger. This may lead to participation in rioting or less respectable means of political resistance, but we contend that unless all share the "burdened virtues," none will flourish. This is the difference between a flourishing trapped in the vacuum of individualistic virtue and that of flourishing contingent on communal solidarity. If more of us would be willing to take up the "burdened virtue" of outrage at injustice, perhaps this would hasten the dismantling of systems of domination and exploitation, making a fuller flourishing more attainable to all.

Notes

1. For a succinct recounting of the shooting, the controversy surrounding it, and the community, police, and legal responses that unfolded over the ensuing months, see the *New York Times* Q&A piece "What Happened in Ferguson?," August 13, 2014, updated August 10, 2015, http://www.nytimes.com/interactive/2014/08/13/us/ferguson-missouri-town-under-siege-after-police-shooting.html?_r=0.

2. For an overview of some of this public commentary on the rioting in Ferguson, see Jermaine M. McDonald, "Ferguson and Baltimore according to Dr. King: How Competing Interpretations of King's Legacy Frame the Public Discourse on Black Lives Matter," *Journal of the Society of Christian Ethics* 36, no. 2 (2016): 141–58. McDonald offers perceptive analysis of how Dr. King's statements and convictions have been variously leveraged in this public discourse.

3. Amy Goodman, interview with Osagyefo Sekou and Jelani Cobb, "Riot as the Language of the Unheard: Ferguson Protests Set to Continue in Fight for Racial Justice," DemocracyNow.org, November 25, 2015, http://www.democracynow.org/2014/11/25/riot_as_the_language_of_the.

4. Martin Luther King Jr., "The Role of the Behavioral Scientist in the Civil Rights Movement," *Journal of Social Issues* 24, no. 1 (1968), reprinted in the *APA Monitor* 30, no. 1 (1999).

5. Nancy E. Snow, "Virtue and the Oppression of Women," in *Feminist Moral Philosophy*, ed. Samantha Brennan, *Canadian Journal of Philosophy* S28 (Calgary: University of Calgary Press, 2002), 34.

6. Vic McCracken, ed., *Christian Faith and Social Justice: Five Views* (New York: Bloomsbury, 2014). This volume is structured as a debate between five Christian approaches to justice, including liberation theology and virtue ethics. For the purposes of this essay, we focus narrowly on liberationist (and liberative feminist) critiques of virtue ethics. A fuller portrait of virtue ethics may be gained by also reading virtue ethicist Elizabeth Phillips's contributions to *Christian Faith and Social Justice: Five Views*, ed. Vic McCracken (New York: Bloomsbury, 2014). Notably, as a virtue ethicist, Phillips critiques liberation theology on certain points, yet, overall, she demonstrates more appreciation than wariness toward liberationist perspectives, and she does not perceive these two approaches as necessarily in opposition.

7. Miguel De La Torre, "Liberation Theology and Social Justice: A Defense," in *Christian Faith and Social Justice: Five Views*, ed. Vic McCracken (New York: Bloomsbury, 2014), 91.

8. Miguel De La Torre, "Virtue Ethics: A Liberationist Response," in *Christian Faith and Social Justice: Five Views*, ed. Vic McCracken (New York: Bloomsbury, 2014), 166, 169.

9. Laura Stivers, "Virtue Ethics: A Feminist Response," in *Christian Faith and Social Justice: Five Views*, ed. Vic McCracken (New York: Bloomsbury, 2014), 171.

10. Katie Geneva Cannon, *Katie's Canon: Womanism and the Soul of the Black Community* (New York: Continuum, 1995), 58.

11. Ibid., 91, 92.

12. Emilie Townes, "Colored Orneriness: A Concerto in Four Movements," Parks-King Lecture at Yale Divinity School, February 23, 2016, http://www.youtube.com/watch?v=IN136LEn-_8.

13. Macalester Bell, "Anger, Virtue, and Oppression," in *Feminist Ethics and Social and Political Philosophy: Theorizing the Non-Ideal*, ed. Lisa Tessman (New York: Springer, 2009), 167.

14. Ibid., 177, italics original.

15. Lisa Tessman, "Feminist Eudaimonism: Eudaimonism as Non-Ideal Theory," in *Feminist Ethics and Social and Political Philosophy: Theorizing the Non-Ideal*, ed. Lisa Tessman (New York: Springer, 2009), 52.

16. Lisa Tessman, *Burdened Virtues: Virtue Ethics for Liberatory Struggles* (New York: Oxford University Press, 2005), 107.

17. Ibid., 130.

18. This definition is a synthesis of the 18 US Code 2102, which states that a riot is a public disturbance involving acts of violence by one or more persons, part of an assemblage of three or more persons which act or acts shall constitute a clear and present danger of, or shall result in, damage or injury to the property of any other person or to the person of any other individual. 18 US Code § 2102—Definitions, Legal Information Institute, accessed November 20, 2016, https://www.law.cornell.edu/uscode/text/18/2102.

19. Alain Badiou, *The Rebirth of History* (New York: Verso, 2012), 22.

20. Ibid., 22–25.

21. Ibid., 33–35.

22. Ibid.

23. Malcolm X and George Breitman, *Malcolm X Speaks: Selected Speeches and Statements* (New York: Grove Weidenfeld, 1990), 167.

24. Natasha Lennard, "The Ferguson Riots Are Not a Shift away from Peace, They're a Challenge to Violence," *VICE News*, August 12, 2014, https://news.vice.com/article/the-ferguson-riots-are-not-a-shift-away-from-peace-theyre-a-challenge-to-violence.

25. Aristotle, *Rhetoric*, book 2, chap. 2, http://www.perseus.tufts.edu/hopper/text?doc=Perseus%3Atext%3A1999.01.0060%3Abook%3D2%3Achapter%3D2.

26. Tessman, *Burdened Virtues*, 122.

27. Joshua Clover, *Riot. Strike. Riot: The New Era of Uprisings* (New York: Verso, 2016), 39.

28. Michel de Certeau, *The Practice of Everyday Life* (Berkeley: University of California Press, 2008), 37.

29. Michel de Certeau, Luce Giard, and Pierre Mayol, *Arts de faire* (Paris: Gallimard, 1998), xvii.

30. Robert Stephens II, "In Defense of the Ferguson Riots," *Jacobin Magazine*, August 14, 2014, https://www.jacobinmag.com/2014/08/in-defense-of-the-ferguson-riots/.

31. "Mike Wallace Interview with Martin Luther King Jr.," *CBS Reports*, September 27, 1966, http://www.cbsnews.com/news/mlk-a-riot-is-the-language-of-the-unheard/.

32. William J. Barber, "Editorial: Charlotte Is Drowning in Systematic Injustice," *NBCNews.com*, September 22, 2016, http://www.nbcnews.com/news/nbcblk/editorial-charlotte-drowning-systematic-injustice-n652541.

33. Tessman, "Feminist Eudaimonism," 47.

34. Tessman, *Burdened Virtues*, 51n15.

35. Ibid., 60.

36. Tessman distinguishes her own approach from those virtue ethicists who theorize flourishing as what is "beneficial to a self-interested individual . . . who is also assumed to subjectively determine what will count as happiness in an assessment of his/her own life."

See Lisa Tessman, "On (Not) Living the Good Life," *Canadian Journal of Philosophy* 32 (supplement vol. 28, 2002): 3–32, at 10.

37. Tessman traces this argument in her essay "On (Not) Living," then offers a version of this argument in chapter 3 of *Burdened Virtues*, "The Ordinary Vices of Domination."

38. Tessman, "On (Not) Living," 29–30.

39. See ibid., 30; and Tessman, *Burdened Virtues*, 77.

40. Tessman, "Feminist Eudaimonism," 54, 51.

41. Ibid., 55–56.

42. Tessman, *Burdened Virtues*, 165.

Resisting the Devil's Instruments: Early Modern Resistance Theory for Late Modern Times

David P. Henreckson

In the midst of religious conflict in the late sixteenth and early seventeenth centuries, a number of prominent Protestant theologians and lawyers wrote on the collective moral obligation to resist systemic injustice. My essay focuses on Johannes Althusius, who offers a theological account of the political community and its obligation to preserve the common good and resist injustice. Thinking alongside Althusius, I will consider not only the conditions that may prompt acts of resistance but also the lawful means and ends of resistance. In other words, how might resistance be carried out rightly? By whom? And to what end? Finally, I argue that we have good reasons to use Althusius's political thought to revive an account of resistance that is internal to the Christian theological tradition—an account that relies on a broader conception of divine justice, covenantal responsibility, and mutual accountability.

THE GOD OF THE EARLY MODERN REFORMED TRADITION HAS sometimes been described as a Leviathan: all-powerful, unaccountable, and utterly free in his dealings with humanity. His chief end is the increase of his own glory. His covenants are made apart from any prior recognition of goodness or merit, depending solely on his sovereign whim. The political theorist Carl Schmitt, in one of his lesser-known works, went so far as to link the rise of covenant theology in the Reformed tradition with the political absolutism of Thomas Hobbes's famously controversial treatise *Leviathan*. According to Schmitt—who is not alone in this judgment—what the early modern absolutists and the early modern Calvinists share is a commitment to the raw, absolute, unqualified, and unchecked power of the sovereign, whether human or divine. To put it in simple terms, the divine Leviathan of the Calvinists begat the human Leviathan of the early modern nation-state.[1]

This narrative, in my judgment, is both too tidy and too provincial to be true. I have addressed the historical inaccuracy of this interpretation elsewhere.[2]

David Henreckson, PhD, is assistant professor of theology at Dordt College, 498 4th Ave. NE, Sioux Center, IA 51250; dhenreckson@dordt.edu.

Journal of the Society of Christian Ethics, 38, 1 (2018): 43–57

At present, my focus is more direct and limited. My first aim in this essay is to show that there is a prominent strand of early Reformed thought that runs directly contrary to the absolutist narrative we have received from Schmitt and others. In fact, I argue that it is the early Reformed tradition, represented here by the important but neglected figure of Johannes Althusius, that gives us one of the earliest examples of a radical, modern, and theological defense of collective political resistance to unjust power.[3]

My second aim is to show how this early modern Protestant tradition offers resources to analyze not only the conditions that prompt acts of resistance but also the lawful means and ends of resistance. In other words, how might resistance be carried out rightly? By whom? And to what end?

My final aim is less historical and more constructive. Many recent works in political theology and Christian ethics invoke the theme of resistance as central to the work of social criticism. However, many of these accounts reflect the disciplinary influence of recent social theory rather than theological ethics. As a result, they sometimes lack the orienting normative concerns that have historically motivated Christian ethicists and moral theologians. I wish to use the resources of Althusius's political thought and this neglected radical strand of the Protestant tradition to revive an account of resistance that is internal to the Christian theological tradition—an account that relies on a broader conception of divine justice, covenantal responsibility, and mutual accountability. Simply put, Althusius and his contemporaries can offer us something that social theorists like Walter Benjamin, Michel Foucault, and Judith Butler—for all their insights—cannot: an account of radical politics that is both theologically rich and historically grounded in the Protestant tradition.

The Problem of Resistance

In the Christian tradition, theological reflection on the possibility of political resistance to injustice extends back at least to Thomas Aquinas and Augustine, not to mention the ancient and late antique sources that informed their views. Sketched in very broad terms, the premodern theological tradition acknowledged that all political authority derives from God, following Paul's argument in the locus classicus of Romans 13. "Political powers do not bear the sword for no reason," and Christian subjects have a divine mandate to obey them. At the same time, premodern theologians were fully aware of exceptional cases. Tyrants, demagogues, and oligarchs are not a modern invention, of course. What should Christians do when confronted by tyrants and their perverted systems of governance? Premodern theologians argued that, while political subjects are generally obligated to obey the command of a political superior as if it came from God, the command is morally binding only if it is just and lawful. A magistrate's command to commit theft, murder, or any other act prohibited by the moral law must not be obeyed. In this sense, what I will call a passive or indirect form of resistance would be considered legitimate. Aquinas even goes so far as to suggest the legitimacy of some sort of political resistance to tyranny: "A tyrannical government is not just, because it is directed, not to the common good, but to the private good of the ruler. . . . Consequently, there is no sedition in disturbing a government of this kind."[4] Aquinas does not, however, provide an account of the mechanism for popular resistance, nor does he articulate a doctrine of popular sovereignty that would support such a collective undertaking.[5]

If we look ahead to the first and second generation of Protestant reformers, we can find this account (which I am generically calling the premodern view) well represented among the leading Protestant theologians. For instance, like Aquinas and other premoderns, John Calvin allows that Christians might resist an unjust authority through indirect means. They might call on lesser magistrates to intervene on their behalf. They might repent of whatever sin prompted God to judge them with the scourge of tyranny in the first place. They might flee the country (this was of course a common occurrence during the religious wars of the sixteenth century). Or they might simply choose not to obey the unjust command and prepare themselves for the consequences. Still, Calvin thinks the subject may not actively, or directly, resist the office of civil rule itself. To resist directly, by force of arms, would be to upset the whole order of divine-human governance. This sort of action would be an impiety that welcomes chaos.[6]

According to Calvin and the premodern tradition, therefore, a Christian subject might choose not to obey an unjust command, and she might choose not to participate in an unjust political system, but she would have no means to chasten or contest the system itself. This sort of resistance to structural sins and injustice is prohibited. The sword belongs to the divinely appointed human sovereign, who alone is the agent of divine wrath and justice.

An Early Modern Solution to the Problem of Resistance

By the turn of the seventeenth century, many Reformed thinkers had become discontent with a merely indirect doctrine of resistance. The reasons for this shift are many, but one of the most important turning points was the massacre of thousands—perhaps tens of thousands—of French Protestants in the weeks following St. Bartholomew's Day in 1572. Suspicions ran deep that members of the French royal family were involved in plotting the horrific event. The historians Harro Höpfl and Martyn Thompson mark the massacre as the pivotal moment that forced early Protestant political thinkers to develop a more comprehensive doctrine of resistance centered on the theological concepts of covenant and contract.[7] Prior to the massacre, leading Protestants had hoped to persuade the French royal family to embrace a policy of toleration. Theodore Beza, Calvin's successor in Geneva, appeared repeatedly before the French court over many years, pleading the Huguenot cause in the face of what he saw as unjust persecution: "Sire, it belongs to the Church of God, in whose name I speak, to endure blows and not to inflict them. But it will also please your Majesty to remember that she is an anvil that has worn out many hammers."[8] Beza's metaphor has an ominous subtlety about it, but even this threat of divine vengeance rang hollow in the aftermath of the massacre. An indirect doctrine of resistance no longer sufficed. As Höpfl puts it, the massacre in 1572 "effectively meant the end of the project for an evangelical conversion of the whole of France: the issue now was survival."[9]

Reformed thinkers such as Beza, and later Althusius, began asking whether there might be certain unjust actions that a political ruler could commit that would not only negate any moral obligations to obey her command but also—if sufficiently unjust or impious—divest her of office. And if there were such acts, how would we recognize them?

Beza attempted to answer these questions in his treatise *On the Right of Magistrates*, written soon after the St. Bartholomew's Day massacre. Following the premodern tradition before him, Beza claimed that whenever a political ruler issues an immoral command, one that directs his subjects to commit injustice or impiety, the command lacks binding force. Up to this point, we have not progressed any further than Aquinas, Calvin, and the preceding theological tradition.

However, Beza then goes on to criticize absolutist theorists—that is, proponents of arbitrary and absolute power—arguing that they "so far exalt the authority of kings and supreme rulers as to dare maintain that they have no other judge but God alone to whom they have to render account (*rationem reddere*) of their deeds."[10] In other words, the absolutists acknowledge that princes may sin and perpetrate injustice in the political community, but they assume that only God has the authority and agency to chasten and correct an unbridled magistrate. The people may pray for divine help. They may call on other political powers to intervene. But that is all. Beza, however, is not content to leave it at this. In fact, he thinks that the idea that an unjust magistrate is answerable only to God is utter folly and impiety. So he asks his readers: "Is there no other remedy for injustice?"[11]

Both Beza and Althusius believe that other remedies do exist, and that these remedies may be not merely permissible but even at times obligatory. Beza answers his own question directly: "I deny that . . . it [is] illicit for a people oppressed by obvious tyranny to protect themselves from their enemy by just remedies, in addition to prayer and penitence."[12] What these just remedies are, beyond seeking the help of other civil or foreign magistrates, is not always clear. What is significant, though, is the fact that Beza reclassifies the unjust magistrate as the "enemy" of the oppressed people. By retitling the person who formerly held the office of "prince" as an "enemy," Beza has found a way around the received interpretation of Romans 13 and other scriptural texts that require Christians to obey political authorities. Christian subjects should of course obey their princes and kings, Beza argues, but why should they be expected to obey their enemies?

Beza does not provide much detail about how to identify the moment at which a legitimate prince becomes a tyrannical adversary. However, if we now turn to Johannes Althusius, we can find a thoroughly theological answer to Beza's question. First, however, recall the precise terms of Beza's criticism of his absolutist rivals. Proponents of absolute power argued that earthly princes were accountable only to God. No matter how heinous the offense, only the divine sovereign may call earthly rulers to account. Beza suggests that this is a false, perhaps even impious, doctrine; however, he does not offer an extensive alternative account. Althusius does.

In his most influential work, a treatise titled *Politica Methodice Digesta*, Althusius picks up the thread of Beza's argument.[13] When the absolutists claim that earthly princes are accountable only to God, Althusius argues, they offer us a false hierarchy of political relations. According to the absolutists, the prince owes obedience to God, as do the people, but both parties are "debtors to God alone." In other words, there is no covenantal accountability horizontally, between earthly rulers and the people—only vertically, between the divine sovereign and the earthly ruler.[14]

According to Althusius, who follows Beza in this regard, this is an unjust and even impious political doctrine. Drawing on his own Reformed theological tradition, Althusius argues that God enters into a mutual covenant with *both* the prince and the people. All are unified in the same covenantal fellowship; therefore, within the terms of this fellowship, the prince and the people are also obligated to render justice to each other and to God for the sake of the common good. In other words, the people have at least as much of a stake in the political covenant as the prince. The people, alongside the prince, are codebtors before God, responsible for pursuing justice in the political community.[15]

But exactly *how* might the political community go about identifying what this justice looks like? What is the standard for right relations between the political ruler and his subjects? Althusius's initial answer is deeply theological and also runs quite to the contrary of the stereotyped picture of the Calvinist God offered by Schmitt and others. He argues, if we want to distinguish just from unjust political relationships, we must look to the paradigmatic relationship between the divine sovereign and his creatures. God is the perfectly good lawgiver who issues directives for the well-being—or salvation—of his people. The terms of this relationship find their rationale in the faithful love of the sovereign for his people and their fulfillment, first, in the people's recognition of God's goodness and, second, in their reciprocating love for God and neighbor. God would not, and in fact could not, be unfaithful or unjust to his beloved people. Althusius applies this point to the political order by means of an a fortiori argument: if even God, who is all-powerful, cannot sin by acting against what is just in relation to his creatures, how much more is the earthly ruler bound to this standard?[16] No just power can be absolute. No good power can be arbitrary.

What happens then if a prince acts unjustly, breaks covenant, and the prayers and patience of the people go unanswered? What happens when power-hungry popes, priests, oligarchs, and magistrates arbitrarily dominate their subjects, destroying the proper goods and fellowship that individuals ought to be able to enjoy together? The conditions are such that the social bonds that ought to provide for the mutual enjoyment and communication of goods no longer exist. Althusius, like Beza, names this condition as tyranny.

Here, at last, we arrive at Althusius's primary innovation, the point at which he is willing to go beyond what I have termed the doctrine of indirect resistance that had long been part of the premodern theological tradition. In effect, Althusius identifies the *people* themselves—and not their rulers and magistrates—as the principal human party of the covenant, the party who bears the primary responsibility for preserving right order. As a collective, covenanted body, the people have authority—given to them by God himself—to hold tyrannical princes to account. They may hold an unjust ruler responsible, name his sins publicly, call for repentance, and even authorize public "vindicators" to mount an armed resistance to an "incurable" tyrant. According to these terms, magistrates and rulers are merely administrators or stewards of the political community and its common goods. And as administrators, they may be deposed as the people see fit.

This new conception of popular political agency carries with it a rather strenuous moral obligation: we are all mutually bound to seek the common good and to challenge those figures or institutions that break covenant and twist our shared forms of life toward unjust ends. In fact, Althusius claims, the people—as codebtor before God—are "held responsible for the fault" of the prince and "[share] his sins" if they do not hold the covenant-breaker accountable and "*resist* and *impede* him" so far as possible. God, the initiating party to the covenant, stands as vindicator: "He will cast Israel down because of the sins of Jeroboam."[17]

How to Recognize Tyranny

It is one thing to claim that it is legitimate for the people to resist an unjust ruler. It is another matter to have the practical wisdom to identify a tyrannical ruler and the forms of systemic injustice that give rise to such a figure. I noted in the previous section that Beza, Althusius, and others made a normative distinction between a true ruler and a tyrant.[18] Resistance is prohibited in the former case but permitted—potentially—in the latter.

For Althusius, as we have already seen in some detail, tyranny is defined as the contrary of just and morally upright political rule. In other words, it is the privation of good rule: "Through tyranny, the foundations and bonds (*vincula*) of the covenantal fellowship are obstinately, persistently, and incurably destroyed and overthrown, against the ruler's pledged faith and professed oath."[19] Althusius, like earlier proponents of resistance, denies that a ruler who perpetrates these tyrannical conditions is the sort of ruler that Paul has in mind in the epistle to the Romans. A tyrant is not a minister of God but is better described as an instrument of the devil (*sed diaboli instrumentum dicitur*).[20] What is owed to this sort of ruler?

For Althusius, this is not just a rhetorical question, and his answer is not as straightforward as we might have expected. We might expect Althusius to authorize any and all acts of resistance to someone he describes as diabolical. Or perhaps we might assume that the existence of tyranny puts an end to preexisting social commitments and moral norms, essentially authorizing popular revolution. But Althusius's answer is more complex.

In an appendix to the *Politica*, added in the second edition in 1610, Althusius analyzes the various species of tyrannical rule so that his readers can better identify the right response in particular cases. Tyrants may be instruments of the devil, but not all diabolical agents are the same, nor should they be resisted each in the same way. Here Althusius reminds his readers that not all failures or imperfections of rule are tantamount to tyranny—or, to be more precise, tyranny in its absolute or paradigmatic sense. In less extreme cases, Althusius cautions, virtuous citizens should not act rashly. Some rulers may be unjust in one aspect of their office but not others. Some rulers may suffer from a failure of will in performing their duties. And others may have started down a tyrannical path but may still be turned away from their destination by wise counselors. Many individual sins and imperfections can and should be tolerated in order to preserve political fellowship. Althusius draws an analogy between political and marital covenantal relationships: the individual sins of a magistrate do not necessarily abrogate his authority *in se*, "just as a marriage is not dissolved by every misdeed committed by one spouse against another, except for adultery, since this is directly contrary to the nature" of the fellowship.[21]

To determine the right responses to political injustice, therefore, we have to consider tyranny in its various forms. Borrowing from earlier Protestant and medieval sources, Althusius distinguishes between "fundamental" and "administrative" tyranny. The former concerns the foundational laws, religious oaths, and social bonds that make the community a cohesive political body.[22] We might describe this as constitutional tyranny, or tyranny in extremis, in which the tyrant breaks the oath she made to the political community—and to God—thereby destroying the social order and impeding the relevant public figures from the performance of their duties.[23] If a ruler were to commit treason, for instance, or plot against her own people, such actions would violate the very foundation of the political order.

The second form of tyranny concerns the unjust or impious administration of the community's goods. It is much more common and takes more complicated forms than the first. In this species of tyranny, the ruler is still technically fulfilling his office, serving as administrator of the goods of society, but doing so in a perverse way—at the expense of his people. The improper administration of goods might be general in nature, as in the exercise of absolute power, or more specific. Althusius here provides a catalog of vices and behaviors that characterize this latter form of administrative tyranny. This catalog provides examples to help his readers recognize injustice when it is cloaked under some other description. Among other things, the tyrant is one who corrupts social practices, luxuriates in material comforts at public cost, permits crimes to go unpunished, and nourishes factions and wars to weaken the collective strength of his subjects.[24] If this list sounds familiar to us today, Althusius would not be surprised: tyranny is a perennial condition that encroaches wherever a community has become vicious or unvigilant.

Identifying Tyranny's Remedies

Besides articulating the distinction between a true ruler and a tyrant, Althusius and others made a second breakthrough in early modern political thought: a new conception of popular political agency, supported by a theological account of divine power and goodness. The political community, as a whole, is authorized by God to hold the ruler to account. It may recognize certain persons, whether individual magistrates or an authorized assembly, as "public" figures with the authority to resist the unjust actions of a tyrant.

At the beginning of this essay, I noted that the premodern theological tradition had the resources to distinguish between just rule and tyrannical rule, even allowing that it may be permissible for someone—it is not entirely clear who—to contest the latter. However, the premodern theological tradition did not offer an explicit account of how legitimate acts of resistance might be carried out, nor did it have a doctrine of popular political agency—as Althusius does—which would authorize the political community to engage in these acts.

While I have argued that Althusius and many of his Protestant peers did make political and theological advances on these points, we still need to consider the mechanisms for resistance. In other words, how might a people go about resisting a tyrant and various forms of structural injustice? More precisely, how might a people resist tyranny in a just and righteous manner so they do not fall prey to the temptations of absolute and arbitrary power?

Early modern theologians like Althusius and Beza were fully conscious of the temptations that often accompany acts of social and political resistance. The tyrant is an existential threat to the political community, but some acts of resistance may themselves threaten to undermine the common good of fellowship if carried out imprudently, rashly, or maliciously. Oftentimes it is better to endure unjust conditions in patient hope that acts of forbearance, rather than resistance, may better serve the common good of the community. If we resist wrongly, social trust breaks down, and the fellowship we hoped to preserve may instead wither away through our rashness.[25]

With these temptations in mind, it is important to consider the practicalities of resistance—a moral task that the early modern Protestants took quite seriously. This involves considering a series of practical, prudential questions of the following sort: Is this the right time or place to resist? What sort of resistance is called for? Will an act of resistance result in greater injustice than the present circumstances? What previous commitments and promises are relevant? To resist lawfully, we must be ready to make judgments on these matters.

Here is it crucial to emphasize that, for Althusius and even the most radical of his Reformed contemporaries, acts of resistance do not occur in anything like a Schmittian state of exception. Preexisting moral norms are not suspended, nor are the principles, institutions, and communal bonds that made the political community something valuable in the first place. That is to say, acts of resistance are not acts of revolution but rather restoration. In fact, as I argue in the next section, acts of resistance may be judged as legitimate, in part, insofar as they aim at protecting the common good of fellowship in the community.

How, then, should we go about identifying the proper criteria of lawful resistance to various species of tyranny? To make these sorts of judgments, Althusius directs us toward a traditional form of moral inquiry: the criteria of lawful resistance are the *who, what, where, when,* and *why* of the action.[26] When considering the legitimacy of political resistance, as in traditional accounts of just war theory, each of these considerations bears on the rightness of the undertaking.

First, the *who*: there must be an authorized representative of the political community. Althusius, following Calvin and others, refers to this officer as an ephor, a lesser magistrate, or some authorized public agent. This public agent is someone who bears responsibility for resistance to injustice and to whom the people ought to join themselves, adding their own strength, resources, and counsel.[27] Here it is crucial to note that when Althusius restricts acts of resistance to this class of public agents, he is not explicitly identifying a particular legal or political office. He is referring, rather, to a general species of public office that holds the supreme ruler to account for his or her actions. This species of public office may occupy a different place in the social hierarchy across different constitutional systems.[28] In other words, the people may look to any number of public figures—a prince, a duke, a city elder, or any authorized assembly of the people—for vindication. The democratic implications of this last option may be more obvious to us than it was to Althusius, but it is worth underscoring.

Second, and immediately related to the first point, the *what* and *where*: jurisdiction matters when determining the right course of action. "What is to be done collectively by the public agents," Althusius argues, is best done through a deliberative process of mutual consent between the people and its authorized administrators. Deliberation must be careful, patient, and arrive at some sort of practical consensus. In other words, public figures must take care not to overstep their own authority and prosecute a tyrant in ways that go beyond their administrative purview or are disagreeable to the community's representatives.[29] In straightforward terms, this means that public administrators must not act "beyond the boundaries" of the scope or scale of their office. At the same time, Althusius's comments about jurisdiction reflect his belief that authoritative public action must arise from *within* the community. Correction and resistance are internal matters.

Third, the *when*: as the people go about identifying the right occasion to resist, and what measure of force should back up the act of resistance, several things must be considered. How serious and inflexible is the tyranny? Have all other remedies been exhausted? And how have the injustices of the tyrannical ruler been made public to the political community? On this final point, Althusius indicates that three forms of public recognition are central: recognition of tyranny's existence, its extent, and the means by which the tyrant has previously been challenged. This last point is crucial for Althusius since there must be a record of admonishment and public correction prior to any formal act of forcible resistance. If these conditions are satisfied, as I detailed earlier, the unjust ruler must be held to account. Ideally, the public agents will call an assembly, but if they fail to do so, Althusius grants that "public avengers and deliverers should be constituted ad hoc by the people itself."

Finally, the *why*: the rationale for lawful resistance is the restoration of fellowship. Althusius writes that a tyrant must be resisted so long as the unjust conditions endure, whether in words, deed, or dissembling, and so long as "he acts contrary to the declared covenant." On these terms, lawful acts of resistance must continue "until the republic is returned to its original condition."[30] The remedy of resistance aims at the restoration of health to the political body and perseveres until this end is accomplished. In other words, the people, having diagnosed the disease that plagues the body, may prescribe the appropriate remedy—even if that means deposing a tyrant, or calling for forcible resistance to unjust power.

Early Modern Resistance and Late Modern Problems

What does this mean for contemporary theological ethics? Are there reasons to view these early modern ideas as something more than just historical relics? Is there still life in these traditional, white, European, Calvinist bones?

I want to draw out two practical, and I think increasingly relevant, implications of early Reformed resistance theory for contemporary Christian ethics. The first implication concerns covenantal responsibility and arises out of Althusius's doctrine of mutual accountability. As I argued earlier, if we read Althusius carefully, we will encounter a strenuous moral exhortation: individuals cannot stand idly by when they witness systemic injustice in the church or political society. This may seem a trite moral maxim, easily endorsed by any right-thinking citizen. But I believe that Althusius's point runs deeper than this. He means to implicate us in the deepest, most complicated sins of our communities—simply by virtue of our membership in these communities. In effect, he tells us, insofar as you take yourself to be—and are recognized as—a member of a particular community, you bear a covenantal responsibility for its goods and ills, its virtues and vices, its justice and injustice. By participating in the life of whatever community you belong to (by choice or by birth), you are under a relentless obligation to seek its good and to ensure that other members of the community are able to do likewise.

We often fail to fulfill this obligation, and in multiple ways. It may be relatively easy to identify the occasions in which we fall short by actively committing injustice against a neighbor. It is more difficult, but no less important, to identify the occasions in which we sin not only by commission but also by omission: "by remaining silent, defaulting, dissembling, permitting, or enduring" the sins and crimes of an unjust ruler or institution. Again, he stresses, the obligation to resist injustice and to set things right obtains to the community as a whole. Factions or parties within the political community cannot simply shirk responsibility or shift blame to their rivals; all are codebtors before God. If anyone stands by while Jeroboam worships idols and slaughters the innocent, they partake in his sin—and his judgment. If we are truly going to claim popular political agency, we must also have a keen sense of our personal and collective responsibility for the shared life of the political community.

If Althusius is right about this, there are two related issues that must be addressed. First, acts of resistance must be regarded as internal to the community itself. In other words, resistance arises from within the community, for the sake of the community. Such acts may be regarded as righteous and just only if they are duly authorized, and this authorization comes from the political community that God has called into being. If someone claims to be a liberator but does not derive her authority from the community or make herself accountable to the community, she lacks the authority to act justly on its behalf. The second related issue regards complicated questions about self-identity, mutual recognition, and the status of liminal persons who may not be fully recognized—or valued—by the communities they find themselves in. Whose voice *counts* in the community? I raise this issue here not to solve it once and for all but rather to suggest that Althusius's discussion of broad-based political agency may be more democratic than he would have cared to admit. If everyone has a responsibility to care for the common good and to ensure that every other member of the community is also able to participate in this fellowship, then the boundaries of inclusion may be more expansive and more porous than Althusius himself may have realized. It is possible to see glimmers of this possibility in some surprising niches of Althusius's writings.[31] The work that remains for contemporary Christian ethicists is to make explicit what was only implicit in the best parts of this strand of early modern thought. Protestant political thought is not a closed canon, and the heirs of Augustine, Aquinas, Calvin, Beza, and Althusius should feel authorized to direct the tradition toward new places and to address questions that would not have occurred to their theological forebears.

There is a second implication of early modern resistance theory, which builds on the first. If the demanding responsibilities of political life are to be carried out faithfully, members of the community will need to find ways to cultivate a set of discrete political virtues to sustain these efforts. Early moderns like Althusius paid a great deal of attention to the virtues that must be in evidence among a people and its rulers if a republic is going to survive, let alone flourish. These virtues, Althusius argues, must be cultivated in homes, congregations, civic communities, and workplaces before they can do the work on a larger political or electoral stage. While it may seem quixotic to campaign on an exhortation to virtue—for good reason these days—I think Althusius is correct. Perhaps ironically, it is on this point that Althusius falls back on the wisdom of the ancients and the medievals: a rightly ordered republic, one in which all members are able to pursue the common good, needs virtuous citizens and exemplars. And what are some of these virtues? They include the prudence to recognize the difference between justice and injustice, the tolerance to live well with those we find objectionable, the piety to honor the people, institutions, and traditions that made us who we are, and the courage to sacrifice for the sake of fellowship and call tyrants to account.

It is also important to account for the flipside of this matter: all too often acts of resistance are undertaken by the vicious or those ill-equipped to rightly order the means and ends of these acts. Those lacking in prudence will misjudge their circumstances or the conditions needed for successful resistance. Those lacking the virtue of tolerance will not be prepared to respond appropriately to those actions or people they find objectionable. Those lacking in piety may become demagogues. Those lacking in courage will habitually conform to the demands of individuals or institutions that exercise undue economic power or social pressure. In many of these cases, vicious agents of resistance and their fellow social critics might turn out to be a remedy more pernicious than the disease.

If we are to recover this early modern doctrine of resistance for contemporary purposes, we need to take note of Althusius's anxiety about the ways that resistance can go wrong. But at the same time, it is important to remember that righteous acts of resistance can often be identified by examining their primary ends and means. Do acts of resistance aim to preserve or restore the fellowship of the community? Or do they instead aim to shore up private goods and partisan interests? Are acts of resistance being carried out virtuously by representative individuals who act with prudence, courage, and charity? Or are they being carried out carelessly, rashly, and with ill intent?

These questions are not easily answered. And in a political context like our own, consensus answers will be even harder to come by. I find this reality regrettable—perhaps even cause for lament—but not paralyzing or sufficient grounds for resentment. The temptation to despair or to resort to some form of apocalyptic impatience may seem quite strong to us now. But insofar as political fellowship is still recognized as valuable, whether by our fellow citizens or by God, we have cause to hope. So long as there are those who devote themselves to cultivating the virtues needed to live well with each other, to pursue just relations despite the personal cost, there is reason to continue to look for restoration.

If we want to repurpose an early modern doctrine of resistance for our own late modern troubles, this is where we must start: doing the hard, slow work of moral formation, correction, and confrontation. The work of virtuous, rightly ordered resistance could begin on the smallest of scales: in homes, classrooms, congregations, or similar civic communities. Perhaps from those seedbeds we will see the outgrowth of something more expansive. However, regardless of the context, we can hope to see the public work of resistance being carried out by virtuous citizens who recognize themselves as codebtors before God and neighbor for the common good of fellowship with each other. This invaluable good is something worthy of our attention, our struggle, and our sacrifice.

Notes

1. A similar, more recent version of this historical narrative can be found in Brad Gregory's *The Unintended Reformation: How a Religious Revolution Secularized Society* (Cambridge, MA: Harvard University Press, 2012).

2. David Henreckson, "The Immortal Commonwealth: Covenant, Law, and the Common Good in Early Modern Protestant Thought" (PhD diss., Princeton University, 2016).

3. While Althusius remains one of the lesser-known leading figures of the early modern Protestant tradition, his political thought has garnered attention recently. See Nicholas Wolterstorff, "The Right of the People to a Democratic State: Reflections on a Passage in

Althusius," in *Understanding Liberal Democracy* (Oxford: Oxford University Press, 2012), 227–44; and Luke Bretherton, *Resurrecting Democracy: Faith, Citizenship, and the Politics of a Common Life* (Cambridge: Cambridge University Press, 2015).

4. Thomas Aquinas, *Summa theologiae*, trans. Fathers of the English Dominican Province (New York: Benzinger Brothers, 1917), II-II, q42a2.

5. Compare also Aquinas's claim that the subject of civil friendship (that is, the subject in which we find the fundamental good of the fellowship) is the ruler of the people, not the people itself, *Summa theologiae* II-II q26a2. This is the reason, he thinks, why citizens owe the ruler obedience. For early moderns like Althusius, as I argue below, Aquinas's account would need to be significantly altered.

6. My distinction between direct or active resistance, on one hand, and indirect or passive resistance, on the other, is not absolute. There may, of course, be actions that seem to fall somewhere on the spectrum between the two categories. I find the distinction helpful, however, in distinguishing between direct popular contestation of the existing social order (as I elaborate below) and forms of resistance in which the people ask for the intercession of other authority-bearing figures (e.g., God or lesser magistrates). I address some aspects of this distinction in my essay, "Rights, Recognition, and the Order of Shalom," *Studies in Christian Ethics* 27, no. 4 (November 2014): 453–73.

7. Harro Höpfl and Martyn Thompson, "The History of Contract as a Motif in Political Thought," *American Historical Review* 84, no. 4 (October 1979). See also John Witte, *The Reformation of Rights* (Cambridge: Cambridge University Press, 2007), 81–87.

8. *Histoire ecclésiastique des églises réformées au royaume de France*, ed. G. Baum and E. Cunitz (1580; repr., Paris: 1884), 1–6.

9. Harro Höpfl, "The Ideal of *Aristocratia Politiae Vicina* in the Calvinist Political Tradition," in *Calvin and His Influence, 1509–2009*, ed. Irena Backus and Philip Benedict (Oxford: Oxford University Press, 2011), 56.

10. Theodore Beza, *De Jure Magistratuum* (Ioannem Mareschallum Lugdunensem, 1576), 80–81.

11. Ibid., 11.

12. Ibid., 17. Notably, the Henry-Louis Gonin translation describes this in terms of a "right" to resist, but this vocabulary is absent from the original Latin passage.

13. Johannes Althusius, *Politica Methodice Digesta* (Herborn 1614). The first edition was published in 1603, then substantially revised in 1610 and 1614.

14. Ibid., XXVIII.23–4, 582.

15. Ibid.

16. Ibid., XXXIX.8, 946. Althusius repeats versions of this a fortiori argument in multiple passages: "Even almighty God is said not to be able to do what is evil and contrary to his nature," XIX.11, 330. Further, we do not consider God "to be less powerful because he is intrinsically unable to sin" (*Nam Deus non eo minus potens censetur, quod per se peccare non possit*), XXXVIII.72, 914.

17. Ibid., XXVIII.22, 581. Althusius believes that earthly rulers have a corresponding obligation to hold the people accountable to the terms of the covenant. If a prince were to fail to correct his people for breaking covenant with God, the prince would be liable for divine judgment as well as the people. The difference in this case, however, is that the earthly ruler acts as merely an administrator over the people. Althusius does not address what should happen if (a) the people break covenant with God, (b) the ruler attempts to correct the people, and (c) the people respond by deposing him.

18. A number of excellent scholarly works have addressed the political importance of theological debates over Paul's claim in Romans 13 and other scriptural loci classici. Notable works on this topic include Daniel Toft, *Shadow of Kings: The Political Thought of David Pareus, 1548–1622* (PhD diss., University of Wisconsin-Madison, 1970); G. Sujin Pak, "Luther, Melanchthon, and Calvin on Romans 5 and 13," in *Reformation Readings of Romans*, ed. Kathy Ehrensperger and R. Ward Holder (New York: T&T Clark, 2008); and the critical edition of Peter Martyr Vermigli's influential "Commentary on Romans 13," in *The Political Thought of Peter Martyr Vermigli*, ed. Robert M. Kingdon (Geneva: Librairie Droz, 1980), as well as the later works contained in that edition.

19. Althusius, *Politica*, XXXVIII.1, 883.

20. Ibid., 884.

21. Ibid., 885.

22. Ibid., 886. He identifies the biblical Omride queen Athaliah, the French king Charles VI, and Philip II of Spain as examples of this form of rule.

23. Ibid., 886. The English translation strangely drops Althusius's characterization of the oath as ordered to "religion."

24. See Althusius, *Politica*, XXXVIII.10–20. This catalog is not translated in the modern English edition.

25. See Beza's discussion of this in *De Jure Magistratuum*, 29.

26. The following summary is taken from Althusius, *Politica*, XXXVIII.46, 904.

27. Althusius, *Politica*, XXXVIII.49.

28. Some of Althusius's recent interpreters have jumped too quickly from this political analysis to particular jurisprudential claims. Althusius's *Politica* is fundamentally a work of politics, not jurisprudence (cf. his later work *Dicaeologicae*), and the point of talking about the "ephors" is not to identify a particular class of individuals in northern Europe but to say, in effect: in political communities, it is the right of those who justly represent the *populus* to defend it against tyrants for the sake of the common good. Robert von Friedeburg offers a contrasting interpretation in *Self-Defence and Religious Strife in Early Modern Europe. England and Germany, 1530–1680* (Burlington, VT: Ashgate, 2002), 116–18. He repeats this interpretation of Althusius's ephorate in *Luther's Legacy: The Thirty Years War and the Modern Notion of "State" in the Empire* (Cambridge: Cambridge University Press, 2016), 175 and n37, relying on what I take to be Henning Arnisaeus's critical misreading of Althusius. While von Friedeburg and I differ on whether Althusius's ephors necessarily identify a determinate constitutional office, we agree that for Althusius the right to resist does not come from heredity (as in earlier resistance literature, such as Philip of Hesse), but by virtue of the office one holds.

29. Althusius, *Politica*, XXXVIII.53, 906.

30. Ibid., XXXVIII.63, 910.

31. For instance, in his discussion of religious freedom (not a topic on which Althusius is usually considered open-minded), the careful reader can find evidence of a broadly prudential defense of toleration. Althusius cautions magistrates against enforcement of orthodox religion in ways that would imperil the commonwealth (particularly a commonwealth with no homogenous religious identity). In these circumstances, the civil ruler "ought to tolerate the dissenters for the sake of public peace and tranquility, winking (*conniveo*) his eyes" for the sake of the political and ecclesial communities, XXVIII.66, 602–3. The common good of peaceful fellowship takes priority to the extent that dissent can and should be tolerated.

Can Love Walk the Battlefield? A Reply to Nigel Biggar

Vic McCracken

This essay considers more closely Nigel Biggar's account of the role love plays in orienting and qualifying the moral experience of just warriors. The evidence that Biggar employs is highly selective and belies a more complex picture of the motivations of soldiers, the experience of killing, and the moral ends of training for modern warfare. This essay argues that a more ambivalent account of love can be reconciled more easily with recent research on the experience of moral injury among combat veterans and is a more useful starting point for grounding the Christian community's service to combat veterans.

IN HIS 2012 AUTOBIOGRAPHY, *AMERICAN SNIPER*, CHRIS KYLE offers a firsthand account of his experiences during the Iraq War.[1] A member of US Navy SEAL Team 3, Kyle is widely recognized as the most lethal sniper in US military history, with more than 150 confirmed kills. Late in his book Kyle turns his attention to how war affected him personally:

I'M NOT THE SAME GUY I WAS WHEN I FIRST WENT TO WAR.

No one is. Before you're in combat, you have this innocence about you. Then, all of a sudden, you see this whole other side of life.

I don't regret any of it. I'd do it again. At the same time, war definitely changes you.

You embrace death.

As a SEAL, you go to the Dark Side. You're immersed in it. Continually going to war, you gravitate to the blackest parts of existence. Your psyche builds up its defenses—that's why you laugh at gruesome things like heads being blown apart, and worse.

Growing up, I wanted to be military. But I wondered, how would I feel about killing someone?

Now I know. It's no big deal.[2]

Vic McCracken is an associate professor of ethics and theology at Abilene Christian University, ACU Box 29417, Abilene, TX 79601; vbm95u@acu.edu.

Journal of the Society of Christian Ethics, 38, 1 (2018): 59–76

Coming to terms with the necessity of killing in war, Kyle reflected on his own eventual death, which tragically came on a Texas gun range shortly after the publication of *American Sniper*. Kyle was shot to death by a fellow soldier suffering from posttraumatic stress disorder. "I am a strong Christian," he wrote: "Honestly, I don't know what will really happen on Judgment Day. But what I lean towards is that you know all of your sins, and God knows them all, and shame covers over you at the reality that He knows. . . . But in that backroom or whatever it is when God confronts me with my sins, I do not believe any of the kills I had during the war will be among them. Everyone I shot was evil. I had good cause on every shot. They all deserved to die."[3]

While Kyle's words may be hard to accept for those who have never experienced combat, they are at least understandable. For soldiers, war is not an ethereal abstraction but a deeply personal, life-altering experience. However, for nearly two millennia Christians have observed that killing one's enemy sits, at best, uncomfortably within a tradition that points to Jesus Christ as the starting point for our moral lives. Christ calls followers to love their enemies (Mt 5:44) after all. Is it possible to love an enemy while staring at him through the end of a sniper scope? How realistic is it to insist that soldiers must love those whom they are commanded to kill?

In the face of such questions, the Christian community can be most grateful for the 2014 publication of Nigel Biggar's book *In Defence of War*.[4] In this book Biggar argues that the violence of the just war is best understood as a faithful enactment of Christian love. In just wars Christians need not jettison forgiveness, compassion, or regard for the enemy's well-being. The Christian just war tradition conceives the violence of the just war as an expression of love for the neighbor and the unjust aggressor.[5] While this argument is not novel, what is novel is Biggar's unflinching attempt to wrestle with the ambiguities that attend the moral experience of soldiers.[6] Is it realistic to claim that soldiers who regularly inflict violence, destruction, and death on the enemy do so as an act of love? At first glance, such a claim seems preposterous, an academic fantasy spun out of the ivory tower to assuage our collective moral conscience. But Biggar insists that, no, this claim is not a utopian fantasy but a realistic possibility. A close inspection of the moral experience of soldiers vindicates the Christian just war tradition. Love truly can walk the battlefield.

In this essay I consider more closely Biggar's account of the role that love plays in orienting and qualifying the violence of war. In the first part, I briefly summarize Biggar's descriptive account of just warriors whose violence is, in his view, a faithful enactment of Christian love. In the second part I identify three problems with Biggar's argument, which relies on a highly selective appropriation of source material. I argue for an alternative reading of this material that is more ambivalent about the moral motivations of soldiers, the experience of killing in war, and the moral ends of training for modern warfare. I conclude by pointing to two ways that this more ambivalent posture improves on Biggar's defense of the Christian just war tradition.

Christian Forgiveness and the Kind Harshness of the Just Warrior

Biggar's argument intends to justify the death-dealing violence of just warriors. However, Biggar's portrait of the just warrior begins not with violence but forgiveness.[7] Critics often argue that Christian forgiveness is incompatible with the violence of war. Biggar disagrees, asserting that too often critics mischaracterize the nature of forgiveness, which is not a single act but a process that encompasses two distinct moments in our relationship with the enemy. First, there is the "moment of compassion." In this moment forgiveness requires us to temper our resentment, to acknowledge that we ourselves are sinners, that we share a common humanity with our enemy. We are all created in God's image, and forgiveness-as-compassion leads us to yearn for reconciliation with the wrongdoer. Forgiveness-as-compassion also requires us to avoid the excess that too often attends our natural desire for vengeance. In this respect, forgiveness is unconditional and unilateral; it requires nothing of our enemy.

Christian forgiveness also encompasses a second moment in our relationship with the enemy, the "moment of absolution." In this moment forgiveness is granted as a result of the repentance of the wrongdoer. In granting absolution to the one who has perpetrated evil, we acknowledge the restoration of right relationship between neighbors that can result only from the sincere admission of sin. Forgiveness-as-absolution, unlike forgiveness-as-compassion, is not unilateral but is itself conditional, premised on the repentance for wrongdoing that we can only yearn for in the moment of compassion.

Understanding forgiveness not as a singular act but as a process offers a constructive starting point, says Biggar, for understanding the moral experience of soldiers fighting a just war. During just wars Christians find themselves caught between these two moments, living in the morally ambiguous space between unconditional compassion toward the enemy and the conditional absolution that forgiveness will permit only in response to the enemy's repentance. And this is the point: in this space between compassion and absolution, Christian love inspires the just warrior to embrace both resentment and violence as appropriate, even necessary responses to ongoing moral atrocity. Appropriate resentment finds its fitting form in the violence of the just warrior who rejects the excesses of vengeance and embraces instead a retributive violence that is limited, tempered by compassion, and yearning for the moment of absolution. As Biggar says, "Forgiveness, properly understood, includes the proportionate expression of resentment and retribution. Resentment and retribution are hostile forces: they seek to coerce the wrongdoer—to stop him, to make him conscious of the evils he causes, to urge repentance on to him. Therefore, forgiveness qualifies, rather than excludes, coercion; and coercion sometimes takes physical form."[8]

So what does Biggar's account of forgiveness mean for soldiers? The portrait that Biggar paints is of soldiers who, while motivated by resentment of injustice, refuse to embrace malevolence. Echoing Augustine, Biggar describes the violence of the just warrior as a sort of "kind harshness" directed against the enemy.[9] Exorcised of vengeance, the violence of war should be "benevolently retributive," a violence that "aims to uphold the dignity of the injured and contradict the offence of the perpetrator."[10] The goal of this violence is to move the enemy toward the moment of repentance and eventual reconciliation. The just warrior must embrace violence as a regrettable but necessary means for coercing another who is also a child of God.

Most provocatively, Biggar offers a creative reinterpretation of the principle of double effect that points to a striking conclusion about the act of killing in war. While soldiers may foresee that their violence will likely lead to the death of their enemies, just warriors must never *intend* the death of those they are targeting. Biggar's argument here depends on his specific definition of intention. To *intend* something is to *desire* it. Biggar argues that soldiers must never *desire* the death of their enemies: "No one should *choose to want* or *intend* to damage or destroy such precious life, for to do so would be to vitiate the agent's heart and will, to corrupt his moral character, to jeopardize his fitness for life beyond death, and to increase the likelihood of his committing further malevolent harm in the world."[11]

Biggar illustrates his point by drawing attention to a scene from the 2003 film *Master and Commander* in which a sailor is ordered to cut the broken mast of his ship in order to save the ship from sinking even though a fellow sailor is clinging to the wreckage and will likely drown. When the sailor cuts the mast free from the ship, does he intend to kill the sailor? No, says Biggar.[12] He intends only to save the ship and its crew, and the death of the fellow sailor is something that he accepts with deep reluctance. He accepts that the death of the sailor is the consequence of his action, but he intends (i.e., he *desires*) only the well-being of the crew. The logic applies to the conduct of soldiers in war, who must accept with regret the death of the enemy as the unintended side effect of a violence intended to motivate repentance.

Biggar's description of the just warrior is clear enough, but is it realistic? Biggar believes that it is. Drawing from the written histories, recorded memoirs, and a few personal interviews of frontline soldiers from World War I to the Second Iraq War, Biggar finds evidence enough to conclude that his constructive account of the moral sentiments of just warriors is a possibility on the modern battlefield. Biggar observes that the motivations of soldiers often fall short of the malevolence that is fundamentally opposed to Christian love. Some soldiers perceive the enemy as little more than ciphers, "anonymous figures to be dealt with as expeditiously as possible," observes military historian Richard Holmes.[13] World War I veteran Ernest Jünger describes his feelings toward enemy soldiers in just this way: "Throughout the war . . . it was always my endeavor to view my opponent without animus, and to form an opinion of him as a man on the basis of the courage he showed. I would always try and seek him out in combat and kill him, and I expected nothing else from him. But never did I entertain mean thoughts about him. When prisoners fell into my hands, later on, I felt responsible for their safety, and would always do everything in my power for them."[14]

Hatred of the enemy is far more common among civilians than soldiers who experience the act of killing as "the unpleasant duty of the executioner," says World War II veteran Patrick Bishop.[15] On the battlefield, there are even occasions for compassion between soldiers. In his personal interview of one veteran of the 1982 Falklands War, Biggar tells of the soldier's recollection following a ferocious battle in which British paratroopers were "cradling wounded Argentine soldiers in their arms."[16] Solidarity with the enemy is a possibility.

Most prominently, when describing the motivations behind their violence, soldiers often point to the love they have for their comrades, not hatred of the enemy. Biggar quotes Second Iraq War veteran Patrick Bury's testimony of a personal exchange he had with a fellow soldier while stationed in Helmand Province:

> "I love you, boss. I'd do anything for you. . . . I'd take a bullet for you." He looks at me. It is not often that a man tells another he loves him. Especially in front of other men. . . . But Matt has called it by its true name, love. . . . And sometimes, out here, you get a glimpse and you understand. You understand why soldiers charge machine guns or hold out to the death while others escape. Love. For love melts fear like butter on a furnace; it transcends it.[17]

Quoting John 15:13, Biggar observes that such love is morally laudatory: "Greater love has no man than this, that a man lay down his life for his friends."[18]

Regarding the intention of soldiers, Biggar asserts that there is considerable evidence that soldiers are reluctant to harm the enemy. To validate this point, Biggar draws from S.L.A. Marshall's influential research during World War II, which concluded that only 15 to 25 percent of US riflemen actually shot their guns at the enemy, with the majority of soldiers either posturing or firing their weapons over the head of enemy soldiers.[19] A study of the British military similarly concluded that the potential number of deaths possible given the firepower of nineteenth- and twentieth-century soldiers far exceeds the actual number of deaths. Reluctance sometimes leads soldiers to avoid killing; other times this reluctance qualifies killing itself, with soldiers sometimes describing the act of killing as an "unwelcome task" that they embrace with a degree of disgust.

The evidence leads Biggar to conclude that the reluctance to kill demanded by the Christian just war tradition is, in fact, what we often find among soldiers.[20] Thus love can walk the battlefield.

Love on the Battlefield: Form without Substance

I find it hard to feel anything but appreciation for the clear sympathy and compassion Biggar demonstrates toward soldiers who have lived in the morally fraught maelstrom of war. Biggar shows the utmost of respect toward soldiers, and he correctly observes that there are examples of soldiers who embrace the virtues of self-sacrifice for others, care and concern for their comrades, and even compassion toward the enemy. There is much to appreciate here.

But what are we to say of the substance of Biggar's argument? Here it will help to consider the two claims at the heart of Biggar's case for the just warrior. The first is a normative claim about what the Christian just war tradition expects of soldiers in battle: just warriors should feel resentment in the face of injustice and may embrace retributive violence as long as this violence is proportionate, nonmalevolent, and leaning toward absolution. The second is a descriptive claim about what the empirical evidence suggests is possible on the battlefield: in modern warfare there is ample evidence that proportionate, nonmalevolent violence is a realistic possibility. Normatively, Biggar believes his account of the just warrior is an accurate reflection of the values and norms of the Christian tradition. Descriptively, Biggar believes the evidence proves that these expectations are not utopian.

Although I am aware that Christian pacifists will find reasons to critique Biggar's normative defense of retributive violence, I am more concerned with the descriptive case that Biggar makes for the experience of soldiers. I note three problems here. The first problem is intrinsic to arguments built around anecdotal evidence. Biggar seems to believe that even a single example of compassion toward the enemy is enough to vindicate the realism of love in war. In my view this sets the epistemic bar far too low for the Christian just war tradition. Individual anecdotes may or may not reflect the overall character of war violence, after all. Biggar would object, rightly, to a caricature of war based on anecdotes of soldiers executing prisoners, torturing combatants, collecting trophies from the dead, and reveling in the sheer pleasure of violence, though these stories are readily available. Should we be any less suspicious of the felicitous story that Biggar tells of just warriors whose violence is rooted and grounded in love?

The fundamental question is not whether there are examples of compassion and nonmalevolence among soldiers. It is whether these examples are exceptional or representative of the common affections, actions, and dispositions of just warriors. To fully vindicate the possibility of love on the battlefield, what we should hope to see is evidence that compassion and nonmalevolence are not exceptional but are themselves the distinctive and pervasive features of conduct among soldiers that have been formed by the just war tradition that Biggar defends. But Biggar makes no claim that these examples actually reflect what most soldiers experience in war. Indeed, such a case would demand a much fuller qualitative study of the moral experience of soldiers. Biggar seems content to offer up a few examples as proof of the possibility of love on the battlefield. A case built around stories of compassion toward the enemy and nonmalevolent killing runs the risk of cherry-picking anecdotes that fit most comfortably into the story that we want to believe about war.

Looking more closely at the sources that Biggar himself employs, there is some evidence that concerns about cherry-picking stories are warranted here. Consider Joanna Bourke's book *An Intimate History of Killing*.[21] In this book-length history of modern warfare, Bourke offers up a searing portrait of the moral experience of soldiers, a sort of phenomenology of killing in war. "The characteristic act of men at war is not dying, it is killing," says Bourke, and she is intent on placing killing front and center of her story.[22]

Bourke relies on the same source material as Biggar, but her exhaustive portrait of soldiers departs substantially from Biggar's cursory case for love in war. While Biggar sees in this material evidence of soldiers embracing the act of killing as a form of kind harshness toward the enemy, Bourke sees ample evidence to the contrary. In her first chapter, "The Pleasures of War," Bourke observes that modern soldiers frequently experience the act of killing as intensely gratifying. "Time and time again," she observes, "in the writings of combatants from [World War I, World War II, and the Vietnam War], we read of men's (and women's) enjoyment of killing."[23] Bourke details soldiers describing the act of killing enemies in war as "gorgeously satisfying," or "sickening yet exhilarating butchery," with commanders praised for their capacity to maintain "a spirit of the 'joy of slaughter' in their troops."[24]

Like Biggar, Bourke acknowledges the existence of what she calls the "warrior ethos," a myth that calls soldiers to show respect for the enemy and encourages them to "kill cleanly, kill quickly, kill efficiently, without malice and brutality."[25] But while Biggar elevates this ethos as quintessential to the character of just warriors and emphasizes its presence on the contemporary battlefield, Bourke describes the almost inevitable decline of this ethos in modern warfare, facilitated in large part by the practice of mass conscription in which civilian soldiers quickly came to see the moral scruples of this ethos as impossible to realize in battle. Notes Bourke, the body count serves as a standard unit for measuring combat effectiveness in modern warfare. Technology and propaganda function as tools meant to obscure the humanity of the enemy, to render him anonymous in order to ease the killing task.

Biggar is aware of Bourke's text, citing it two times, but his appropriation of her book misses the larger thrust of her history. First, he quotes Bourke when she chronicles a survey of American soldiers in World War II who identify solidarity with fellow soldiers and family as their primary motivation for fighting, not vindictiveness.[26] Second, he cites a story that she recounts of fraternizing among World War I soldiers during Christmas 1914 as evidence that soldiers can feel kinship with the enemy.[27] Biggar is correct to draw attention to these incidents, which lend some support to the story he tells about love in war, but I fear that Biggar mistakes the forest for the trees. Bourke's book is harrowing precisely because these occasional moments in which soldiers are lifted from the ordeals of war pale when juxtaposed alongside the day-to-day banality, misery, and horror that are at the foreground of her history.

In response, Biggar might well say that his argument does not intend to offer up an empirical description of how most soldiers experience war. He is simply describing what the Christian just war tradition expects of just warriors and presenting some evidence to show that these demands are within the realm of possibility. To be fair to Biggar, he does acknowledge that vindictiveness, anger, hatred, and "the sheer pleasure of destruction" can sometimes motivate soldiers.[28] He is a Christian realist, and he acknowledges that the ecstasy of war sometimes leads soldiers to embrace feelings and actions that are, in his words, "morally dubious."[29] Nonetheless, the sum of Biggar's argument seems to be that, as long as there is some anecdotal evidence that soldiers sometimes embrace violence without malevolence, sporadically show compassion toward enemy soldiers, and on occasion express regret for the killing that must be done, this vindicates the possibility of love on the battlefield. This makes Biggar's argument roughly analogous to that of the tobacco advertiser who insists that cigarettes are safe because some smokers do not get cancer.

I see no simple way to resolve whether Biggar's empirical evidence is sufficient to make the case for the possibility of love on the battlefield, so let's set aside for the moment concerns about the anecdotes that Biggar employs. The second problem with Biggar's case may be seen if we consider an obvious question: What sort of training would be sufficient to form soldiers capable of killing in a way that their retributive violence is a natural extension of their own compassion toward the enemy? Biggar argues correctly that whether the powerful emotions of the battlefield can be appropriately governed is dependent on "the military discipline instilled by training, and especially upon the quality of leadership in the field."[30] However, if this is the case, it is quite surprising that Biggar himself spends no time reflecting on the actual process by which modern soldiers are trained for war. This absence implies some confidence on Biggar's part that contemporary combat training *is* effective in cultivating a moral disposition that allows love to walk the battlefield.

But this confidence is misplaced. Just how misplaced it is can be seen if we reconsider Biggar's discussion of the intention of soldiers at war. Biggar asserts that soldiers must never intend to kill their enemy, and he cites the Marshall study to support his claim that there is a widespread reluctance to kill among soldiers. As noted above, the Marshall study concluded that during World War II only 15 to 25 percent of US riflemen fired their weapons at the enemy. For Biggar, this study proves that the moral disposition that is appropriate for just warriors is in fact what we often find among soldiers.

But in treating the Marshall study in this way, Biggar neglects to consider the larger role that this study played in reshaping the combat training methods employed in preparing soldiers for war. As David Grossman observes in his book *On Killing*, the US military was deeply troubled by Marshall's findings.[31] When 75 percent of soldiers fail to fire their weapons at the enemy, this is not mere evidence of an appropriate reluctance to kill; it is a fundamental threat to combat effectiveness. Although Marshall's research on the low firing rates of American soldiers during World War II has been roundly discredited for being methodologically flawed and perhaps even fabricated, his conclusions about the ineffectiveness of combat soldiers were deemed accurate by military leadership following World War II and prompted a dramatic revision to the techniques and ethos of combat training.[32]

As described by Grossman, modern combat training is not only concerned with equipping soldiers with the essential skills of their profession but is itself a form of moral training that cultivates a disposition in which soldiers are enabled to kill on command. The intent is to root out this reluctance to kill, that quality of character that Biggar points to as evidence of the right intention of soldiers. Today soldiers are exposed to both classical and operant conditioning techniques when training for war. In live-fire exercises, soldiers are subjected to simulations intended to mimic conditions on the modern battlefield, with soldiers firing at targets made to look as human as possible. "Soldiers are highly rewarded," says Grossman, "and recognized for success in this skill and suffer mild punishment (in the form of retraining, peer pressure, and failure to graduate from boot camp) for failure to quickly and accurately 'engage' the targets—a standard euphemism for 'kill.'"[33]

Moreover, modern combat training also aspires to cultivate the "offensive spirit," a capacity to embrace killing without regret. After all, to entertain regret is to leave open the possibility that a soldier might refuse to fire in the heat of the moment. Gwynne Dyer describes what Grossman calls the "boot camp deification of killing" during the Vietnam era, with soldiers regularly participating in the training chant, "kill, kill, kill, kill." While most soldiers recognized this as "meaningless hyperbole," Dyer describes the important role that these rituals played in helping soldiers to wage war: "It does help to *desensitize* them to the suffering of an 'enemy,' and at the same time they are being indoctrinated in the most explicit fashion (as previous generations were not) with the notion that their purpose is not just to be brave or to fight well; it is to kill people."[34]

Such training was, according to Grossman, "almost unheard of in World War I, rare in World War II, increasingly present in Korea, and thoroughly institutionalized in Vietnam."[35] The effects of this training are clear. A study by R. W. Glenn concluded that the firing rate of soldiers during the Vietnam War approached 95 percent—testimony to the efficacy of these revised methods.[36]

To be clear, the point is not that contemporary combat training cultivates hatred in soldiers. Like Biggar, other scholars have presented comparable evidence of soldiers who are capable of killing without feeling hatred toward the enemy. Nonhatred is as much a pragmatic concern as a moral one in the military. Notes Bourke, "Blood-lust, rage, and hatred were liable to make men's hands tremble when shooting at the enemy . . . troops who were too aggressive were liable to overrun their objectives and sustain heavy casualties."[37] The goal of training is to desensitize soldiers to the act of killing, conditioning them in ways that shield them from the humanity of the enemy they are required to kill.[38]

Notably, such training is intended to protect the psychological well-being of soldiers themselves. A growing body of research has established a positive correlation between the act of killing in war and suicidal ideation.[39] Grossman quotes military biographer Richard Holmes in asserting the necessity of such training: "A soldier who constantly reflected upon the knee-smashing, widow-making characteristics of his weapon, or who always thought of the enemy as a man exactly as himself, doing much the same task and subjected to exactly the same stresses and strains, would find it difficult to operate effectively in battle. . . . Without the creation of abstract images of the enemy, and without the depersonalization of the enemy during training, battle would become impossible to sustain."[40]

But if this is the case, then Biggar's claim that there is a natural reluctance to kill is simply wrong. It would be more accurate to say that this reluctance to kill evidenced prior to World War II has prompted new, more effective methods that aim to overcome this reluctance. If this combat training is successful, then it raises fundamental questions about whether such formation is at odds with what Biggar asserts is necessary for love to walk the battlefield: a moral disposition in which soldiers embrace a resentment that recognizes the full humanity of the enemy and accepts the need for violence with regret and hope for repentance.

This leads us to the third problem with Biggar's descriptive case for the just warrior. The problem is not found in Biggar's claim that soldiers may kill without hatred. The problem is that Biggar assumes that because soldiers can act violently without malevolence, this is evidence that love is present to qualify their violence. This conclusion rests on an either/or assumption about what motivates killing in war: either hatred or love. But are these the only ways of understanding the moral experience of killing in war? This either/or dichotomy loses sight of the range of moral possibilities that lie between love and hate.

Is it the case that the absence of malevolence entails the presence of love? I do not believe so. To not hate is not the same as to love. An analogy here will be helpful to illustrate the point. Consider the role that retributive violence has played in the family. Comparing the violence of the just war to corporal punishment in the home might seem outlandish at first glance, but Augustine himself frequently appeals to the family as a metaphor for understanding the retributive violence of the state. In a sermon preached in 418, for example, Augustine lauds corporal punishment as a form of harsh mercy directed by the father toward his erring son. When the son remains defiant, "you apply the rod, you impose punishment, you inflict pain, but you also look to his welfare. Many by love, many by fear are corrected, but what they arrive at through fear and trembling is love. . . . Look, the father is devoted in his beating, by beating his son he is merciful."[41] In his commentary on the Sermon on the Mount, Augustine describes the just ruler in similar fashion, a ruler who accepts the responsibility of punishment "with the disposition of a father punishing his little boy."[42]

While corporal punishment is today a source of controversy among researchers who have raised important questions about its efficacy and harms, spanking and other forms of retributive violence are pervasive historically and in the present.[43] Setting aside for the moment this moral debate, the logic of corporal punishment is quite similar to the logic that Biggar offers to explain retributive violence in war, and Biggar himself makes this connection explicit at the beginning of his book, pointing to the punishment that a parent metes out on a "willfully errant child" as an illustration of the moral aims of violence in just wars.[44] In both cases the violence is intended as a response to a moral wrong. In both cases the goal is to motivate the wrongdoer—the unjust aggressor or the child who has gone astray—to repent.

Now consider two scenarios. In the first scenario a child has done something morally wrong. The parent is deeply upset. Angered by his child's offense, the parent feels an intense and malevolent rage toward the child and promptly spanks him. In this scenario, it seems obvious that the malevolence that motivates the parent's retributive violence is in conflict with love. Indeed, we have every reason to fear that malevolent rage might lead this parent to pursue a violence that is disproportionate, even abusive. In the case of war, Biggar is surely correct that soldiers motivated by malevolent rage act in ways that are fundamentally opposed to Christian love, and they similarly open themselves to the risk of embracing a violence that is disproportionate. When Biggar argues that soldiers may embrace violence against the enemy without hatred, he is saying that this is not inevitable. Here also, I believe he is correct.

But now consider a second scenario. Imagine that a child does something morally wrong. As in the first scenario, the father is resentful of his child's wrongdoing and spanks him, but this time the father feels no malevolence. Indeed, imagine that this father feels nothing at all toward the child—neither malevolence nor affection. Imagine that the father is not motivated at all by feelings of compassion toward his child. Yes, the father is careful to avoid any hint of abuse, but he does so not out of a personal regard for the child but out of a desire to avoid entanglement with Child Protective Services. Concerns about the ultimate well-being of the child are far from his mind. For him, corporal punishment is simply a practice intrinsic to his role as the child's father. The child is somewhat inconsequential to the task, in fact. The father is simply "doing his job," living up to the social expectations appropriate to his parental role. The child is little more than a "cipher," an object that, when disciplined, allows the father to realize these expectations.

What would we say of the parent in this scenario? On the one hand, it is hard to say that this parent is embodying hatred; malevolence is missing here. On the other hand, it would be absurd for us to insist that because the parent is nonmalevolent, he is showing love toward his child. Indeed, in this case we would be right to conclude that the relationship between the parent and child is strange, even perverse. This is a relationship that is devoid of the substantive feelings and motivations most basic to love: a regard for the well-being of the other, a sense of reluctance for the need for discipline, a regret for the pain that the father knows the son will experience, and a yearning for repentance. In his actions, the father is embodying neither love nor hate but something between love and hate.

What does this have to do with war? My point is that even if the anecdotes that Biggar deploys exemplify the possibility of killing without hatred, this in itself does not necessarily point to the conclusion that love is present to guide and qualify the retributive violence of soldiers. Whether love is playing this critical role will depend on whether soldiers who kill are themselves internally motivated by compassion toward the enemy, a recognition that the enemy is a child of God, and a justifiable resentment tinged with regret and yearning for absolution.

But this is where Biggar's case falls short. As previously noted, Biggar well observes that on the battlefield the enemy often functions as little more than a "cipher" for combatants who are simply living up to the expectations appropriate to their role, to be "good soldiers." This seems to me an example of retributive violence that is closer to what we see in the second scenario above, a retributive violence that is nonmalevolent but also lacking the most basic affections that even Biggar himself insists are at the heart of Christian love. This, I suggest, is what we see more commonly in the experiences of soldiers at war: a moral disposition that lies between love and hate.

Chris Kyle, America's most lethal sniper, offers a useful example that illustrates the point. When Kyle says of those he killed, "They all deserved to die," we might agree with Biggar that this assertion is a manifestation of appropriate resentment of injustice. While we may flinch from the bluntness of Kyle's words, we should expect severe resentment from a soldier in a position where he regularly observes insurgents planting improvised explosive devices and putting innocent lives at risk. As a whole, *American Sniper* rarely includes examples of Kyle demonstrating sheer, malevolent hatred toward the enemy, and there are occasional glimpses of regard for the enemy's well-being. Kyle's memoir also offers vivid, sometimes heartbreaking evidence of his affection for the soldiers alongside whom he fought, something that Biggar is correct to praise.

However, what is most striking about *American Sniper* is the casual manner that Kyle employs when describing his own feelings about the violence of war. How does he feel about killing someone? "It's not a big deal." Recounting his memories of the early days of his first deployment in Iraq, Kyle's description exudes no reluctance, regret, or remorse for the killing that lay ahead. "Man this is going to be good," he says. "We are going to kill massive amounts of bad guys. And I'm going to be in the middle of it."[45] Kyle's battlefield memories frequently revolve around the details of his profession—the range of his longest kill shot, the feeling of staring through the end of a sniper scope and aiming center mass, the smooth squeeze of the trigger, and the surprise as the gun pulls and the bullet makes its way to the target.[46] The enemy is almost a nonperson here, an object far from view. "After the first kill, the others came easy," he says. "I don't have to psych myself up, or do anything special mentally—I look through the scope, get my target in the crosshairs, and kill my enemy before he kills one of my people."[47] This is his profession; killing is simply part of the job.

Kyle acknowledges that the military rules of engagement serve to clarify the limits of permissible violence in war, and he insists that throughout the war he always followed these rules. Biggar might ask us to take this as evidence of how, amid the brutality of war, love remains present to qualify the violence of soldiers. However, this claim loses sight of Kyle's own perception of the purpose and consequence of these rules. Kyle describes the rules of engagement as legalisms that are drawn up by lawyers who are trying "to protect admirals and generals from the politicians."[48] For him, these rules do not well reflect his own sentiments about his responsibilities in war, nor do they account for the consequent risks these rules posed to him and other soldiers:

Do you want us to conquer the enemy? Annihilate them? Or are we heading over to serve them tea and cookies?

Tell the military the end result you want, and you'll get it. But don't try and tell us how to do it. All those rules about when and under what circumstances an enemy combatant couldn't be killed didn't just make our jobs harder, they put our lives in danger.[49]

If the rules of engagement exemplify what it means to instantiate the qualifying power of love over violence, it's not clear whose love is made manifest here. Certainly, it is a stretch to say that it is the soldier's.

Kyle exemplifies what I think is a more accurate picture of what we see among soldiers in war, a violence that, while not motivated by personal hatred, is also lacking the moral qualities that are basic to Christian love. And this is what we should expect if Grossman's description of combat training methods and goals is accurate. Kyle epitomizes the formative ends of combat training. He is a capable executioner, not a mournful warrior, and what he exemplifies, while not malevolence, is something between love and hate, something resembling the form of love without its substance.

Conclusion: The Price of Love

Let's return to the original question: can love walk the battlefield? Biggar sees in the lives of soldiers enough to offer a confident yes to this question. By contrast, I argue that the evidence points us to an answer that is less confident, more ambivalent about what is possible among soldiers, even soldiers prosecuting a just war. Love can walk the battlefield in the sense that soldiers need not be motivated by personal hatred and can often be motivated by love for their comrades. But to not hate one's enemy is not the same as to love them, for love entails not only the rejection of malevolence but also an unmitigated recognition of the humanity of our enemy that leads us to embrace violence with regret and remorse. Here I believe the evidence suggests that modern combat training strives to cultivate a disposition that undermines these affections among soldiers.

Undoubtedly some will see in this critique more reason to question the viability of the Christian just war tradition, but I do not go this far. I remain persuaded by Biggar's case for the just war even if I am not yet persuaded that his empirical case well captures the moral ambiguities and tragedy intrinsic to its prosecution. Rather than questioning Biggar's defense of war, I suggest that a more ambivalent account of the moral experience of soldiers improves Biggar's argument in two crucial ways.

First, recognizing that even just wars entail a moral price in the lives of soldiers who fight them calls Christian just war advocates to embrace war with much greater reluctance than is apparent in Biggar's book. Recently Tobias Winright and E. Ann Jeschke have warned us of the risks inherent in a stream of the Christian just war tradition that treats the just war as a "positive good" rather than a "lesser evil."[50] Such views valorize war in a way that obscures the moral tragedy of war, and they also potentially encourage the relaxation of the constraints that limit our violence. These concerns seem relevant when applied to Biggar's defense of the Christian just war tradition, which leans toward the sort of valorization that Winright and Jeschke critique. It is notable that in Biggar's three-hundred-page book he offers up not a single example of how application of the *jus ad bellum* criteria led him to conclude that a historical war fought by the United Kingdom or the United States was, all things considered, unjust. While it is not entirely clear what to make of this, rhetorically this absence, when coupled with his expansive defense of the justifiability of the recent war in Iraq, suggests a willingness on Biggar's part to embrace war all too quickly; it is much easier to embrace war, after all, when one assumes an easy reconciliation of love and violence.

Second, a more ambivalent posture about the possibility of love on the battlefield better positions the Christian community to respond compassionately to soldiers when they return home from war. Over the last two decades therapists and Christian ethicists have focused a growing body of research on the problem of moral injury among soldiers.[51] We see moral injury in soldiers who experience intense feelings of shame and guilt because of actions they have done, failed to do, or observed being done in war. Such feelings are not confined to those who violate the rules of war but may persist even among soldiers who engage in justifiable violence.[52] Such feelings make sense in a moral context, where soldiers experience real tension between war violence and internalized moral norms. Shame and guilt make much less sense in the context of an account of war that assumes that love and violence are easily reconciled.

A more tragic, ambivalent vision of the moral experience of soldiers invites us to reconsider liturgical practices that are rooted in an acknowledgment that the act of killing, even when killing is necessary, is itself a morally fraught practice that is in tension with Christian love. Bernard Verkamp has explored at great length the ancient Christian practice of imposing penance on soldiers returning home from war, arguing that this practice reflects Christian misgivings about the act of killing.[53] Verkamp suggests that medieval Thomistic appeals to the common good as the telos of justifiable war contributed to the decline of this practice, overcoming "any lingering theological suspicions on the moral status of killing."[54] Biggar's confident defense of love on the battlefield similarly suggests a movement away from those misgivings that animated this Christian practice. When just warriors return from war, they themselves may be the ones in need of absolution, or at the very least in need of religious communities capable of providing safe space for them to grieve, recover, and confess.

Finally, a more ambivalent posture about the possibility of love on the battlefield points us to a return of sorts to the insight of Reinhold Niebuhr. "Creative love must express itself not only in trust but in sacrifice," writes Niebuhr.[55] In the Christian just war tradition, love must remain a guiding norm that orients and constrains the violence of war. However, just war advocates should acknowledge that war, even a just war, entails real moral sacrifice. Creative love may motivate the just war, and it may offer a ground for the establishment of moral norms that constrain war's violence. But there is a tragic irony here when we, motivated by a love that provokes our resentment in the face of grave injustice, send the just warrior to wage war. He is there now, on the battlefield, staring through his sniper scope, aiming center mass, watching as the body of his enemy falls, and reloading, preparing his next kill shot, all the time embodying something between love and hate, the just warrior sacrificed for love's sake.

Notes

1. Christopher Kyle, *American Sniper* (New York: HarperCollins, 2012).
2. Ibid., 377.
3. Ibid., 378.
4. Nigel Biggar, *In Defence of War* (Oxford: Oxford University Press, 2014).
5. Ibid., 61.
6. See, for example, Paul Ramsey, *The Just War: Force and Political Responsibility* (Lanham, MD: Rowman & Littlefield, 1983).
7. Biggar, *In Defence of War*, 61–69.
8. Ibid., 72.
9. See Augustine, *Epistle*, 138.13–14.
10. Biggar, *In Defence of War*, 71.
11. Ibid., 101; emphasis original.
12. Ibid., 94.
13. Ibid., 78, quoting Richard Holmes, *Dusty Soldiers: Modern Soldiers at War* (London: Harper Press, 2006), 317.
14. Ibid., quoting Ernst Jünger, *Storm of Steel*, trans. Michael Hoffmann (London: Allen Lane, 2003), 58.
15. Ibid., 83, quoting Patrick Bishop, *Fighter Boys: Saving Britain 1940* (London: Harper Collins, 2003), 336.
16. Ibid.
17. Ibid., 80, quoting Patrick Bury, *3 Para* (London: Harper Press, 2007).
18. Ibid., 79.
19. Marshall's research is cited in Dave Grossman, *On Killing: The Psychological Cost of Learning to Kill in War and Society*, rev. ed. (New York: Back Bay, 2009).
20. Biggar, *In Defence of War*, 104–5.
21. Joanna Bourke, *An Intimate History of Killing* (London: Basic Books, 1999).
22. Ibid., xiii.
23. Ibid., 18.

24. Ibid., 19.

25. Ibid., 37.

26. Biggar, *In Defence of War*, 79, quoting from Bourke, *Intimate History of Killing*, 142.

27. Ibid., 83, quoting from Bourke, *Intimate History of Killing*, 136.

28. Ibid., 88.

29. Ibid., 85.

30. Ibid., 89.

31. Grossman, *On Killing*, 2–3.

32. See Roger Spiller, "S.L.A. Marshall and the Rate of Fire," *RUSI Journal* 133, no. 4 (Winter 1988): 63–71.

33. Grossman, *On Killing*, 255.

34. Dyer, quoted in ibid., 253.

35. Ibid.

36. Cited in ibid., 36.

37. Bourke, *Intimate History of Killing*, 156.

38. Grossman, *On Killing*, 177.

39. See Shira Maguen, David D. Luxton, Nancy A. Skopp, Gregory A. Gahm, Mark A. Reger, Thomas J. Metzler, and Charles R. Marmar, "Killing in Combat, Mental Health Symptoms, and Suicidal Ideation in Iraq War Veterans," *Journal of Anxiety Disorders* 25 (2011): 563–67.

40. Richard Holmes, *Acts of War*, as quoted in Grossman, *On Killing*, 186.

41. Augustine *Sermon* 13.9. Translation taken from *Sermons; The Works of Saint Augustine: A Translation for the 21st Century*, vol. III/1, trans. Edmund Hill (New York: New City Press, 1990).

42. See Augustine, *Commentary on the Lord's Sermon on the Mount*, trans. Denis J. Kavanaugh (New York: Fathers of the Church, 1951), I.20.63. I am indebted to Phillip Wynn, *Augustine on War and Military Service* (Minneapolis, MN: Fortress Press, 2013), 178–79, for these observations.

43. See Murray A. Straus and Denise A. Donnelly, *Beating the Devil out of Them: Corporal Punishment in American Families and Its Effects on Children* (New Brunswick, NJ: Transaction, 2001).

44. Biggar, *In Defence of War*, 4.

45. Kyle, *American Sniper*, 120.

46. Ibid., 151–52.

47. Ibid., 132.

48. Ibid., 274.

49. Ibid.

50. See Tobias Winright and E. Ann Jeschke, "Combat and Confession: Just War and Moral Injury," in *Can War Be Just in the 21st Century?* (Maryknoll, NY: Orbis, 2015), 169–87.

51. See Sheila Frankfurt and Patricia Frazier, "A Review of Research on Moral Injury in Combat Veterans," *Military Psychology* 28 (2016): 318–30. In the field of Christian ethics, see Warren Kinghorn, "Combat Trauma and Moral Fragmentation: A Theological Account of Moral Injury," *Journal of the Society of Christian Ethics* 32, no. 2 (2012): 57–74. See

also E. Ann Jeschke, "The Moral Trauma of America's Warriors: Why We Must Treat Combat Posttraumatic Stress Disorder as a Bio-Psycho-Social-Spiritual Phenomenon," *Nova Law Review* 37 (2013): 547–78.

52. See Winright and Jeschke, "Combat and Confession," 171.

53. Bernard Verkamp, *The Moral Treatment of Returning Warriors in Early Medieval and Modern Times* (Scranton, PA: Scranton University Press, 2006).

54. Ibid., 47–48.

55. Reinhold Niebuhr, *Love and Justice*, ed. D. B. Robertson (Louisville, KY: Westminster/ John Knox Press, 1957), 243.

Exploitative Labor, Victimized Families, and the Promise of the Sabbath

Angela Carpenter

Families and children are hidden victims of labor exploitation in the US economy across the economic spectrum. The Sabbath commandment, however, provides a theological basis for resisting this structural evil. In Karl Barth's discussion of the commandment, Sabbath rest not only limits the scope of economic activity in human life but also sets the stage for reflection on the meaning and purpose of work. As a recurring reminder that human life is a gift to be lived in joyful fellowship with God and neighbor, Sabbath observance can be a crucial practice to orient work toward the flourishing of individuals, families, and communities.

IN JULY OF 2015 DEBRA HARRELL, A MCDONALD'S EMPLOYEE, was arrested for allowing her nine-year-old daughter to play at the park while Harrell was at work. The case received substantial news coverage at the time as one in a string of incidents that brought questions of parental supervision and the intervention of authorities into the public eye. While most commentators focused on the question of appropriate state interference with parenting decisions, many also noted the less-than-ideal parenting choices forced on low-wage workers in the contemporary US economy.[1] A McDonald's hourly wage is hardly sufficient to pay for childcare, and not all workers have reliable family members who are willing or able to help. Unlike most developed nations, public subsidies for childcare in the United States are patchy and difficult to access. In the contemporary work climate, what were Harrell's options?

On the surface, Harrell's situation is worlds apart from that of the wealthy businessman portrayed in the 2014 Cadillac commercial "Poolside." The actor in this ad extols the virtues of America's hard-work ethic, chastises the French for taking excessive vacations, and enjoys material goods like his new Cadillac not as the reason for his work but as an upside nonetheless. As the white male actor says, "It's pretty simple. You work hard. You create your own luck. And

Angela Carpenter, PhD, is an assistant professor of religion at Hope College, Lubbers Hall, 126 East 10th St., Holland, MI 49423-3516; carpenter@hope.edu.

Journal of the Society of Christian Ethics, 38, 1 (2018): 77–94

you gotta believe, anything is possible." With its message of autonomy, the vision of work depicted in the ad hardly seems vulnerable to exploitation, yet I will argue that common assumptions regarding work and human life in both of these scenarios allow for systemic exploitation of labor in the US workforce. Furthermore, this exploitation victimizes not only the workers themselves but also families and especially children. In response, I propose that the observance of Sabbath rest, as a theological and not just a secular practice, has the potential to disrupt the assumptions about human work on which this exploitation depends.

This argument proceeds in two stages. First, I investigate the exploitative labor practices in the United States and their implications for families and children. While labor exploitation can be found in more severe forms globally, within the developed world the United States is noteworthy for its minimal labor regulations and its thin network of social support for parents. In addition, labor exploitation in the United States, while most noticeable in lower socio-economic strata, can be found across the economic spectrum. I contend that its pervasiveness is due to underlying assumptions about labor in our economy and culture. Dominant culture suggests that employment constitutes a primary means of establishing personal identity and bestowing value on persons. From an economic perspective, a default assumption is that market forces should carry a greater weight in decisions regarding labor practices than human flourishing or the health of social institutions such as families.

The second part of the essay draws on Karl Barth's exposition of the Sabbath commandment in *Church Dogmatics*. For Barth, the primary significance of the Sabbath is not to provide protection for workers to limit the worst abuses of economic power. Instead, the rightly informed practice of the Sabbath calls into question the very assumptions on which the exploitative labor I describe in the first part depends. I conclude by considering how a conscious and reflective participation in this distinctly theological practice can undermine the assumptions on which labor exploitation is grounded.

Exploitative Labor and Victimized Children in the Contemporary US Economy

In the United States, labor exploitation is most noticeable and egregious among low-income hourly workers in the growing service sector. Among these workers, the most obvious aspect of exploitation is the fact that the wages are often insufficient to meet basic needs. An adult worker supporting a family of four needs to earn roughly $12 an hour just to rise above the poverty level. At present, more than a quarter of the US workforce earns less than this, and 28 percent of these workers have children. Forty percent of single mothers earn less than $12 an hour, and 22 percent of all US children live in a household with a parent earning less than $12 an hour.[2]

The extensive literature regarding the ill effects of poverty on children is, of course, widely known and hardly needs to be rehashed here. What is noteworthy, however, is how little the US government presently does, compared to other nations with similar economies, to try to neutralize poverty's effects.[3] Without government support, millions of low-wage workers like Debra Harrell are forced to make difficult choices between earning a living and providing safe care for their children.

Low wages and the corresponding effects of poverty are only the most obvious form of systemic labor injustice wreaking havoc on American families. A variety of other features of low-wage jobs also signal the underlying assumption that these employees should be treated primarily as workers without lives or responsibilities that would ever take precedence over the demands of their jobs. Low-wage jobs tend to have minimal or nonexistent benefits such as health insurance or paid leave. Among service-sector jobs, for instance, only 39 percent of workers have paid sick time, only 20 percent have personal time, and only 53 percent have paid vacation.[4] When you add to this the crisis of quality, affordable childcare, the challenges of combining work in the service sector with life as a parent are profound.[5] Benefits such as these enable workers to not only care for children when the need arises but to cultivate strong and healthy parenting relationships by being present with children in important life events. The provision of these minimal benefits implies that employees are persons with complex lives and not simply laborers.

Another feature of low-wage jobs that contradicts the complex humanity of workers is nonstandard work scheduling. In the current 24/7 economy, roughly 20 percent of the US workforce has some form of nonstandard schedule. The majority of these workers do not adopt a nonstandard schedule by choice and end up missing key time for family activities like eating meals together or assisting with homework. Furthermore, the formal childcare network is generally operative only during standard working hours, forcing nonstandard workers to rely on family members, friends, or neighbors. While such care can be excellent, workers in this situation are more likely to be pressured into relying on persons they do not fully trust or who are not fully committed to the task. A robust body of literature over the past few decades has thoroughly documented the precise risks involved for families where one or more parents works a nonstandard schedule. From infancy through adolescence, having a parent who works a nonstandard schedule correlates with an increased risk of adverse academic, behavioral, and psychological development, even when factors such as socioeconomic status are controlled.[6]

Nonstandard schedules have been a reality in the service sector for some time, but new scheduling technologies are currently used in ways that increase demands on workers' time and heighten the stress surrounding childcare. Employers use computer programs to track demand for services and then schedule shifts to best match consumer demand. Workers impacted by these technologies not only work outside the hours of 6:00 a.m. to 6:00 p.m. but their schedule varies from week to week, often with little notice. This "just in time scheduling" frequently requires employees to call in every morning to see if their services are needed. The Economic Policy Institute estimates that a minimum of 10 percent of the current workforce operates with this sort of irregular work schedule.[7] Within the past few years coverage in the popular media has brought this new form of worker exploitation to the attention of the general population, and workers have seen some modest concession from individual employers, but these technologies continue to be widely used throughout the service sector.[8]

The pressure that unpredictable schedules impose on workers and their families is substantial. The worker's time is never her own. She is always potentially a phone call away from having employee responsibilities that she cannot refuse. Childcare in these circumstances generally cannot be arranged with licensed providers, and even if the childcare industry were capable of adjusting to these workers' needs, it would hardly be in the best interest of children. A routine schedule with a consistent set of childcare workers is one of the most important criteria for emotional security when children are in an institutional setting.[9] Once again, parents who are subject to this kind of work schedule are forced to cobble together care from family and friends, who participate with varying degrees of enthusiasm. Meanwhile parents' relationships with their children lack the consistency of routine that developmental experts have long held to be crucial for children's health and well-being. In addition to causing problems with childcare and parent–child relationships, irregular and unpredictable schedules make it difficult for workers to arrange transportation, balance work with school, or participate in other relationships and activities that are part of ordinary human lives. In extreme cases, this sort of management practice effectually claims the whole of the employee's life for work.

For most low-wage workers, random or nonstandard schedules are more of a problem than overwork. In fact, workers complain about reductions in their hours—and, consequently, their pay—as retribution for actions like staying home with a sick child. At the same time, the dearth of full-time employment does pressure some low-wage workers to seek multiple jobs and, thus, longer hours. Others at the managerial level might still make a very low salary, just over the current $23,660 minimum that prevents them from being subject to time-and-half overtime, and subsequently be forced to work much longer than forty hours a week.

None of these employment practices in the low-income sector is particularly surprising. The decline of unions in the US workforce means that market-driven labor practices are increasingly unregulated. Low-wage workers are generally less educated and have little access to power and influence by which they might work for change. And, naturally, unionization among these industries is highly discouraged. But the systemic and structural injustices—and their repercussions for children and families—are not limited to low-wage employees. The ongoing debates surrounding work–life balance and gender among educated professionals indicate that many careers in higher socioeconomic strata are often inconsistent with other life responsibilities, especially care for dependent family members.

While, among lower-income workers, an excess of hours is discouraged by overtime law, for most salaried workers there are no legal limits to the number of hours in the work week.[10] The work expectations for many professionals were set at a time when a one-income household was the norm, with a stay-at-home adult, the wife, available to care for the home and family. This picture of the American family has changed substantially, but the work expectations for careers have not. Today, 25 percent of salaried workers report working sixty or more hours a week. An additional 25 percent work fifty to fifty-nine hours per week.[11] While many of these workers technically have provisions like sick leave, vacation time, and family leave (the lack of which constantly threatens the livelihood of many lower-income workers), whether they can use such provisions without professional consequence is a matter of intense public debate. The fact that women continue to constitute a minority of workers in the upper echelons of most professions is suggestive of structural impediments to combining family life and professional success.

This argument, which rejects the dominant narrative that women choose family over work or that women are unable to balance work and family, has become more visible in the past few years. Anne-Marie Slaughter's recent book, *Unfinished Business*, has suggested for a popular audience that the problem with work–life balance is not a problem with *women* but rather a problem with *work*. The working world of the twenty-first century, she argues, is inhospitable to the responsibilities for care faced by the majority of workers, including men. Slaughter's basic argument is supported by a growing body of academic research.[12] Harvard business professor Robin Ely and colleagues, for instance, found that in one consulting firm, both men and women expressed dissatisfaction with seventy-hour workweeks and 24/7 accessibility to work through communication technologies. In this case, both men and women were leaving the firm at the same rate. Among those who stayed, however, men tended to suffer in silence or covertly adjust their schedule while women took work–life accommodations and saw their chances for promotion decline. The problem, according to Ely's analysis, was not the inability of women to balance work with family but the culture of overwork that affected men and women alike.[13]

Scholars such as Slaughter and Ely helpfully identify the structural exploitation of labor in the professional class, but they tend to overlook an important facet of this exploitation that distinguishes it from the dilemmas facing low-wage workers. In the case of many career-oriented professionals, long hours are not technically required, but the work environment and its culture enlist the worker's participation in the exploitation of labor. In these cases, it is not enough to analyze institutional and legal structures without also attending to how these interact with the psychological dynamics of elite American workers.[14]

The high-powered world of American finance is an excellent site to analyze this dynamic not only because it is visible in the extreme work habits of Wall Street bankers but because so many workers begin in finance and subsequently move to other influential fields, including politics, business, or academia. Sociologist Alexandra Michel's twelve-year ethnography of investment bankers illustrates the way that organizational structure and worker choice combine to create a culture of extreme overwork.[15] In the two banks Michel studied, power differentials were deemphasized and bankers were given tremendous autonomy to set their own work schedules. The workplace, however, was always open and provided a variety of conveniences such as meals, fitness facilities, and dry cleaning. While such practices had the stated goal of facilitating work–life balance and allowing workers time with family, their actual effect was the opposite. Rather than freeing up time for spouses or children, these structures created the illusion that all time was for working. Bankers were technically free to work whenever they chose, but they chose to work virtually nonstop. Competition between bankers and a personal identity that associated self-worth with high productivity ultimately served to heighten work hours under the auspices of autonomy.

The personal costs that Michel details as a result of such a grueling work pace eventually forced most bankers out of the field by their mid-thirties. When these employees entered other segments of the economy, however, they took this autonomous work ethic with them. A focus on results rather than a work schedule, for instance, pressured workers in other settings to compete with one another for bonuses and promotions based on output. Instead of working less and spending time with family, employees were pressured to work more and more. For many, this culture of work became a central part of their identity and was emulated by colleagues. As one former banker told Michel, "The more you work, the more of a hero you were. But I found that this is true everywhere. Even the people I meet randomly at the gym, they cannot appreciate my skills. . . . But they do understand and have awe for hard work."[16]

Michel's analysis suggests that the culture of work in elite settings can have a spillover effect throughout society. On a practical level, a 24/7 work culture creates a heightened demand for services from low-wage workers. The identities and ideals cultivated by elite workers also set the stage for work expectations on a broader cultural level. It is the business and political elite who set the labor practices and legal restrictions for the economy as a whole. In a survey of more than two thousand managers and executives around the world, more than three-fourths thought the best workers were those without many personal commitments, and over half thought a high commitment to personal and family lives was inconsistent, for both men and women, with a high commitment to work.[17] It is hardly surprising when these elite workers make judgments about other socioeconomic strata through the lenses of their own work–life culture. A 2014 Pew survey, for instance, found that more than half of the most financially secure Americans agreed with the statement "Poor people today have it easy because they can get government benefits without doing anything in return."[18] Like the Cadillac man, these workers tend to associate affluence with hard work and poverty with laziness. Such sentiments, however, are not limited to the wealthy. In the United States, a full 73 percent of the population say it is "very important"—a 10 on a 10-point scale—to work hard to get ahead in life. By comparison, only 49 percent of Germans and 25 percent of French say the same.

While wealthier professionals have greater financial resources to mitigate the harmful effects of long and irregular hours on children, and they have the option of one parent scaling back on career objectives, the stress of work can still take a toll on marriages and children.[19] The psychology of work and identity, however, does not simply lead to competition between work and family. It is also passed on to children as they develop their own sense of identity and self-worth. Psychologist Suniya Luthar has explored the unique pressures facing adolescents in wealthy families, and her research suggests that maladjustment among upper-middle-class and wealthy youth rivals or surpasses that of youth in poorer communities.[20] According to Luthar's reading of upper-middle-class families, children come to internalize from a very early age the significance of wealth for their ultimate happiness and believe the path to wealth is attending an elite university followed by a lucrative career. Therefore, these children are subject to enormous pressure from parents, peers, their schools, and ultimately themselves. Luthar's research indicates that adolescents in this demographic are significantly more likely to use cigarettes, alcohol, and hard drugs. These trends only continue in college.[21] Upper-middle-class adolescents also have rates of delinquency similar to inner-city youth and exhibit rates of depression and anxiety higher than the national norm. Luthar's work links these disturbing outcomes among adolescents to a combination of stress, limited parental supervision, and children's perception of their parent's approval coming from achievement and success rather than from their character or from unconditional parental love.[22] She summarizes her findings saying, "It is no surprise, therefore, that among our children the driving sentiments are essentially . . . 'I can, therefore I must, achieve: strive for the top, to attain what my parents achieved. This is the central imperative life goal; nothing else is as important. Without such success, I will be left behind as a failure, as others soar to great heights.'"[23]

In the higher socioeconomic strata, it seems that the insatiability of the modern economy thus colludes with a particularly troubling set of psychological dynamics that are present in parents and passed on to their children. The competition inherent in the economic structures feeds on a deep insecurity and an insatiable need to prove one's worth by succeeding at ever-higher levels. These dynamics are also not limited to the most financially lucrative professions but can be observed to varying degrees in middle-class careers such as public service or in academia.

It is worth pausing here to note that while the types of systemic exploitation in the US labor force differ according to socioeconomic class, a set of common assumptions supports this exploitation. First, there are assumptions about work and time. In a modern economy the patterns of work are increasingly such that the worker's time is continually at risk of being claimed by work. New technologies in particular have helped to erase the limitations that were previously placed on an employers' ability to claim the time of workers. This is not simply an issue of too many hours being claimed by work. Rather, it is a lack of any theoretical limits to working time and what this suggests regarding the importance of other aspects of life. This means that any time in a person's life is increasingly liable to the claims of work, suggesting that human life is for the sake of work, rather than work existing for the sake of human life and flourishing.

Underlying this trend is a further assumption about the meaning and primacy of work in establishing human identity and value. Increasingly, we see labor practices that presume a person is identified with her work and that work in turn validates the person. The person apart from work has no meaning or value that enables us to think about the appropriate scope of work. We see this in the way that the basic provisions for a meaningful life apart from work are denied to low-income workers, with the denial of a living wage, sick time, vacation time, and appropriate flexibility to care for loved ones. We also see this in professional classes where workers consent to dedicating more and more of life to work so that they can attain ever-greater markers of success such as promotions, bonuses, and awards. It's an assumption that is almost theological in character. Joan Williams, one of the leading researchers on work–life balance, characterizes this employee who is defined by and always available for work as the "ideal worker." Williams writes, "The belief in the ideal worker way of working is so deep that even when you introduce evidence that contradicts it, people just don't buy it. It shows you that what's operating is much deeper. It's not about the rational weighing of evidence. We're talking about work as people's religion."[24]

Despite these common assumptions that shape the exploitation of labor across the economic spectrum, there is also a crucial difference regarding the workings of personal agency. For the lower-income worker, the exploitation is imposed and inescapable. Economic realities at present leave little alternative. The professional worker, however, is psychologically formed and pressured to collude in the exploitation of labor, which of course can be imposed externally as well. This worker's own desires and choices are enlisted in the effort to exploit her labor.

Barth's Theology of the Sabbath

Thus far I have argued that labor exploitation takes very specific forms in the contemporary United States and has as its hidden victims the families and children of workers. In this second part of the essay, we turn to one of the oldest forms of limitation on human labor—the practice of the Sabbath. While resistance to exploitation must ultimately take many and varied forms, I argue that Karl Barth's exposition of the Sabbath in *Church Dogmatics* provides a foundation for challenging the basic assumptions about the role of work in human life. Observance of the Sabbath can thus be seen as a practice of resistance to the quasi-theology that undergirds exploitation. The structure of this analysis begins by looking at the way in which Barth's understanding of Sabbath contests the claims on human time that we have observed in the contemporary labor market. From here I turn to the alternative vision of human identity and its relation to work that Barth believes is recalled and instantiated in Sabbath observance. I conclude with some practical reflections on what Sabbath observance as a practice of resistance might entail in a contemporary setting.

Barth begins his discussion of the "Holy Day" with a broader point about the meaning of human life. To be human, Barth says, is to be in a position of freedom and responsibility before God.[25] This divine–human covenant relationship is the most basic and fundamental meaning of human existence. Such a posture, however, cannot simply be considered in the general and abstract. To make this existence possible, God also commands a particular existence from humanity, a particularity that Barth explores under the heading of the Sabbath command, which, he contends, "explains all the other commandments."[26] In contrast to a labor context where the use of workers' time—any of their time—is increasingly within the control of employers, Barth claims that the whole of a person's time is claimed by God for freedom and responsibility before God.[27] Because all of time is claimed by God, a specific time and a particular act are claimed in the Sabbath command.[28]

Barth's exegesis of the text in Genesis suggests that the command of the Holy Day is based on the fact that human time begins not with working or with the observation of divine working but with rest, celebration, and freedom. Humanity is created on day six, and therefore the first thing that human beings do is participate in the divine celebration of rest and joy in the goodness of creation. For Barth this means that the divine–human relationship, the existence of the human person as constituted for freedom and responsibility before God, is not an optional "add-on" to creation but rather is woven into its very fabric as the beginning of human time. "To the creation itself," Barth writes, "there belongs also this particular event of the seventh day, the 'rest' in which the living God both confronted and also associated Himself with the cosmos and man in the cosmos."[29] Barth connects this sequence of rest before work with his gospel/law thesis in which gospel takes priority to law. The fact that human time begins with rest means that human experience begins with the gospel. Only after this gospel rest is the commission to work—which Barth maps onto law—applicable.

Socially, the implications of this temporal ordering are profound. It means that rest, not work, sets the initial context for human activity, and it is to rest, not work, that this activity is repeatedly oriented. As Barth puts it, "the first word said to him, the first obligation brought to his notice, is that without any works or merits he himself may rest with God and then go to his work."[30] For Barth, this means that Sabbath is the true time by which we understand all other time. We cannot think about and understand the working day without first understanding the Holy Day. It is the latter that provides the standard for human life and thus for grasping the true meaning of work.[31]

Within this framework, the regular practice of observing Sabbath rest reconfigures the person's understanding of the passage of time and thus of human activity that takes up this time. The Holy Day is a "recurring interruption," a break in the passage of time and ordinary activity that requires the adherent to pause her own striving and reflect on God's saving activity that always comes before and establishes her own working. Barth writes, "The command of God introduces free grace into the human scene, taking up time in the midst of the succession of human undertakings and achievements."[32] This reconfiguration of time through a recurring interruption is ultimately also eschatological. The Holy Day is both beginning and end, evoking the final day of God's activity that will bring an end to human working as well as evoking the day of each person's death, when her own activity is seen clearly in its limited character.[33] The Sabbath is thus a continually recurring interruption of ordinary activity and work. It forms a person in the recognition of God's gift as both the foundation and limit of her own activity.

It is worth pausing here to consider how this practice and its theological rationale challenge contemporary assumptions regarding time and work. Barth's description of the Sabbath as a recurring interruption includes but also goes beyond the idea of limit—its intent is not to divide human time into sections such that employers can claim a certain portion, whatever that might be, as their legitimate sphere. The implications of Sabbath time are instead much more totalizing. And the limit to the ordinary activity we call "work" is so that we can recognize and internalize this comprehensive claim. The interruption and limit are not to establish a boundary to "work time" as opposed to "leisure time." Instead, they function to constantly reiterate the comprehensive divine claim. All time belongs to God. This totalizing assertion puts the question of human meaning in relation to God at the center of how we think about human activity in time. God claims all of time precisely so the whole of human life can be freedom for God and responsibility before God. Any absolutizing of employer claims to time are therefore unjust usurpations of this divine claim. They fail to see the human person as created fundamentally and completely for this freedom and responsibility. The human person is not for work. The person is for God, and work must fit within and serve this prior covenantal relationship.

With respect to the professional classes, who collude in the coopting of time, the function of Sabbath observance as a practice of resistance seems clear. Even though most Christian communities today don't make much of Sabbath observance beyond participation in worship, one can see how such a practice, engaged in with the kind of intentionality and reflection Barth envisions, could facilitate new patterns of thought with respect to time and human activity. By taking a day away not only from the office but also from work emails and phones, the illusion of constant responsibility to one's employer or to unlimited professional expectations is interrupted. By focusing this day, through worship and rest, on the primacy of grace in human life, the Sabbath reorients human activity not to a job or an employer but to ultimate freedom and responsibility before God.

For the hourly worker, however, who ordinarily has no choice in such matters apart from abandoning his or her job, the issue is more complex. Can Sabbath observance still function as a practice of resistance to the exploitation of time in this context? Barth addresses this question at a few points in his discussion. First, he criticizes the Sabbath legislation of earlier eras as being "blatantly adapted to the requirements and claims of the ruling classes."[34] The Sabbath, he says, was in practice not for all humans but instead allowed the ruling classes to claim the labor of "domestic servants and other dependents." In contrast to this socioeconomic stratification, Barth argues that in scripture the Sabbath is given to the person in community and not as an isolated individual. Thus, actual Sabbath legislation might indeed be needed to protect against the compulsion of some workers by others who require their services.[35] I return to this question in a moment but for the present simply observe that resisting the coopting of time involves more than individual Sabbath observance. It also requires the support of social structures that afford all community members the same responsibility and freedom before God. And it may indeed call for structural change that goes beyond the traditional observance of Sunday rest in resisting the absolute claims of employers on worker time. In the words of biblical scholar Walter Brueggemann, Sabbath calls for sponsoring a "system of rest" rather than a "system of anxiety."[36]

We have seen, then, how Sabbath observance in Barth's analysis calls for a specific perspective on time and human activity within it, one that undermines the expansive claims of contemporary employers on worker time. Barth's insistence that the Sabbath is a way for grace to occupy time in the midst of human activity also has deeper implications for the identity and self-worth of the one who observes the Sabbath. By "taking up time" and "interrupting" ordinary activity, Sabbath observance is an opportunity for grace to reconfigure human identity and value. Barth gets at this transformation through what he calls "renunciating faith," by which he means a faith in God that results in the person's renunciation not only of the self but of "all that he thinks and wills and effects and achieves." It is this kind of faith that is for Barth the "comprehensive content of the Sabbath commandment."[37]

But how can the observance of the Sabbath instill such a kenosis and, perhaps more importantly, does it thereby eliminate the possibility for legitimate human working? The connection between rest and identity is grounded in the relationship Barth detects between human activity and human self-worth. Barth thinks that most of us, most of the time, look to what we do rather than who we are before God as the source of our value. He also thinks that this is a perfectly rational self-understanding and not in itself an aspect of human corruption. "For in what possible self-understanding can man fail to posit, affirm and express himself, and as far as he is able represent and help and justify himself."[38] In contrast to this ordinary self-understanding, Barth argues that it is through the regular cessation of work that a person concretely, in the course of everyday life, makes space to consciously recognize and affirm the grace of the divine "yes." What is always true of genuine human activity—that it is established by grace and directed toward grace—must be consciously recognized on a recurring basis. To truly do justice to one's own work, one must actually, in lived existence, observe and confront the origin of human activity in God's gift. The weekly limit on human working forces just such a confrontation. With the interruption of work by the imperative of rest, the person is not allowed to assume that his own capacities are sufficient. He is not even allowed to assume that these capacities are in fact his own. Limitation in the form of a command to rest points the person to the commanding God "who is gracious to man in Jesus Christ."[39] The Sabbath rest directs a person away from what he does for himself and toward what God does for him. It thus forces the recognition of human activity as a gift, one that is dependent on, and not in competition with, a prior divine working.

The interruption of Sabbath rest, with its recognition of human limitation and grounding of human activity in grace, does not thereby negate human capacity for work or the divine commissioning to make use of that capacity.

Instead, Barth insists that the Sabbath command does not forbid a person "to speak an active Yes of his own to himself and human society. It even commands him to do so." Rather, what the Sabbath forbids is that one "try to live by the Yes which he can say to himself or others or to the cosmos."[40] In other words, the Sabbath functions to frustrate and subvert an identity characterized by self-sufficiency by reminding the person that who and what she will become is ultimately not her own accomplishment. Rather, all human identity and accomplishment have their origin in God's gift, and one should therefore never imagine "that what is going to become of him, his future and that of his fellow-men, lies in his own power."[41] This recurring frustration of a false human grasping is ultimately what Barth means by the "renunciating faith" that forms the comprehensive content of the Sabbath. By recalling one's origin and establishment in grace, one gives up any other basis of self-understanding.

If the Holy Day is genuinely celebrated, if it is a rest from work, a day of joy, an opportunity to reflect on and receive God's grace, a time of human fellowship, and a rejection of the desperate human grasping for performance-based approval, then the "renunciating faith" of the Sabbath does not undermine authentic human working but rather supports it. The human "yes" displayed in authentic activity and working on behalf of human society is liberated from any role it might play in establishing worth or value. One need not enslave oneself to work for the sake of establishing the self as master over it. Instead one can work with a sense of peace regarding the outcome. Barth writes of such a liberated worker, "As he is busy on the everyday, he will also rest; as he fights on the everyday, he will also be at peace; as he works on the everyday, he will also pray. At the same time he will both grasp completely and let go completely. At bottom, he will never be anxious on the working day. Why not? *Nostri non sumus sed Domini.*" (We are not our own, but the Lord's.)[42] Workers are liberated in that they can work diligently and with devotion to the tasks to which they have been called, but they can also work with complete trust and abandon.

To observe the Sabbath, in Barth's analysis, is thus to resist the basic assumption that human value is derived from or supported by human labor. Not only are human beings not "for" work but work is not for humanity, if by that we intend to say that work enables the person to judge the worth of self or others. Work is for humanity in a different sense. It is the gift that allows that human person to speak a "yes"—a word of grace—to self and others that corresponds to God's "yes."[43] To collude with the culture of competition for ever-greater work and ever-greater human accomplishment is to distort our understanding of human purpose and the proper role of work within that purpose. This may be one of the few times when Barth's exclusive use of masculine pronouns is less of a problem from a feminist perspective. For it is emphatically not a matter of allowing women to "balance" work with life, but it is a reorientation and delimiting of work for everyone, perhaps most especially for the wealthy businessman in the Cadillac commercial. Ideally such a reorientation carries with it a reverse "spillover" effect to the one I analyzed with respect to overwork. Those who are able to resist a culture of work do so not simply on a personal level. Rather, it is resistance to an ideology that values human activity and human accomplishment—labor and its products—over the humanity of those who work.

Indeed, as Barth describes it, the practice of Sabbath rest is given not to the individual but ultimately to the community.[44] This includes, naturally, the communal practice of worship, the content of which should be the "the joy which should be to all people" rather than a series of religious or moral ideals under the guise of the gospel.[45] But it also, for Barth, involves time for relationships, for deliberate human fellowship that might not take place otherwise. Building on Barth's brief comments regarding the potential for exploitation of a subset of workers on the Sabbath, I would argue that it must also be seen as a ground or source of communal protest. I think here of those low-wage workers like Debra Harrell, who work extremely hard yet remain in or near poverty and who do not receive sick leave, family leave, vacation days, assistance with child care, or scheduling accommodations to care for family members. Just as the Sabbath insists that human dignity is a gift that precedes any activity for the elite professional, the same is true for the working class. For low-wage workers, however, because the unlimited scope of work tends to be imposed on them without their consent, the communal observance of the Sabbath calls for reflection on how work might be appropriately limited for all workers. What labor structures would allow grace to take up space in a collective imagination as the ground of all human identity and value?

I cannot answer such questions comprehensively here, but before making some initial suggestions, it is worth noting that the underlying aim, that of making genuine Sabbath rest available broadly across society and not just among the middle and upper classes, is firmly part of the biblical mandate. As Brueggemann notes, the Israelites are not commanded to rest until they are liberated from the economic oppression of Egypt. In other words, those who are oppressed are not blamed for their inability to observe the Sabbath. Likewise, when the law is given to Moses, it contains within it recognition that the rest of some—namely, children, slaves, and even animals—is under the control of others. So the command is not only to rest but to allow others to rest as well.[46] As Barth intuits, without developing as thoroughly as one might like, authentic observance of the Holy Day must therefore be communal and structural as well as personal and freely undertaken.

What, then, might be the structures that would make rest more widely available? The question must be asked both at the interpersonal and familial level as well as at the level of broader society. First, we would do well to consider the ways in which our own choices demand the work of others so that we might enjoy rest. Should Sabbath observance perhaps include a cessation not merely of work but also of consumption? The issue is particularly important in the household, where unpaid care work, much of which cannot be deferred to another day, falls disproportionately on women. Genuine Sabbath observance must be a matter of household members collaborating to achieve an equitable and mutual practice of rest, which must include any children in the rhythms of work and rest as well. For example, can essential tasks like meal preparation be made restful by being simplified and undertaken as a form of fellowship and celebration? Julie Hanlon Rubio's work on family practices helpfully lays a theoretical foundation that could support more extensive reflection on family Sabbath observance.[47] Not only is Sabbath given to the community, but ultimately it will be authentically observed only if it is practiced together rather than by each person in isolation.

The same principle applies when considering the broader society. To observe the Sabbath is paradoxically to work toward the possibility of equitable observance, to identify and resist the ways that work makes absolute claims not just on the self but on all persons. In the secular, 24/7 economy of the twenty-first century, the Sabbath laws of a bygone era are not likely to return. Nor is it clear that such legislation on its own would address the particular violations of the Sabbath that we encounter. Structurally, we are allowing employers to make absolute claims on the time of workers that are not resolved by granting a day off. For the lower-income worker, the problem is just as much knowing when one will work and whether one will get enough hours as it is not being allowed a day off. Socially and structurally, we also assume that many of the benefits essential to ordinary and dignified life must be earned through the right kind of work. In these circumstances, communal observance of the Sabbath should also take the form of advocacy and support for basic worker rights like sick leave, a living wage, accommodations for care responsibilities, and reasonable, consistent work schedules. These kinds of structural changes are essential to resisting a culture that idolizes work and thereby diminishes human persons.

It might, of course, be objected that these initiatives are standard for the liberal democracies of Western Europe and its predominantly secular culture. Do we really benefit from a specifically theological argument for this kind of advocacy? Addressing the complicated question of European secularity is a topic for another essay, but minimally it should be noted that we cannot abstract European social ideals from centuries of Christian culture. In our own context, however, religion is still a factor in public discourse. Why not therefore make a theological argument for those inclined to hear it? One might point to the success of AIDS advocacy during the George W. Bush administration as one example of where such theological arguments have had some success.[48] Given the ongoing debates about work and family life in the broader culture, we may even find that some of our secular citizens will also be receptive to aspects of a theological analysis of work and authentic human purpose.

Notes

1. Bryce Covert, "McDonald's Fires Mom Who Was Arrested for Letting 9-Year-Old Play in Park Alone," *ThinkProgress*, July 22, 2014, http://thinkprogress.org/economy /2014/07/22/3462704/debra-harrell-fired/.

2. David Cooper, "Raising the Minimum Wage to $12 by 2020 Would Lift Wages for 35 Million American Workers," Economic Policy Institute, July 14, 2015.

3. Lillian Mongeau, "Why Does America Invest So Little in Its Children?," *Atlantic*, July 12, 2016, https://www.theatlantic.com/education/archive/2016/07 /why-does-america-invest-so-little-in-its-children/490790/.

4. U.S. Department of Labor, "Employee Benefits Survey," March 2015. http://www.bls .gov/ncs/ebs/benefits/2015/ownership/private/table32a.htm.

5. On the issue of childcare quality in the US, see Brigid Schulte, *Overwhelmed: Work, Love, and Play When No One Has the Time* (New York: Sarah Crichton Books, 2014), 97–116.

6. Jianghong Li, Sarah Johnson, Wen-Jui Han, Sonia Andrews, Garth Kendall, Lyndall Strazdins, and Alfred Michael Dockery, "Parents Nonstandard Work Schedules and Child Well-Being: A Critical Review of the Literature," *Journal of Primary Prevention* 35 (2014): 53–73.

7. Lonnie Golden, "Irregular Work Scheduling and Its Consequences," Economic Policy Institute, April 9, 2015.

8. For coverage in popular media, see Jodi Kantor, "Working Anything but 9 to 5: Scheduling Technology Leaves Low-Income Parents with Hours of Chaos," *New York Times*, August 13, 2014; Brian Nearing, "On Call Scheduling Benefits Employers, Can Leave Workers Scrambling," *Times Union*, November 16, 2015; and Seth Freed Wessler, "Shift Change: 'Just-in-Time' Scheduling Creates Chaos for Workers," *NBC News*, May 10, 2014.

9. For a review of the literature on optimal childcare conditions, see Sarah Blaffer Hrdy, *Mother and Others: The Evolutionary Origins of Mutual Understanding* (Cambridge, MA: Belknap Press, 2009).

10. President Obama's new overtime regulations are designed to change this reality for millions of workers by raising the income threshold to $47,476. At present, a federal judge has blocked this rule from taking effect as planned on December 1, 2016.

11. Lydia Saad, "The '40-Hour' Workweek Is Actually Longer—By Seven Hours," *Gallup News*, August 29, 2014, http://www.gallup.com/poll/175286/hour-workweek-actually -longer-seven-hours.aspx.

12. See Joan C. Williams and Heather Boushey, "The Three Faces of Work-Family Conflict: The Poor, the Professionals, and the Missing Middle," Center for American Progress, January 25, 2010; and Heather Boushey and Bridget Ansel, "Overworked America: The Economic Causes and Consequences of Long Work Hours," Washington Center for Equitable Growth, May 16, 2016. Brigid Schulte also surveys much of this literature in *Overwhelmed*, 71–96.

13. Robin Ely and Irene Padavic, "Work–Family Conflict Is Not the Problem. Overwork Is," *Huffington Post*, last updated January 23, 2014, http://www.huffingtonpost.com/robin-j -ely/workfamily-conflict-is-no_b_4221360.html.

14. Several authors writing on the work–family interface recognize the power of cultural dynamics yet overlook the way human autonomy and desire is enlisted as a mechanism for exploitation. Heather Boushey, for instance, observes that some professionals overwork voluntarily, but she does not probe why they might make this choice or its cultural

ramifications. Boushey and Ansel, "Overworked America," 31. Likewise, Slaughter insists that her aim is to revalue care, not devalue competition. Anne-Marie Slaughter, *Unfinished Business: Women, Men, Work, Family* (New York: Random House, 2015), 121. Slaughter never asks, however, if care can be valued without questioning the scope that competition for professional success occupies in conceptions of the good life.

15. Alexandra Michel, "Participation and Self-Entrapment: A 12-Year Ethnography of Wall Street Participation Practices' Diffusion and Evolving Consequences," *Sociological Quarterly* 55 (2014): 514–36.

16. Ibid., 528.

17. Schulte, *Overwhelmed*, 79.

18. "The Politics of Financial Insecurity: A Democratic Tilt, Undercut by Low Participation," Pew Research Center, accessed January 2, 2017, http://www.people-press.org/2015/01/08/the-politics-of-financial-insecurity-a-democratic-tilt-undercut-by-low-participation/#political-values-and-partisan-choices.

19. Williams and Boushey, "Three Faces of Work-Family Conflict"; and Boushey and Ansel, "Overworked America."

20. Suniya S. Luthar, Samuel H. Barkin, and Elizabeth J. Crossman, "'I can, therefore I must': Fragility in the Upper-Middle Classes," *Development and Psychopathology* 25 (2013): 1529–49.

21. Ibid., 1530.

22. Ibid., 1532.

23. Ibid., 1545.

24. Quoted in Schulte, *Overwhelmed*, 89.

25. Karl Barth, *Church Dogmatics*, ed. Geoffrey M. Bromiley and T. F. Torrance (Edinburgh: T&T Clark, 1956–1975), III/4, 47.

26. Ibid., 53.

27. While such a statement might initially sound simply like an alternative form of tyranny and human subjugation, Barth takes great pains here and at other points throughout *Church Dogmatics* to avoid such a conclusion. Here the covenantal intent of the divine claim—that it is for freedom and responsibility before God—is crucial. God's claim of the whole of time is directed toward the potential for human freedom whether this freedom before God is exercised in "joyful acceptance or denial." Barth, *Church Dogmatics*, III/4, 47.

28. Ibid., 49.

29. Ibid., 52.

30. Ibid.

31. Ibid., 51.

32. Ibid., 54.

33. Ibid., 58.

34. Ibid., 66.

35. Ibid., 69.

36. Walter Brueggemann, *Sabbath as Resistance: Saying No to the Culture of Now* (Louisville, KY: Westminster John Knox, 2014), 30.

37. Barth, *Church Dogmatics*, III/4, 59–60.

38. Ibid., 58.

39. Ibid., 53.

40. Ibid., 54.

41. Ibid.

42. Ibid., 72.

43. Ibid., 53.

44. Ibid., 70.

45. Ibid., 69.

46. Brueggemann, *Sabbath as Resistance*, 40–41.

47. Julie Hanlon Rubio, *Family Ethics: Practices for Christians* (Washington, DC: Georgetown University Press, 2010).

48. Sheryl Gay Stolberg, "In Global Battle on AIDS, Bush Creates Legacy," *New York Times*, January 5, 2008, http://www.nytimes.com/2008/01/05/washington/05aids.html.

Raising Our Kids: Social and Theological Accounts of Child-Rearing amid Inequality and Mass Incarceration

Kathryn Getek Soltis

There are 2.7 million children with an incarcerated parent, resulting in profoundly negative consequences for these children and society at large. Whether this is viewed as an injustice, however, depends on our account of parenting. This essay argues for an understanding of child-rearing as contributive justice, correcting for an overly privatized concept of parenting and specifically challenging the invisibility of parents and children in our criminal justice system. After examining the sources of the more private, children-as-pets account of parenting, I consider accounts of child-rearing that emerge from the Catholic theological tradition, noting both the promising directions and the obstacles. This analysis is then applied to the realities faced by children of incarcerated parents, revealing the urgent need to see child-rearing as integral to any system of justice.

WITH THE 2015 PUBLICATION OF ROBERT PUTNAM'S *OUR KIDS*, new attention has been directed to the inequalities faced by American children. Putnam identifies a threefold threat from the growing opportunity gap among our youth: threats to our economy, democracy, and values.[1] He maintains that we ignore the plight of poor children, and this imposes economic burdens on the entire society. At the same time, class differences in political voice delegitimize democracy and exacerbate alienation. Finally, Putnam warns about the erosion of our values, undermining the professed belief in equal worth and opportunity. Significantly, Putnam notes that past successful responses to similar threats involved a "commitment to invest in other people's children." In short, we must see all kids as our kids.

In order to establish this robust sense of collective responsibility, policies must be revised and moral imagination must be expanded. At present, child-rearing is largely regarded as a private activity. Yet a model of parenthood that

Kathryn Getek Soltis, PhD, is the director of the Center for Peace and Justice Education and an assistant professor of Christian ethics at Villanova University, 800 Lancaster Ave., Villanova, PA 19085; kathryn.geteksoltis@villanova.edu.

Journal of the Society of Christian Ethics, 38, 1 (2018): 95–112

is set apart from the interests of society is incompatible with justice. A clear example is mass incarceration, through which the United States removes and stigmatizes millions of parents. Seven percent of all children under eighteen—more than 5 million children—have a parent who went to jail or prison.[2] Research suggests that mass imprisonment has more impact on social inequality through these children than from its effects on the men and women who are actually incarcerated.[3] Here is a structural failure to recognize child-rearing as a public concern and a matter of justice. For the sake of all our kids, we must challenge and revise the language that disassociates parenting from the common good. In what follows, I argue that an account of child-rearing as contributive justice is able to correct an overly privatized conceptualization of the family. First, I examine the sources of this private account of parenting. Second, I look to the accounts of child-rearing that emerge from the Catholic theological tradition, noting both the promising directions and the obstacles. Third, I put forward a vision of parenting as contributive justice. In the fourth and final section, I show how a contributive justice approach is particularly important in the context of mass incarceration.

A Private Vision of Child-Rearing

In her work on family ethics, Julie Hanlon Rubio challenges the strictly private view of family life.[4] She develops her argument by taking to task dominant cultural narratives of marriage that are turned in on themselves, "diminishing the necessity and importance of the rest of the . . . world."[5] There are parallel cultural narratives for parenthood, situating children in the private haven of the family and set apart from society. Even more, these narratives suggest that the decision to raise children is one of personal preference; child-rearing can be likened to "purchasing an expensive luxury item or pursuing a personal leisure interest."[6] In social science literature, this is often dubbed the children-as-pets model, and it is closely associated with a reluctance to provide public assistance to parents.[7] Economist Nancy Folbre explains the phenomenon as follows: "I think I know why so many people seem to think that parents, especially mothers, should pay most of the costs of raising children. These people think of children as pets. Parents acquire them because they provide companionship and love. Therefore, they should either take full responsibility for them or drop them off at the pound. . . . Those who care for them are the ones who get the fun out of them; therefore, they should pay the costs."[8]

Folbre's reference to the "pound" gestures to a structural reality: robust public provisions for the care of children are available in only extreme situations when the rights of a child are being violated brazenly. Thus, the children-as-pets model describes not only individual perceptions but, to a large extent, a structural assumption. Most institutions in the United States regard child-rearing as a private activity, an attitude manifested concretely by the lack of paid parental leave and the inadequacy of affordable, high-quality childcare. The Internal Revenue Service, through its tax credits and exemptions, may be one of the few public agencies that is an exception. Overwhelmingly, our nation's policies and programs designate the care of children as a matter beyond the scope of public responsibility.

The absence of care language in public discourse affirms this private vision. For example, one study found that legislative efforts to subsidize after-school programs carefully avoided the language of care and instead emphasized academic achievement and the prevention of drug use and crime. The study's author took this linguistic strategy to be a sign of the increased devaluation and privatization of care in the United States.[9] Sociologist Barrie Thorne notes that poor parents receive subsidies that are not only highly means-tested but also highly stigmatized.[10]

Thorne places the blame for this privatized vision in two places. First, there is "the fiction of the autonomous individual" who acts out of self-interest and is in all things self-sufficient."[11] A recent book affirms that the care work required to sustain *homo economicus* is typically uncompensated and invisible to economic analysis.[12] Thorne also points to the ideal worker. The American workplace is structured around an ideal male worker who is thoroughly unburdened by caregiving obligations. "He has no need of family-friendly policies like flexible scheduling, part-time work, or telecommuting. The ideal worker doesn't have to find babysitters, deal with school closures on snow days, or otherwise worry about child-care responsibilities."[13]

Thorne's blame is well-placed, yet I suggest three additional reasons for our overly privatized vision of parenting: an emphasis on parental rights, developments in the science of reproduction, and a highly sentimentalized account of childhood. First, child-rearing most often garners public attention in the context of claims to nonintervention, emphasizing the privacy of parenthood. Political discourse on family values is not directly concerned with the good of children but rather about "parents' rights to have children and exercise power over them."[14] Second, birth control and other reproductive technologies portray parenthood as a deliberately chosen status. One can easily opt out or, if one struggles to opt in, an industry is prepared to provide its services. Thus, if child-rearing is a consciously selected life choice, it would seem the responsibilities are not the concern of those who have chosen otherwise.

Third and finally, children have taken on a highly sentimentalized value, thereby increasing focus on emotional rewards granted to individual parents. Viviana Zelizer has demonstrated the striking change in valuation of children in the United States, detailing the "social construction of the economically 'useless' but emotionally 'priceless' child."[15] Children were once economic assets, providing both labor and security for parents later in life. However, standards for their valuation shifted from transactional terms to the realm of sentiment and emotion, a realm that emphasizes private, intimate relationships. Social scientists have suggested that the positive emotional rewards of parenting compensate for the hefty economic liability that children now present. As of 2013, average parents in the United States could expect to spend more than $245,000 per child to raise them to age eighteen, a figure that includes neither postsecondary education costs nor the economic value of parental labor.[16] One study suggests that idealizing myths that exaggerate the private emotional rewards of child-rearing are used by parents to rationalize the high cost of raising children. Those same exaggerated emotional rewards are used by nonparents to defend against the idea that society unjustly exploits parents.[17] Thus, parents and nonparents alike use (and embellish) the emotional experience of parenthood to distance child-rearing from public responsibility.

Alternative visions of parenthood have been proposed by the social sciences. Instead of the children-as-pets model, there is the children-as-public-goods model. This view highlights the ways that society benefits from parental investment in raising children who will grow up to be workers, taxpayers, and citizens.[18] Theological accounts of parenting have the potential to strengthen these alternative visions by integrating them into overarching conceptions of social responsibility and by giving special attention to the dignity and vulnerability of children. However, as noted below, theological accounts have the potential to reinforce private visions of parenting as well.

Catholic Theological Accounts of Child-Rearing

Promising language related to families and parenting is provided by some official documents of the Catholic Church as well as the excellent work of contemporary theologians. Yet some of these resources are embedded within frameworks and language that can be counterproductive. I begin with the apostolic letters arising from synods on the family to identify some of the promising contributions.

Pope John Paul II's letter "On the Family" is clear that the family has a social mission: "It does not live closed in on itself, but remains open to the community, moved by a sense of justice and concern for others, as well as by a consciousness of its responsibility towards the whole of society."[19] As the first and vital cell of society, the family is where "citizens come to birth" and learn the social virtues that animate "the existence and development of society itself."[20] For John Paul II, a key task for the family is participation in the development of society, which includes familial practices of hospitality, political intervention, and worldwide solidarity, especially those shaped by the preferential option for the poor.[21] The letter addresses the social role of the *family* more than it considers the nature of child-rearing explicitly, yet it makes clear that the formation of children has social significance.[22]

"The Joy of Love," the most recent apostolic letter on the family, issued by Pope Francis in 2016, echoes many of these ideas. The family is described at one point as "a hub for integrating persons into society and a point of contact between the public and private spheres."[23] Quoting from the Final Report of the 2015 Ordinary Synod of Bishops, Pope Francis speaks of the family as an agent of pastoral activity through varied forms of witness including solidarity with the poor, protection of creation, commitment to the promotion of the common good, and transformation of unjust social structures.[24] The social relevance of family life finds another mention when the family is considered as an educational setting, training us "how to live together in this greater home."[25]

These specific statements from "On the Family" and "The Joy of Love" can help shape an alternative to the privatized, children-as-pets vision of parenting. However, these statements do not represent the overall emphasis of the two apostolic letters, nor do they represent the overall emphasis of Catholic theological discourse on the family. These statements about the social significance of family life are generally overshadowed by extensive attention to affectivity and the sacrament of marriage. As a result, the potential public contribution of a Catholic theological vision of parenting is greatly diminished, if not at times muted altogether.

When it comes to family, justice is mentioned in passing; love is explored in depth. "On the Family" discusses the need for children to be enriched by a sense of true justice but "also and more powerfully by a sense of true love." For Pope Francis, it is through the family's capacity to love that it can confront social inadequacies. He concludes that "social love . . . is what truly unifies the spiritual meaning of the family and its mission to others."[26] Justice in these writings is rightly understood as deeply consonant with love. However, the deliberate choice to engage a concept like "social love"—implying perhaps a replacement or upgrade of "social justice"—makes it more difficult for these documents to generate public recognition of the family's contributions to the common good.

The ubiquitous concern with conjugal love is a particular obstacle for linking family—and therefore child-rearing—to a public discourse about justice. *Gaudium et spes* largely reduced family life to a discussion of marriage, and that tendency remains strong in official documents today. For example, in the Final Report of the 2015 Synod on the Family, a section titled "The Christian Teaching on Family" is nearly completely focused on marriage.[27] When discussing wounded families, the synod has in mind failing marriages. At one point baptism is mentioned as a key sacrament to understand the mission of the family to extend outside itself. But similar references to baptism occur at only three other points in the entire report. In contrast, matrimony or sacramental marriage/union is mentioned twenty-five times. There is a theological rationale given for this: "[The family's] vocation receives its ecclesial and missionary form from the sacramental bond which consecrates the indissoluble, conjugal relationship between a husband and a wife."[28] Pope Francis's "Joy of Love" reflects this emphasis. To his credit, he does acknowledge that at times the Church has engaged in "excessive idealization," proposing "a far too abstract and almost artificial theological ideal of marriage."[29] Still, children and the raising of children receive visibility through the lens of marriage, characterized as reflections of love and signs of conjugal unity.[30]

An exaggerated concern with marriage impacts perceptions of parenting. With the conjugal bond at the family's core, the most urgent threats to family well-being are threats to marriage. The well-being of children is contained within the frame of these individual marriages, so child-rearing is made implicit and invisible. When the Catholic tradition emphasizes a child's right to be born into a real family, it is difficult to think of the welfare of all "our kids" because child welfare seems to rely on differentiated, private experience dependent on the couple's conformity to moral standards.[31] Furthermore, when the tradition refers to children as "the ultimate crown" of marriage, children appear to belong to the intimate sphere of the couple and are distanced from the gaze of public concern.[32] An extensive theological emphasis on marriage as the lens for family—and thus for raising children—is a reinforcement of a privatized vision of parenting.

When these documents do engage parenthood, it is typically in terms of the reception of children as gifts or in an affirmation of parental rights. Both resonate more with a private, children-as-pets model. First, the dominant framework is to see children as gifts, an effective antidote to a parent's individualistic desires.[33] Even while gift language helps to decenter the parental self, it does not urge social engagement. Second, there is a long tradition of affirming parental rights in a way that sets families apart from the larger society. At the end of the nineteenth century in *Rerum novarum*, the Church expressed its concern with the "pernicious error" of civil government intrusion in family.[34] While greater openness emerged, a defensive posture still remains. Despite calls for the state to assist and support the family, theological warnings continue to identify parental roles and rights under attack from external forces (e.g., schools, the media).[35] Parental rights have merit, but if they emerge as a frame to think about child-rearing, they direct emphasis to a decidedly private—not public—sphere.

Theological accounts of parenting that emerge out of official documents of the Catholic tradition contain promising resources to shape a more public, social vision of family and child-rearing. However, the tradition actually tends to reinforce a privatized vision. These documents have not offered sufficient language to impact social policy or expand the moral imagination toward the common good. The language of gift, mission, and vocation are theologically rich, but what can the Church say to all parents of good will and the institutions that have the responsibility to support them? In the context of mass incarceration, children's needs are invisible if the inmate's marital status becomes the focus of family ethics. Parental rights can be viewed as among those stripped away by punishment, and an inmate-parent can be seen as failing to honor the gift of children. The Catholic tradition calls the family to justice work, but it struggles to identify such work internal to the activity of raising children.[36] Scholarship by contemporary theologians provides a promising association between parenting and justice. Building off their work, I argue that child-rearing should be regarded as an act of contributive justice.

Julie Hanlon Rubio has written importantly about the dual vocation of parents.[37] She argues that Christians must live out their calling both at home and in the world. Rubio identifies discipleship as the appropriate framework for the calling of the Christian parent, and discipleship cannot be satisfied by a life of putting family above all else. In her later volume, *Family Ethics*, Rubio explores various daily practices—such as eating, serving, and tithing—that demonstrate how the "household is a unique locus of personal choices of social significance."[38] Families, Rubio contends, must actively resist injustice with these everyday practices.[39]

Lisa Sowle Cahill has written on a Christian social perspective of family. She notes that a domestic church image of family ties into the larger systemic agenda of Christian social ethics, including transformation of oppressive and exclusionary institutions.[40] Yet, as she later observes, this depends on the proper understanding of "church."[41] She asserts that "family roles should promote social well-being by educating for economic and political participation, including respect for the rights and fulfillment of the responsibilities to others that are part of the common good."[42]

Mary Doyle Roche has made a powerful case for the recognition and proper regard of children's participation in social life, especially the economic aspects of it. She argues that participation is constitutive of justice for children. Accordingly, she articulates an ethic of the common good for children in the context of consumer culture. Roche notes a communal responsibility for ensuring children's well-being and children's duty to serve the common good.[43]

Cristina Traina has declared as false the "American assumption that parents are solely responsible for raising all the children they bear or who otherwise end up in their care."[44] She highlights the need to fulfill social obligations to children by fulfilling them to parents, and she presses for social structures that will facilitate the vocation of parents to care for their children. Similarly, Christine Firer Hinze attests to a lack of common accountability for children. In concluding an essay on wage justice, she notes that "we must think in fresh ways about the responsibilities of child-rearing. . . . Changes in the public valuation of children will . . . be required."[45]

These theologians, in various ways, point us in the direction of a more children-as-public-goods approach to parenting. They suggest that the practices of families have social significance and should be used to educate children for economic and political participation. In addition, society is accountable for sharing in the responsibilities toward children and must therefore adopt policies that better support those who raise them. This notion of social responsibility is especially relevant for confronting mass incarceration as it impacts children. In the next section I seek to sharpen these theological contributions with the explicit language of contributive justice.

Parenting as Contributive Justice

Justice, particularly as it is invoked in the Catholic social tradition, can be identified under three categories: distributive, commutative, and legal.[46] In Aquinas, legal (or general) justice is the virtue that directs other virtues toward the good of the community.[47] Very simply put, commutative justice concerns the relationship between individual members of society, and distributive justice concerns the proper relationship of the common good to individual members. Legal justice, on the other hand, concerns the relationship of individuals to the common good.

This category of justice was given the name contributive in the US bishops' pastoral letter *Economic Justice for All*: "Persons have an obligation to be active and productive participants in the life of society and that society has a duty to enable them to participate in this way. This form of justice can also be called 'contributive,' for it stresses the duty of all who are able to help create the goods, services, and other nonmaterial or spiritual values necessary for the welfare of the whole community."[48] For David Hollenbach, contributive justice means that citizens must "act in ways that lead to meeting the basic material needs of their fellow citizens, to the generation of jobs for the unemployed, to overcoming patterns of discrimination and exclusion, to the support of environmental quality, and to building up the general sense of community in society as a whole."[49] The language and examples used by the bishops and Hollenbach suggest contributions made outside of the family, related more to public structures and the wider community. Yet Rubio has already pointed us to concrete activities within the family that make contributions to "goods, services, and . . . values necessary for the welfare of the whole community." By this description, the specific work of child-rearing is an activity of contributive justice. It builds up the community by helping children to integrate into society. Parenting is contributive justice because it is the work of forming new members of the community to recognize their capacity and responsibility for participation. When parents/guardians neglect or abuse children instead, those children are profoundly violated, as is justice itself.

Language is critical if policy changes are to be won and moral imaginations are to be transformed. A society that characterizes child-rearing as contributive justice can offer extensive public support for parenting because it ultimately redounds to the good of the community. Therefore, any schema of justice (e.g., provisions for affordable housing, fair wages, immigration policy) must prominently include the impact on child-rearing in its calculations. In addition, the language of contributive justice shapes moral imagination. It directs parents to orient their child-rearing toward participation rather than individual advantage. And it reminds all members of the critical significance of child welfare for the good of society.

A few caveats may be in order. First, I do not claim that contributive justice is the exclusive framework for child-rearing. The language of love, gift, vocation, and so on have important roles to play. Yet contributive justice can help correct privatizing tendencies, and the language of justice signals how child-rearing is a basic concern, relevant for the whole of society. Second, my invocation of justice in parenting has not engaged a gender analysis, but there are connections that could be pursued separately. Third, I am sympathetic to Rubio's assertion that a public vocation is needed for Christian discipleship. I emphasize the public character of raising children to counter the narrative that it is a private activity, not to claim that raising children is wholly sufficient work for a public vocation. Fourth and finally, my appeal to justice is not meant to replace the category of care but to offer language that helps us to account for the profoundly social significance of caregiving.

In the assertion that parenting is an act of contributive justice, there are two related claims. First, parents contribute directly to the common good in the raising of their children. And, second, as an activity of fundamental public significance, parenting belongs within policy discourse on provisions for justice. In the final section, I apply these claims to parenting in the context of mass incarceration.

Parenting and Mass Incarceration

Sixteen-year-old Kmani Baxter's father is in prison. He has not seen him in thirteen years. He has not hugged or touched his father since he was just three or four years old. Youth advocate Nell Bernstein says few people sympathize with incarcerated parents. She commonly hears that inmates don't deserve to have kids. She says, "Who knows if there [are] parents who don't deserve to have kids—in or out of prison. But I haven't met a kid who doesn't deserve to have a parent."[50] Bernstein runs a support and leadership development program for kids like Baxter who have an incarcerated father or mother. These and other programs can be lifelines for children facing not only the loss of a parent but all that very often comes with it: severe economic strains, emotional trauma, weakened family structures, intense social stigma, and more.

Sometimes lip service is paid to maintaining family bonds, but the reality is that the criminal justice system does not factor child-rearing into its mission. The needs of inmates who are parents fall beyond the scope of the prison's institutional responsibility; the needs of the children of these inmates are even less visible. For prisons and jails, the mission is custody, safety, and order. Facilitating family relationships is not a fundamental objective. Contact with family is a threat—or, at best, a hassle—for a facility seeking to maintain control of everything and everyone passing through its gates. In an institution committed to security and order, family contact is regarded as a privilege that can be leveraged to secure inmate compliance. These institutions do not cultivate relationships, but—if one behaves—they *permit* contact, albeit under constrained and closely monitored conditions. Mail will be opened and searched before it gets to an inmate. Phone calls are available, even as the exorbitant cost burdens families who are already financially strapped. Visits happen, but travel can be costly, as can be the time away from work needed to get there. Inmates may be shipped off to remote facilities even when ones closer to family are available. These decisions are based on factors that serve custody, safety, and order—not general familial bonding and certainly not the opportunity to raise one's child.

"Secondary prisonization" describes the humiliation and trauma linked with visitation when adults and children undergo searches and are subject to prison authority.[51] Recent work is beginning to explore how "children learn the norms of the jail, adapt to its strictures, and are subject to its disciplinary controls."[52] Zoe Willmott's mother was locked up when she was four. Seeing her mother meant a great deal, but she recalled, "It was hard to go to. It was stressful. I cried a lot. I had nightmares about being in prison all the time."[53] One formerly incarcerated father recalled how the cramped visiting rooms were additional obstacles: "nothing about how contact with family is structured is conducive to building relationships."[54] In response, he helped to create a children's visiting area at his facility and worked to establish weekend-long family fun day events to assist father–child bonding. Another program reached out to the schools and arranged for the incarcerated fathers to receive copies of their children's report cards. These and similar efforts have made real differences in the lives of children and parents. However, they represent limited and local efforts of individual inmates, prison administrators, and members of the community. It remains the case that there is a structural failure to address the needs of children and parents who interact with the criminal justice system.

A tremendous amount is at stake for the children of incarcerated parents. In Putnam's *Our Kids*, he collects extensive research to show the powerful and long-lasting effect of childhood experiences.[55] If children experience chronic or severe stress, they are "less able to solve problems, cope with adversity, and organize their lives."[56] Extreme stress results in biochemical and anatomical changes that "impair brain development and change brain architecture at a basic level."[57] One long-term study showed that improving social skills and social trust (as early as seven years old) can powerfully enhance opportunity: "When kids and their parents are given a 'dose' of sociability . . . the kids stay in school and out of jail, and do much better economically over the long run. Conversely, a childhood 'dose' of social isolation and distrust . . . significantly compromises their prospects."[58]

Putnam touches on parental imprisonment only briefly in his book, but in his concluding remarks he notes that "incarceration, especially parental incarceration, was part of the story of virtually every poor kid we met in this study."[59] Tragically, the reality of mass incarceration makes this observation unsurprising. It is common knowledge that the United States incarcerates a scandalously high number of its citizens and does so in a manner that fuels racial oppression and ensures the suffering of the poor. Only relatively recently has attention turned to the reality of parental incarceration and what that means for raising our children.

More than half of the men and women behind bars (more than 1.2 million inmates) are parents of children under age eighteen.[60] There are 2.7 million minor children with a parent behind bars, which amounts to more than 3.6 percent of all children.[61] One study puts this in perspective, particularly given the comparative amount of public attention and research, by noting that only about 1 percent of children are on the autism spectrum.[62] The ubiquity of parental incarceration is indeed stunning. The numbers amount to 1 in every 28 children in the United States. That figure was 1 in 125 in 1980.[63] Within these statistics is crushing racial inequality. One in 9 black children, or 11.4 percent, have an incarcerated parent. This compares to only 3.5 percent of Hispanic children and 1.8 percent of white children.[64] The cumulative statistics are worse. For a white child born in 1990, there was a 1 in 30 chance of experiencing paternal incarceration by age fourteen. For a black child, the chance was 1 in 4. If the father dropped out of high school, the chance for a black child to experience paternal incarceration rose to just over 50 percent.[65] The weight of the burden of parental incarceration falls on younger children. Almost a quarter (22 percent) of children with a parent in prison are under age five, and the majority (58 percent) are younger than ten, with eight years old the average age.[66]

Conventional wisdom used to be that men and women who went to prison or jail were unfit parents.[67] However, studies consistently show that, even while some children may be helped by the removal of a parent, the vast majority are harmed, and significantly so. These facts, combined with Putnam's data about the long-term disadvantages associated with childhood stress and poverty, are disastrous. There is research to suggest that mass imprisonment creates greater social inequality through its impact on children than from its effects on the men and women actually behind the bars.[68] Scholars warn that, even if incarceration rates were dramatically reduced today, the long-term impact of mass incarceration would still be ahead of us; all the children of the prison boom have yet to come of age.[69]

Prominent effects of parental imprisonment on children "involve the strains of economic deprivation, the loss of parental socialization through role modeling, support, and supervision, and the stigma and shame of societal labeling."[70] There are particularly strong negative outcomes for children's mental and behavioral health, and these are linked with outcomes that continue into adulthood.[71] In addition to higher risks for delinquency and crime, children are at risk for educational failure, premature departures from home, early childbearing and marriage, and idleness linked to joblessness.[72] The stigmatization experienced as a result of a parent's imprisonment can lead to similar problems for children, sometimes setting in motion a chain reaction of antisocial behavior.[73]

All this research supports the first claim about the nature of child-rearing: parents contribute directly to the common good in the raising of their children. This is made apparent by the harms that result when parenting capacities are diminished or cut off by way of incarceration. Children suffer emotionally and economically, and they are less able to participate and flourish in their communities. The common good requires parents who care about their children and who are given the opportunity to nurture, protect, provide, and educate. Criminal offenses, even including violent ones like murder, should not automatically deprive a child of a relationship with a parent. Rather, correctional institutions ought to facilitate parent–child relationships in every way possible for all inmate-parents capable of basic healthy interactions. Indeed, it is not simply a private misfortune when institutional structures are indifferent to child-rearing; it is an injustice felt broadly and shouldered by the most vulnerable.

This charge of injustice may seem counterintuitive; the criminal justice system is supposed to be in the business of establishing justice. Yet the system's justice is largely understood as retributive, a version of justice in which the proper relationship of the common good to the individual is defined according to deserved and proportionate punishment. The fatal flaw of a system that relies so heavily on a retributive framework is that it assesses due punishment in a relational vacuum. Even if we can agree that an offender deserves incarceration from society (a judgment that invites rightful skepticism amid mass incarceration), there is little basis for saying that children deserve to be separated from a loved one. Retributive justice articulates why a guilty individual must "pay" but provides little explanation why innocent children bear the cost as well. On the other hand, contributive justice can offer a more consistent account of the matter. Assuming incarceration is an appropriate response to an individual's violation of the common good, the criminal justice system ought to facilitate a reorientation of the individual's relationship to that common good. Given the unique role of parents for the flourishing of vulnerable members of our society, a contributive justice framework would see support of child-rearing as one of the essential goals of a system tasked with establishing justice.

This tension between retributive and contributive visions of justice relates to my second claim, that parenting belongs within policy discourse on provisions for justice. In the wake of mass incarceration, children and their incarcerated parents have not been a priority for correctional systems, social service agencies, or public policy makers. For instance, most states do not have child welfare policies to address parenting issues during imprisonment.[74] Structurally speaking, the realities faced by children of incarcerated parents are invisible. Yet, if child-rearing is a matter of contributive justice, then it must be given serious consideration. Child-rearing would influence the decision of imprisonment or community-based sentencing and would propose a different calculus for where inmates serve their sentence, how time and space are made available under custody, and what sorts of resources were mandated for every facility in this country.[75] This would mean that a host of social institutions—including schools—would be expected to interact with prisons and jails to facilitate parent–child relationships of care and support. One author affirms that the responsibility for "family-oriented prison environments and system-wide change" rests with congressional bodies and state legislatures since these are matters of national interest.[76]

The United States has already demonstrated a strong tolerance for suffering and inequality among its children. Mass parental incarceration implies child poverty and homelessness; it weakens educational outcomes. These outcomes are not peculiar to incarceration. What distinguishes mass parental incarceration is the forcible disruption of child-rearing relationships. Thus, not only a proper understanding of justice but also a proper understanding of the work of parenting is necessary.

If raising children is strictly a private matter, then parental mass incarceration is just the unfortunate reality that some children must face. The implied logic is that if parents cannot be sufficiently responsible to avoid criminal detention, then they will lose access to their children just as they lose access to property and other opportunities while incarcerated. It would seem the disadvantage conferred on these children is not the fault of structures of the justice system but rather a mere byproduct of the need to pursue retributive justice. Theological accounts of parenting that focus on parental rights and children as gifts serve to reinforce this perspective. When children of incarcerated parents suffer, it seems to be simply the sins of their fathers and mothers that are to blame. There are indeed parents who directly harm children, but this does not describe incarceration, which is a socially constructed and imposed hardship.

Private accounts of child-rearing—theological and otherwise—are complicit in obscuring the systemic failures that burden children of incarcerated parents.

On the other hand, if raising children is an act of contributive justice, then parental incarceration is a public concern and crisis. It is especially so for black and brown children who will suffer into their adulthood and bear out the legacy of unbelievable racial and economic injustices. If children are being deprived of central relationships of nurture, protection, and education, then it is the common good that is jeopardized. The disadvantage conferred on these children is structured into the so-called justice system by a willful negligence of the socially significant work of parenting. Parenting construed as contributive justice demands a reformulation of policies and institutional responsibilities, wholly rejecting the isolation of criminal justice from family justice. For example, policies around family visitation would shift radically, a new calculus would be used to discern terms of release, and efforts for prison diversion would see expanded investment and urgency. These would be just some of the terms for public discourse. In addition, how might theological discourse change?

The US bishops include consideration of children of incarcerated parents in their pastoral letter *Responsibility, Rehabilitation, and Restoration*, including their increased risks of imprisonment and the significant racial disparities.[77] These children are designated as victims of crime and are discussed immediately after the direct victims of the offense. Later in the letter the bishops note that solidarity with victims includes the children of the incarcerated. Ultimately, the letter recommends that the church community reach out to families of the incarcerated and minister to their needs. This presentation is problematic on several accounts. First, to identify children as additional victims of the crime is to place blame squarely on the shoulders of the incarcerated parent. This creates an adversarial image and undermines general support for the possibility of continued-though-limited parenting. Moreover, it seems to echo the flawed "conventional wisdom" that all inmates are by definition unfit parents. Second, this presentation exonerates the criminal justice system and other institutions from responsibility in the child's suffering. Such suffering appears to be the direct result of private actions by the incarcerated parent and therefore does not seem to rise to the level of a public matter of justice. The bishops' letter contains no calls to critically examine the system in this way, despite the letter's acknowledgment in a separate context that parents have an irreplaceable and primary role as guides and guardians. Third and finally, the bishops attend to the suffering of the children but do not consider how this reality burdens the incarcerated parent. Were the bishops to take seriously the lens of contributive justice when it came to child-rearing, these children would not be reduced to victims of individual crime nor would the system and society escape responsibility for the way that mass incarceration increases the vulnerability of children, parents, and families.

Conclusion

Simply appealing to child-rearing as contributive justice will neither rewrite policies nor conjure personal conversions. But attentiveness to language and underlying frameworks can suggest how to move our discourse forward and thereby advance moral imagination as well as concrete policy. Strong cultural inclinations toward a privatized, children-as-pets model of parenting must be challenged by theological accounts. The Catholic tradition has served as an example of such resources as well as a cautionary tale of how theological language can reinforce a private view, disconnecting the work of parenting from the concerns of justice. By expanding the social vision of family and drawing on the work of contemporary theologians, contributive justice language establishes the crucial connection between parenting and the common good. And this connection is essential if we are to confront the structures of inequality and injustice that set the terms of life for millions of American children. In acknowledging that parents contribute to the good of society in raising children, we are equipped to enter directly into a discourse on justice that is critical for confronting mass incarceration. Moreover, by acknowledging that raising kids is a work of justice, then justice clearly becomes a matter of raising all our kids.

Notes

1. Robert Putnam, *Our Kids: The American Dream in Crisis* (New York: Simon & Schuster, 2015), 261.

2. Pew Charitable Trusts, *Collateral Costs: Incarceration's Effect on Economic Mobility* (Washington, DC: Pew Charitable Trusts, 2010). Based on research by Bruce Western and Becky Pettit.

3. Sara Wakefield and Christopher Wildeman, *Children of the Prison Boom: Mass Incarceration and the Future of American Inequality* (New York: Oxford University Press, 2014).

4. Julie Hanlon Rubio, *Family Ethics: Practices for Christians* (Washington, DC: Georgetown University Press, 2010). Rubio highlights two other significant contemporary theologians who also explore family ethics: Florence Caffrey Bourg and David Matzko McCarthy. Ibid., 4–6. See Florence Caffrey Bourg, *Where Two or Three Are Gathered: Christian Families as Domestic Churches* (Notre Dame, IN: University of Notre Dame Press, 2004); and David Matzko McCarthy, *Sex and Love in the Home* (London: SCM Press, 2004).

5. Rubio, *Family Ethics*, 17.

6. Richard P. Eibach and Steven E. Mock, "Idealizing Parenthood Functions to Justify Policy Neglect of Parents' Economic Burdens," *Social Issues and Policy Review* 5, no. 1 (2011): 8.

7. Paula England and Nancy Folbre, "Who Should Pay for the Kids?," *Annals of the American Academy of Political and Social Science* 563, no. 1 (1999): 194–207.

8. Nancy Folbre, *The Invisible Heart: Economics and Family Values* (New York: New Press, 2001), 109.

9. Anita Ilta Garey, "Concepts of Care in After-School Programs: Protection, Instruction, and Containment," Berkeley Center for Working Families Working Paper No. 48 (May 2002).

10. Barrie Thorne, "Crisis of Care," in *At the Heart of Work and Family: Engaging the Ideas of Arlie Hochschild*, ed. Anita Ilta Garey and Karen V. Hansen (New Brunswick, NJ: Rutgers University Press, 2011), 157.

11. Ibid., 157–58.

12. Katrine Marcal, *Who Cooked Adam Smith's Dinner? A Story about Women and Economics*, trans. Saskia Vogel (New York: Pegasus, 2016).

13. Brigid Schulte, *Overwhelmed: Work, Love, and Play When No One Has the Time* (New York: Sarah Crichton Books, 2014), 76.

14. Cristina Traina, "For the Sins of the Parents: Roman Catholic Ethics and the Politics of Family," in *Prophetic Witness: Catholic Women's Strategies for Reform*, ed. Colleen Griffith (New York: Crossroad, 2009), 114.

15. Viviana A. Zelizer, *Pricing the Priceless Child: The Changing Social Value of Children* (Princeton, NJ: Princeton University Press, 1994), 21.

16. Mark Lino, *Expenditures on Children by Families, 2013* (Alexandria, VA: U.S. Department of Agriculture, Center for Nutrition Policy and Promotion, 2014).

17. Eibach and Mock, "Idealizing Parenthood."

18. Nancy Folbre, "Children as Public Goods," *American Economic Review* 84 (1994): 86–90.

19. Pope John Paul II, *Familiaris consortio*, Vatican, November 22, 1981, 64.

20. Ibid., 42.

21. Ibid., 42–48.

22. In the encyclical *Laborem exercens* issued by Pope John Paul II just two months prior to his letter "On the Family," child-rearing is included within the broad concept of work. Pope John Paul II, *Laborem exercens*, Vatican, September 14, 1981, 9.

23. Pope Francis, *Amoris laetitia*, Vatican, April 8, 2016, 181.

24. Ibid., 290.

25. Ibid., 276.

26. Ibid., 324.

27. Synod of Bishops, XIV General Ordinary Assembly, *The Vocation and Mission of the Family in the Church and the Contemporary World—Final Report*, 2015, 47–51.

28. Ibid., 36.

29. Pope Francis, *Amoris laetitia*, 36.

30. Ibid., 165. Elsewhere, I have argued for alternative theological foundations for the family. See Kathryn Getek Soltis, "*Gaudium et spes* and the Family: A Social Tradition with Room to Grow," *Journal of Catholic Social Thought* 12, no. 2 (2015): 245–58.

31. On a child's right to be born into a real family, see, for example, *Compendium of the Social Doctrine of the Church* (Washington, DC: United States Conference of Catholic Bishops for the Libreria Editrice Vaticana, 2005), par. 244. Roche and Traina echo this concern that excessive focus on the conjugal bond can obscure the well-being of children. Mary M. Doyle Roche, "Children and the Common Good: Protection and Participation," in *Prophetic Witness: Catholic Women's Strategies for Reform*, ed. Colleen Griffith (New York: Crossroad, 2009), 127; and Traina, "For the Sins of the Parents," 121.

32. Pope Paul VI, *Gaudium et spes*, Vatican, December 7, 1965, 48.

33. For example, see Pope Francis, *Amoris laetitia*, 81, 166, 170.

34. See Ethna Regan, "Barely Visible: The Child in Catholic Social Teaching," *Heythrop Journal* 55, no. 6 (2014): 1022. Quote from Pope Leo XVIII, *Rerum novarum*, May 15, 1891, 14.

35. See Pope Francis, *Amoris laetitia*, 84; and Synod of Bishops, *Vocation and the Mission of the Family*, 67.

36. The documents offer brief, undeveloped platitudes. See Pope John Paul II, *Familiaris consortio*, 45; *Compendium of the Social Doctrine of the Church*, 213; and Synod of Bishops, *Vocation and the Mission of the Family*, 62–63.

37. Julie Hanlon Rubio, *A Christian Theology of Marriage and Family* (New York: Paulist Press, 2003), 98–105.

38. Rubio, *Family Ethics*, 15.

39. Ibid., 58.

40. Lisa Sowle Cahill, *Family: A Christian Social Perspective* (Minneapolis, MN: Fortress, 2000), 129.

41. Ibid., 134.

42. Ibid., 135–36.

43. Mary M. Doyle Roche, *Children, Consumerism, and the Common Good* (Lanham, MD: Lexington, 2009), 92.

44. Traina, "For the Sins of the Parent," 117.

45. Christine Firer Hinze, "Bridge Discourse on Wage Justice: Roman Catholic and Feminist Perspectives on the Family," in *Feminist Ethics and the Catholic Moral Tradition*, Readings in Moral Theology No. 9, ed. Charles E. Curran, Margaret A. Farley, and Richard A. McCormick (New York: Paulist, 1996), 526.

46. See, for example, Charles E. Curran, *Catholic Social Teaching, 1891–Present: A Historical, Theological, and Ethical Analysis* (Washington, DC: Georgetown University Press, 2002), 188–98.

47. Thomas Aquinas, *Summa theologica*, trans. Fathers of the English Dominican Province (Allen, TX: Christian Classics, 1948), II-II.58.6. It takes the name "legal" since "it belongs to the law to direct to the common good" (II-II.58.5).

48. Catholic Church, *Economic Justice for All: Pastoral Letter on Catholic Social Teaching and the U.S. Economy* (Washington, DC: National Conference of Catholic Bishops, 1986).

49. David Hollenbach, *The Common Good and Christian Ethics* (New York: Cambridge University Press, 2002), 196.

50. Bernstein quoted in Kyung Jin Lee, "Kids of Incarcerated Parents Speak Out," *KALW Public Radio—San Francisco*, July 15, 2014, http://kalw.org/post/kids-incarcerated-parents -speak-out#stream/0.

51. Megan Comfort, *Doing Time Together* (Chicago: University of Chicago Press, 2008).

52. Brittnie J. Aiello and Jill A. McCorkel, "'It Will Crush You like a Bug': Maternal Incarceration, Secondary Prisonization, and Children's Visitation," *Punishment & Society*, January 1, 2017, doi:10.1177/1462474517697295.

53. Willmott quoted in Lee, "Kids of Incarcerated Parents Speak Out."

54. Malik Bandy, interview by Kathryn Getek Soltis, January 6, 2017.

55. See especially Putnam, *Our Kids*, 109–17.

56. Ibid., 111.

57. Ibid., 112. See also American Academy of Pediatrics, Early Brain and Childhood Development Task Force, "A Public Health Approach to Toxic Stress," https://www.aap.org /en-us/advocacy-and-policy/aap-health-initiatives/EBCD/Pages/Public-Health -Approach.aspx.

58. Putnam, *Our Kids*, 115.

59. Ibid., 247.

60. Pew Charitable Trusts, *Collateral Costs*.

61. Ibid.

62. Wakefield and Wildeman, *Children of the Prison Boom*, 20.

63. Pew Charitable Trusts, *Collateral Costs*.

64. Ibid.

65. Wakefield and Wildeman, *Children of the Prison Boom*, 33–40.

66. Christopher J. Mumola, *Incarcerated Parents and Their Children* (Washington, DC: U.S. Department of Justice, Bureau of Justice Statistics, 2000).

67. J. Mark Eddy and Julie Poehlmann, eds., *Children of Incarcerated Parents: A Handbook for Researchers and Practitioners* (Washington, DC: Urban Institute Press, 2010), xiv.

68. Wakefield and Wildeman, *Children of the Prison Boom*.

69. Ibid., 12.

70. John Hagan and Ronit Dinovitzer, "Collateral Consequences of Imprisonment for Children, Communities, and Prisoners," in *Crime and Justice*, vol. 26: *Prisons*, ed. Michael Tonry and Joan Petersilia (Chicago: University of Chicago Press, 1999), 123.

71. Wakefield and Wildeman, *Children of the Prison Boom*, 6.

72. Hagan and Dinovitzer, "Collateral Consequences," 148.

73. Ibid., 127.

74. Creasie Finney Hairston, "Prisoners and Their Families: Parenting Issues during Incarceration," in *Prisoners Once Removed: The Impact of Incarceration and Reentry on Children, Families, and Communities*, ed. Jeremy Travis and Michelle Waul (Washington, DC: Urban Institute Press, 2003), 277.

75. See, for example, Ross D. Parke and K. Alison Clarke-Stewart, "The Effects of Parental Incarceration on Children: Perspectives, Promises, and Policies," in *Prisoners Once Removed: The Impact of Incarceration and Reentry on Children, Families, and Communities*, ed. Jeremy Travis and Michelle Waul, 189–232 (Washington, DC: Urban Institute Press, 2003).

76. Hairston, *Prisoners Once Removed*, 277.

77. Catholic Church, *Responsibility, Rehabilitation, and Restoration: A Catholic Perspective on Crime and Criminal Justice* (Washington, DC: United States Conference of Catholic Bishops, 2000).

The Priority of the Affections over the Emotions: Gustafson, Aquinas, and an Edwardsean Critique

Ki Joo Choi

The association of emotions as kinds of affections is not unusual. This essay, however, considers whether the tight association between affections and emotions is conceptually satisfactory and advantageous. Does an emphasis on the boundedness of affections and emotions inadvertently mask their distinctive natures? In turning to Gustafson, Aquinas, and, ultimately, Edwards, I propose that, while affections are not emotionless, noticing their differences can reveal the limitations of the emotions for moral deliberation and draw greater attention to the moral significance of the affections.

IN HIS SEMINAL *ETHICS FROM A THEOCENTRIC PERSPECTIVE*, James M. Gustafson writes that his use of the term "affectivity" "includes 'senses,' attitudes, dispositions, and more particular affections or emotions."[1] In this essay, I am particularly interested in that last component of his statement on affectivity, the association between affections and emotions. "As I use the term," Gustafson writes, "it [affections] refers to emotion."[2] The association of affection with emotion is not unique to Gustafson, although the way he associates both terms, particularly through his interpretation of Jonathan Edwards, has certainly been influential in discussions on the emotions in contemporary religious and theological ethics.[3] Intuitively, Gustafson's approach to affection and emotion as interchangeable terms makes sense and almost seems descriptively necessary. At what point can one say an experience of anger, for instance, is an affection and not an emotion? Can one be only emotively angry and not affectively angry? Does it even make sense to ask that sort of question?

Approaching the affections as emotions offers one way of underscoring and circumventing the kind of conceptual tangles one might fall into when trying to make clean distinctions between the two terms. Gustafson seems to

Ki Joo Choi, PhD, is an associate professor and chair of the Department of Religion at Seton Hall University, Fahy Hall 326, 400 S. Orange Ave., South Orange, NJ 07079; kijoo.choi@shu.edu.

Journal of the Society of Christian Ethics, 38, 1 (2018): 113–129

be well aware of such pitfalls in *Can Ethics Be Christian?*: "Feelings, emotions, affections, sensibilities—these are so uncertain in terms of their references that it might be well not to use the words. . . . One must constantly remember that [those terms] are in experience intimately related."⁴ But does such a close association mean that affection and emotion are essentially distinct, without difference?

In this essay, I want to follow Gustafson's lead in turning to Edwards's approach to the affections. But unlike Gustafson, I see Edwards's language of the affections as offering an important way of differentiating the affections from the emotions. That differentiation is essential, I propose, because it offers a critique of the emotions that has been perhaps obscured by the prominence of Gustafson's account of the affections, especially in relation to his reading of Edwards, but is worth the attention of contemporary religious and theological ethics. A closer inspection of Edwards's account of the affections, therefore, reveals what is at stake in discerning and maintaining the affections as something distinct from the emotions. To make that case, it will be helpful to first turn briefly to Thomas Aquinas.

Why Aquinas? As we will see in the following, Aquinas operates with a notion of emotions that is formally distinct from affections. Rather than providing a detailed study of Aquinas here, my goal is to examine how the basic blueprint of that Thomistic differentiation between the affections and emotions can serve as a kind of reading guide for parsing Edwards's approach to the affections and emotions. Such an ecumenical way of reading Edwards is useful in light of the fact that Edwards, rather surprisingly, rarely refers to the term "emotion" in his magisterial treatise *Religious Affections*. One way of interpreting such relative silence is to take his discussion on the affections as assuming emotions. However, reading Edwards with Aquinas's distinctions in mind reveals how Edwards's account of the affections does not necessarily have to be taken as also meaning emotions.

Yet it is important to note that Edwards's account of the affections and emotions is not simply a Thomistic account; there are important differences between the two. In this essay, I want to call attention to those differences as a way of indicating Edwards's provocative perspective on what emotions are, their cause (the way in which emotions are formed), and the kind of "information," if any, they provide (their cognitive dimension). From the point of view of Edwards's thought, emotions can be construed as having a cognitive dimension. However, Edwards raises critical questions about what emotions actually reveal with respect to one's feelings, desires, values, and, ultimately, thoughts. Those questions cast doubt on the salience and reliability of the emotions for moral discernment and the potential for emotional manipulation and self-deception. It is in discerning how, for Edwards, the affections are bound to but functionally distinct from the emotions that draw out such suspicions. And it is when we approach Edwards with Thomistic definitions and distinctions in mind that such Edwardsean suspicions over the emotions come to clearer light, or so I hope to show.

Thomistic Definitions

At first glance, Aquinas's language of the passions of the soul as emotions seems to obscure more than clarify the relationship between emotions and affections.[5] In question 22 of the *Summa theologica* I-II, Aquinas asserts, "it is evident that the passions of the soul are the same as affections. But affections manifestly belong to the appetitive, and not to the apprehensive part. Therefore passions are in the appetitive rather than in the apprehensive part."[6] Note how he interchanges affections and passions: the affections are appetitive; the passions are appetitive too. Therefore, the passions "are the same as" affections.[7]

As appetitive motions, affections and passions are the same, which is to say that both are powers that tend toward an object in relation to a notion of goodness. But the sameness of the affections and passions becomes more complicated when Aquinas later notes that "passion is more properly in the act of the sensitive appetite, than in that of the intellectual appetite."[8] In line with that differentiation, Aquinas observes that the intellectual appetite or the will "consider[s] the common notion of good" in its capacity to "apprehend the universal" and, thus, moves toward or away from a particular object in relation to that sense of the universal good.[9] In contrast, the passions, as motions of the sensory appetite, "crave" the goodness that is particular to a specific object.[10] In other words, it is the sensory appetite or the passions that orient us to or away from a particular object beyond an intellectual grasp; the passions enable a grasping of an object in such a way that "the object also gets a hold of us" in one way or another.[11]

That "the passions of the soul are the same as affections" only in reference to their appetitive natures is in keeping with Aquinas's delineation of at least two kinds of love. As he asserts, "love differs according to the difference of appetites."[12] There is the movement of love that arises from the sensitive appetite (irascible and concupiscible), wherein love in this sense is a passion.[13] Then there is the movement of love that arises from the intellectual appetite, what Aquinas refers to as intellectual love since "it is in the will."[14] In question 83 of the *Summa theologica* I, Aquinas employs the term "affections" to describe such an intellectual love: "Love, concupiscence, and the like can be understood in two ways. Sometimes they are taken as passions—arising, that is, with a certain commotion of the soul. And thus they are commonly understood, and in this sense they are only in the sensitive appetite. They may, however, be taken in another way, as far as they are simple *affections* without passion or commotion of the soul, and thus they are acts of the will."[15]

It is important to note at this point that, by construing the passions as motions of the sensory appetite, passions are "of the body" or, as he puts it, "found where there is corporeal transmutation."[16] Thus, one might say that a passion involves embodied motion, has a bodily, physiological correlate and expression. "For instance, *anger* is said to be a *kindling of the blood about the heart*."[17] To be oriented to an object emotively (or by the sensitive appetite) is to be so moved where one's skin tingles, forehead sweats, stomach turns, knees weaken, or heart beats excitedly, depending on the emotion. Affections, however, express themselves in a "disembodied" manner. Aquinas suggests as much when he states, "Now there is no need for corporeal transmutation in the act of the intellectual appetite: because this appetite is not exercised by means of a corporeal organ."[18] It is interesting on this account that he says, "When love and joy and the like are ascribed to God or the angels, or to man in respect of his intellectual appetite, they signify simple acts of the will *having like effects*, but without passion."[19] There is this "resemblance" because, unlike human beings, the angels (and God) have no bodies, whereas human beings are soul–body composites.[20]

The corporeal character of the passions solidifies its distinction from the affections. But that leads to two interrelated puzzles. First, if affections are movements of the will and thus are noncorporeal, then why bother referring to them in a way that resonates with the passions, which are by their nature corporeal? In other words, why begin his exploration of the passions, starting with question 22 in *Summa theologica* I-II, with the claim that the passions are the same as affections? What is gained in his theory of the passions by claiming identity with affections? Given that initial claim of sameness, one can ask the question in the converse: what is gained by thinking of the affections as emotions when it is relatively clear that for Aquinas they are not the same all the way down? In view of these questions, it is noteworthy that Diana Fritz Cates prefers Aquinas's language of "simple act of the will" over the affections.[21] There is nothing fundamentally objectionable to Cates's preference for Aquinas's own reference to simple acts of the will in describing, say, joy or love that arises from motions of the intellectual appetite; such a preference certainly makes the distinction between movements of the intellectual and sensory appetites tidier. Yet it is also the case that Aquinas refers to simple acts of the will as affections. That he does raises the question, why?

That question can be asked from a different but ultimately related angle. While the passions can be differentiated from the affections, even though they are similar in terms of their appetitive natures, is a necessary relationship between the two lacking? Given his formal definition of passion and his use of affection to refer to simple acts of the will, in theory it would seem that the connection between affections and emotions is not intrinsic; love and joy, for instance, are either in the sensory appetite or in the intellectual appetite.[22] But is an affective act of love conceivable as passionless? How can an act of the will that expresses itself in love or joy not be corporally, emotively felt? Perhaps for that reason Aquinas chooses to refer to loving and joyful expressions of the will as affections, suggesting that such acts of the will, while different from the passions formally speaking, are not wholly unrelated to the passions at least in one sense, when simple acts of the will, depending on their intensity, "affects" the passions. Aquinas refers to such an occurrence as one of "redundance," "when the higher part of the soul is intensely moved to anything, the lower part also follows that movement; and thus the passion that results in consequence, in the sensitive appetite, is a sign of the intensity of the will, and so indicates greater moral goodness."[23] In another instance, Aquinas refers to this kind of redundance as the "intensely moved" will "overflow[ing] into the sensitive appetite in so far as the lower powers follow the movement of the higher."[24] This can make sense experientially. In making an assertive, conviction-filled choice that we believe promotes our flourishing, "our experience of being perfected in relation to an intelligible good will be accompanied by noticeable bodily changes, such as a heightening of our energy level, a lessening of our awareness of physical discomfort, or a relaxation response."[25] In that way, one can say that the affections, such as love and joy, although they are "intellectual," they are also the "same" as the passions insofar as the passions may intensify the affectivity of simple acts of the will.

To account for the affections and emotions in terms of redundance or overflow underscores, as Cates puts it, their "indirect" connection.[26] That there is at least an indirect connection makes sense in light of Aquinas's insistence on the soul–body composition of the human person; due to that unity, the body and, correlatively, the emotions can hardly be considered ancillary to human life. But in maintaining an indirect connection, Aquinas allows for, I believe, a kind of autonomy to the emotions, but autonomy not in the sense that our emotions are something completely beyond our control. In saying that our emotions have relative autonomy, I mean to convey how Aquinas allows for the movements of the sensitive appetite to be controlled or moderated by the will and, ultimately, the intellect as well as the converse, that is, the capacity of the emotions to inform and influence the will and intellect, positively or negatively.[27] In either case, emotions as something different from affections provide Thomas a way of conceiving the emotions as critical sources of moral deliberation and judgment.

Reading Edwards in Light of Thomistic Definitions

While more can be said of Aquinas's delineation of the affections and emotions, especially in relation to the two sets of questions I outlined above, I now turn to thinking about Edwards in light of our basic sketch of Aquinas's account. My aim is to examine the extent to which basic features of Aquinas's use of the terms "affections" and "emotions" are noticeable in Edwards's thought and, consequently, how Edwards might respond to the two questions that emerge from Aquinas's definition of affections and emotions. That Edwardsean response, I propose, calls attention to the relative irrelevance of the emotions (but not the affections) in a way that Aquinas's account does not.

While the language of appetite is not typical in Edwardsean moral psychology, Edwards's approach to the affections is complementary to that of Aquinas. Consider Edwards's assertion in *Religious Affections* that affections are "more vigorous and sensible exercises of the inclination and will of the soul."[28] I take Edwards's insistence on will and inclination as similar to Aquinas's approach to the will as an intellectual appetite. Human agency is not simply a function of choice, but being able to choose is, as Edwards says, "governed" by ones' likes and dislikes, or the extent to which one is either "inclined or disinclined to what is in view."[29] Thus, like Aquinas, the will is object-oriented and pertains to our capacity to move toward or away (a matter of inclination) from an object based on our understanding or, more precisely, perception of it.[30] Insofar as one's exercise of will and inclination are rooted in the perceptual understanding of, as Edwards puts it, the soul or mind, one's willing and inclining, as John E. Smith describes, expresses or gives insight into the basic orientation or character of one's life.[31] Affections indicate the state of one's will and inclination, the "liveliness and sensibleness of [their] exercise." Without "the vigorous and sensible exercise of the inclination and will of the soul," argues Edwards, human activity would cease: "Such is man's nature, that he is very inactive, any otherwise than he is influenced by some affection, either love or hatred, desire, hope, fear or some other. These affections we see to be the springs that set men agoing, in all the affairs of life, and engage them in all their pursuits: these are the things that put men forward and carry 'em along, in all their worldly business."[32]

If Edwards, like Aquinas, generally locates the affections in the will (and its inclinations), then does Edwards, like Aquinas, locate the emotions elsewhere— namely, in the body? A negative response to the question is not unreasonable given that Edwards, in marrying the affections with will and inclination, underscores the idea that human willing and inclining, or one's dispositions of character, are not simply a function of speculative knowing (or notional knowledge in Edwardsean nomenclature) but sensible knowing (or "heart" knowledge).[33] That distinction between notional and sensible knowledge is meant to convey the reality "that feeling and sense make up the more profound level in human experience."[34] Would that not suggest that for Edwards emotions are located in the same "place" as the affections—that is, in the will and not the body?

The question is not as straightforward as it may seem, however, if we recall that we have been taking the corporeal motions of the passions to mean emotions in Aquinas. To do the same with Edwards is a bit trickier. Edwards refers to passions in only one paragraph of the *Religious Affections*.[35] For now, however, it is important that we do not mistake Aquinas's passions for Edwards's reference to the passions and, in turn, important not to equate Edwards's comment on the passions as somehow pertaining to the emotions, at least not directly or simply.

So, then, for Edwards, where are the emotions located? Are they the same as the affections and, therefore, of the will and inclination, or are they different and, consequently, pertain to something other than will and inclination? Consider first that Edwards on occasion refers to "affections of body" and "affections of soul." This distinction appears in one of his discussions on whether the saints in heaven are capable of experiencing affections (in this case, religious affections). Saints in heaven, he claims, "be not united to flesh and blood, and have no animal fluids to be moved." But that does not mean they cannot experience affections of the soul such as love and joy. When it comes to the saints in heaven, "we are not speaking of the affections of body, but the affections of soul, the chief of which are love and joy."[36] What might the affections of body be if they are not affections of soul, of will and inclination, and, thus, of the mind? That the affections can be experienced in the body is suggestive of Aquinas's notion that the passions or emotions are of the body. Edwards's later reference to "emotion of the mind" furthers this suggestion, and, as such, we can take affections or emotions that refer to the mind as properly "affections" and those that refer to the body as properly "emotions."[37]

Like Aquinas, then, we can say that for Edwards emotions are different from affections and involve changes in the body; they are "constitutions of the body," of bodily sensation.[38] Note that for Edwards the movements of the body or "motions of the blood and animal spirits" are strictly different in their nature from the vigorous exercise of the will and inclination (affections).[39] As Edwards states, "it is not the body, but the mind only, that is the proper seat of the affections." This is so because the body is not capable of thinking, and since affections reflect the soul's perceptual understanding of an object, which forms the basis of the soul's inclination or disinclination to that object, the affections cannot be of the body, only the emotions.[40]

It is at this point that we can start to detect some of the subtle but significant divergences between Aquinas and Edwards. For Edwards, the affections are neither located in the body nor dependent on the movements of the body; this is similar to Aquinas. And echoing Aquinas's notion of redundance between affections and emotions (that the will when intensely moved can spill over to the emotions in such a way that the emotions then buttress the movement of the will), Edwards notes in passing throughout the *Religious Affections* that "the constitution of the body, and the motion of its fluids, may promote the exercise of the affections" insofar as such motion is an effect of or a reaction to the affections in the first place.[41] As he remarks, by the body's "reaction [to love and joy] they may make some circumstantial difference in the sensation of the mind."[42] This is so due to "laws of the union of soul and body."[43]

Those same laws, however, also establish the necessary and not simply reactive "alterations of the motions of [the body's] fluids, and especially of the animal spirits" by the affections.[44] As necessary, the relationship between the affections and the emotions is far more than the indirect connections between the affective expressions of the intellectual appetites and the emotive movements of the sensitive appetites in Aquinas, as noted earlier. Consider the following passage from Edwards:

> All affections whatsoever, have in some respect or degree, an effect on the body. As was observed before, such is our nature, and such are the laws of union of soul and body, that the mind can have no lively or vigorous exercise, without some effect upon the body. So subject is the body to the mind, and so much do its fluids, especially the animal spirits, attend the motions and exercises of the mind, that there can't be so much as an intense thought, without an effect upon them. Yea, 'tis questionable, whether an embodied soul ever so much as thinks one thought, or has any exercise at all, but that there is some corresponding motion or alteration of motion, in some degree, of the fluids, in some part of the body. But universal experience shows, that the exercise of the affections, have in a special manner a tendency, to some sensible effect upon the body, we may then well suppose, the greater those affections be, and the more vigorous their exercise (other circumstances being equal) the greater will be the effect on the body. Hence it is not to be wondered at, that very great and strong exercises of the affections, should have great effects on the body.[45]

A similar passage appears almost at the outset of *Religious Affections*.[46] But the version above has a few notable specifications that are less prominent in the earlier passage. First, the claim of affections having a necessary effect on the body is not a backtracking from the earlier claim that the affections are of the mind and the emotions are of the body. Instead, it is Edwards's way of taking the unity of body and soul seriously not just in a theological sense but in a manner that is consistent with lived experience. Note his insistence, "But universal experience shows . . . ." Last, Edwards is clear that there are different states or degrees of affections, and corresponding to those various degrees, in keeping with the unity of body and soul, different degrees of bodily effects follow: the greater the affections, the greater the bodily, emotive commotion.

It is within this context, of varying degrees of affections leading to varying degrees of bodily effects, that Edwards's one passing paragraph on the passions makes sense. In that one paragraph, Edwards explains, "*affections* and *passions* are frequently spoken of as the same; and yet, in the more common use of speech, there is in some respect a difference."[47] Affections, he claims, refers to "all vigorous lively actings of the will or inclination." Passions refers to "those that are more sudden," but to what does "those" refer? Passions are those "lively actings of the will or inclination" that "are more sudden, and whose effects on the animal spirits are more violent, and the mind more overpowered, and less in its own command."[48] Inasmuch as Edwards suggests that passions are also a kind of vigorous exercise of the will and inclination—albeit exercises that are less in control by the mind—the passions are a kind of deformed, deficient affections that subject the body to great, heightened effects. Thus, passions in an Edwardsean key are not to be taken as Thomistic passions (or what we have been taking as emotions). What Edwards appears to be pointing to with respect to the passions is a situation in which one's will and inclination is of the sort that one is led to emotional hysteria and, correspondingly, wild bodily movement.

That the passions have this kind of frenzied, bodily, emotional effect is in keeping with Edwards's claim that, due to the soul–body unity, varying degrees of affections will necessarily move or alter the body in kind. But I think it would be a mistake to think that such wild bodily effects are consequences of only malformed and irreligious affections (the passions, for instance). Consider the observation that Edwards puts forward on the religious versus nonreligious affections. For Edwards, one's emotional state—the constitution of one's bodily existence—is a consequence of varying degrees of genuine religious affections (the result of which is the indwelling of the Holy Spirit), false religious affections, or even secular affections. As he suggests, someone who is of "gracious and holy affections" can exhibit a kind of body that is emotionally frenzied or dizzied: "No such rule can be drawn from reason: I know of no reason, why a being affected with a view of God's glory should not cause the body to faint, as well as a being affected with a view of Solomon's glory."[49] How could this be the case with respect to the body under the influence of true religious affections? Wouldn't that be the case only for those who have been unduly influenced by excessively dramatic preaching or even the spiritualism of antinomian heresies? No, suggests Edwards, citing scripture, "But man's nature is weak: flesh and blood are represented in Scripture as exceedingly weak; and particularly with respect to its unfitness for great spiritual and heavenly operations and exercises (Matt. 26:41; I Cor. 15:43, and 50)."[50]

If "great effects on the body" can arise from religious as well as nonreligious affections, then the emotional states of the body "are no sure evidences that affections are spiritual; for we see that such effects oftentimes arise from great affections about temporal things, and when religion is no way concerned in them."[51] This is why Edwards, in part, held deep reservations over the kind of religious enthusiasm that accompanied the many evangelical revivals that swept through early eighteenth-century New England, especially those encouraged by the itinerant preaching of George Whitefield, among others.[52] Whether such enthusiasm is a genuine mark of holy conversion and, correlatively, the exercise of true religious affections in the soul or mind is questionable if such enthusiasm can arise from all kinds of affections or perceptual understandings of self and world, and not just genuinely religious ones.[53]

Much of the *Religious Affections* is devoted to naming and mapping out the twelve genuine signs of true Christian life. The relevant point here is that such a project is motivated by Edwards's insistence that the motions of the body alone cannot be a reliable indicator of the kind of affections that orient the soul or mind since "all affections [whether religious or not] have some effect on the body."[54]

Affections or Emotions? An Edwardsean Response

Like my discussion of Aquinas on affections and emotions, Edwards's discussion of the two terms is much more wide-ranging than what I have provided so far. Even so, some conclusions already recommend themselves. When viewing Edwards in light of Thomas's more formal delineation of the affections and the emotions, we are able to see starkly why, for Edwards, affection language can (and must) comingle with the language of the emotions. The nature of that comingling, however, raises the question of whether the emotions for Edwards can be counted as appetitive in the same way as they are for Aquinas.

To be more specific, while the affections may "resemble," to use a Thomistic description, the emotions, they do so, for Edwards, because the emotions (qua movements of the body) are always "affected" by one's particular dispositions, inclinations, or commitments. The picture of the emotions that I am trying to convey here is one in which the emotions are simply beholden to some kind of affections and therefore "activated" by them. On that view, the emotions are simply reflexive features of human experience and not functionally appetitive in the way Aquinas conceives of the emotions. Although the emotions are not the same as the affections, emotions "always accompany them"; they are "only effects or concommitants of the affections."[55] Perhaps another way of putting the point is that for Edwards, the emotions are when the affections are—that is, when we are willing and inclined in a particular direction based on what we perceive or apprehend. Recall an earlier assertion from Edwards: "So subject is the body to the mind, and so much do its fluids, especially the animal spirits, attend the motions and exercises of the mind, that there can't be so much as an intense thought, without an effect upon them."[56] Does this not convey a sense of the body's (and, correlatively, its emotive movements) basic submissiveness to the seat of the affections, to the activity and direction of the will and inclination or, ultimately, the mind? That would certainly be in line with his biblical appeals to the body's vulnerabilities.[57]

The emotions are beholden to the affections and, thus, to what we apprehend. That is the corollary to Edwards's insistence that our apprehensions or perceptions of self and world—if they are of the kind that inclines us toward particular likes or dislikes, preferences, or values—necessarily move the body and therefore are necessarily accompanied by particular emotions, sometimes intensely, sometimes less so. We can understand, then, why Gustafson, as we saw at the beginning of this essay, is able to readily identify affections as emotions. While we are disposed to react or respond to situations based on particular commitments, judgments of value, and so on, those responses are hardly emotionless. As Gustafson notes, "we assume something like this when we say about an event, 'That's going to make him very angry.'"[58] Such a statement assumes continuity between our judgments and emotions, which is captured in the term "affection." But against the backdrop of our discussion of Edwards so far, Gustafson ends up conflating affections and emotions in a way that obscures the fine points of Edwards's understanding of affections and emotions. Gustafson is not alone in that regard. Enlisting Edwards's account of the affections, James E. Gilman strives to affirm "that emotions are powerful moral forces and very often, when properly cultivated, function as reliable moral guides."[59] My reading of Edwards, however, raises the question of what kind of moral guides the emotions represent. As simply consequences of or arising from (necessarily, due to our soul–body nature) some kind of affections, emotions in themselves lack moral content, at least, not independent of the affections and therefore our thinking.

It would not be wholly inappropriate, then, to think of the emotions as nonrational in a sense. At the same time, it would not be wholly inappropriate to claim them as having a cognitive dimension. But cognitive in what sense? That is a tricky question, requiring a good deal of nuance and precision. While emotions are concomitant with our affective knowing, it would not be entirely accurate to say that they are forms of thoughts about the fragility of one's attachments and relationships, as Martha Nussbaum would think of them.[60] While an extended discussion of the convergences or divergences between Edwards and Nussbaum is not possible here, suffice it to say for now that, unlike Nussbaum, Edwards suggests emotions are cognitive only in the secondary or subordinate sense. They can appear to be object-oriented; one's emotions can appear to be in response to some experience of a thing, person, or event and thus seem as if they are expressing or manifesting judgments about them in one sense or another. But the emotive reaction arises from (is an effect of) the object-oriented nature of the soul's affective knowing or perception of reality. As such, emotions lack a cognitive structure; they simply are felt, embodied experiences that are caused by and accompany one's affectivity.

Perhaps the more significant implication of Edwards's claim that emotions (as movements of the body) are only concomitant effects of the affections is that emotions are relative rather than, as Gilman contends, "bearing truths that are universally accessible, comprehensible, and normative."[61] That emotions are relative is perhaps an unsettling claim, especially from a Thomistic perspective, but it conforms to the kind of affective and emotive distinctions that emerge when reading Edwards with Thomas in mind. For Edwards, since movements of the body are not reliable indicators of one's affective dispositions, there is nothing particularly informative in a normative way about a person's emotional state. Recall that, for Edwards, one can be equally emotional from affections that are either religiously or nonreligiously constituted. One's emotional state, therefore, is not indicative of whether one is in fact under the influence of the spiritual sense imparted by the indwelling Spirit or under the influence of some other sort of affective understanding of self and world. The Edwardsean point is simply that while emotions are an intrinsic part of human agency and experience, the composition of one's emotional state is not normatively particular to certain kinds of cognitions and valuational dispositions. That point draws Edwards somewhat closer to a contextual account of the emotions advanced by the psychologist Lisa Feldman Barrett.[62] It also draws Edwards further away from Nussbaum's cognitive construal of the emotions, although Edwards would likely agree with Nussbaum that his approach does not necessarily mean that emotions are ultimately evil and require suppression, as the Stoics argued in their normative philosophy.[63]

That emotions are relative or contextual—that is, not indicative of specific dispositional attitudes—helps to explain why persons may be similarly angry while expressing such emotion in different directions, toward different objects of concern. For instance, take two college students who, in their anger, are both fuming, their hearts beating rapidly, and expressing, both verbally and physically, their frustrations (pulling and tugging their hair, banging their fists on the wall or table, and possibly yelling expletives). While both are emotionally, visibly angry, one is angry toward racially discriminatory policing tactics while the other is unmoved by such violations of civil rights but is angered by something more trivial, such as having two final exams in one day or, perhaps even more trivially, the frequent crashing of her texting app. Perhaps Aquinas would suggest that both are angry because of some common perceived injustice, and in their anger, they "[desire] evil" toward the unjust.[64] Yet their anger does not necessarily reveal why each student is angered by particular, seemingly divergent, conceptions of injustice (the injustice of police brutality versus the injustice of a burdensome exam schedule or a poorly designed smart phone app).[65] An Edwardsean perspective suggests that what explains one person being angry about an app versus another about racist policing requires attending to their affections, which is to say their basic valuational orientations.

The foregoing helps to explain how an emotion can be subject to different aims or put in the service of disparate moral visions. Audre Lorde's classic essay on anger and racism is a noteworthy example of this possibility. She considers different ways in which the anger of black persons, especially black women, can be channeled. She insists that the moral priority or interest of black women's survival and flourishing should be the primary driver of one's anger.[66] That insistence underscores the notion that anger, or emotions generally, is given moral direction under the influence of a particular perception of self and world (in Edwardsean terms, that would refer to affections). Multiple persons can be angry alike in their embodied feelings and expressions, but the direction to which their anger is placed depends on their affectivity, the kinds of values and commitments that orient their selves. Perhaps another way of putting the point is the following. The emotive markers of our embodied existence may be common to all persons so long as we have bodies. But those emotive markers will take on different meanings as a consequence of one's affectivity, which is expressive of one's basic moral orientations. But discerning the particular moral meanings of emotions is not as easy as simply noticing one's anger or sadness— that is to say, one's emotions.

Conclusion

At the start of this inquiry, I noted that while Edwards is often taken as promoting the centrality of the emotions in his emphasis on the affections, he rarely employed the actual term "emotion" in his discussions. But that should not be immediately taken to suggest that a meaningful distinction cannot be had between affections and emotions, as Gustafson, for instance, could be interpreted as implying. Reading Edwards with Aquinas's account of the affections and emotions in mind allows for a differentiation between the affections and emotions in Edwards's thought that would otherwise remain opaque. The key to that differentiation is discerning the body as the locus for the emotions and the will for the affections.

Why that differentiation matters from an Edwardsean perspective also requires discerning Edwards's distinctive construal of how the body (emotions) and will (affections) are related. For Edwards, emotions are bodily feelings that well up in response to affections of some kind. But whether one's emotional state gives access to the content of one's affectivity is questionable since persons with diverse moral dispositions can be similarly emotional. While such a view of the emotions problematizes the prospects of construing the emotions as cognitive experiences at least in some normatively robust way, such an Edwardsean view is valuable in its own rite by calling attention to the downsides of human emotional life.

Those downsides can stand in tension with Edwards's profound attunement to and affirmation of the emotional dimensions of human experience.

That tension, however, underscores the complexity of Edwards's thought and its importance for contemporary discussions on the emotions. For Edwards, human agency is not simply a rational calculation of choices but a function of inclinations, preferences, desires, or judgments that are deeply embodied. His insistence on the term "affection" attempts to capture that more holistic sense of human knowing and doing. But Edwards's profound attunement to the emotional dimensions of human life equally attunes him to the pitfalls of overemphasizing the significance of the emotions. More specifically, if emotions are not reliable indicators of our moral orientations insofar as persons of diverse dispositions can feel the same kind of emotions, then whether or not our emotions are being manipulated or exploited remains a real and persistent threat. How would we know if our emotions are the consequence of being influenced by beliefs, perceptions, or visions that have unduly captured—perhaps even enticed or seduced—our attention and moral imagination? That was in part the kind of lesson Edwards drew from his experiences with revivalism in eighteenth-century New England. A person under the influence of a theatrical evangelist could be just as emotionally enthused about religion as one under the influence of a more conventional pastor.

That lesson is as important today as it was almost three centuries ago. Emotions are intrinsic features of human life; human life without them would be less than human. But as important as they are, emotions can be deceiving; we can be falsely led or manipulated into feeling emotions for the wrong reasons and would hardly be aware of being unduly swayed simply by paying attention to or examining our emotions. The morally righteous person can be angry just as the unrighteous. Thus, while emotions give our beliefs and convictions color, depth, and vitality, we do well to follow Edwards in looking to something other than the emotions to gain insight into our fundamental convictions about the world. For Edwards, we ought to look at our actual moral habits, choices, and practices and then assess what those reveal about ourselves, focusing less on our emotional lives. For Edwards, it is the focus on the affections as something involving but ultimately differing from the emotions that calls attention to that seemingly paradoxical but significant reality: while the emotions are essential, they are also morally unreliable.

Notes

I thank the anonymous reviewers and SCE audience for their probing questions. Special thanks to Kevin Jung, Lisa Sowle Cahill, and Edward Collins Vacek, SJ, for their insights and extended conversation.

1. James M. Gustafson, *Ethics from a Theocentric Perspective*, vol. 1, *Theology and Ethics* (Chicago: University of Chicago Press, 1981), 198.
2. Ibid., 199, cf. 119, 229.

3. For his interpretation of Jonathan Edwards, see ibid., 171–78. See Diana Fritz Cates, *Aquinas on the Emotions: A Religious-Ethical Inquiry* (Washington, DC: Georgetown University Press, 2009); Diana Fritz Cates, "The Religious Dimension of Ordinary Human Emotions," *Journal of the Society of Christian Ethics* 25, no. 1 (Spring/Summer 2005): 35–53; James E. Gilman, *Fidelity of Heart: An Ethic of Christian Virtue* (Oxford: Oxford University Press, 2001); and Paul Lauritzen, *Religious Belief and Emotional Transformation: A Light in the Heart* (Lewisburg, PA: Bucknell University Press, 1992).

4. James M. Gustafson, *Can Ethics Be Christian?* (Chicago: University of Chicago Press, 1975), 43; cf. Cates, *Aquinas on the Emotions*, 44.

5. In this essay, I follow Diana Fritz Cates's lead in taking Thomistic passions (*passiones*; *passio*) as emotions. She notes that while some argue that Thomistic passions are noncognitive and, therefore, non-emotions, she argues that insofar as passions are object-oriented in Thomas's thought (passions are caused by an apprehension of an object), passions translated as emotion makes sense. Cates, *Aquinas on the Emotions*, 74–75n1.

6. Thomas Aquinas, *Summa theologica* II (I-II), trans. Fathers of the Dominican Province (New York: Benzinger Bros., 1948), Q. 22, Art. 1, 692. Hereafter cited as ST I-II.

7. The murkiness of Aquinas's use of the terms "passion" and "affection" appears elsewhere too, primarily as a matter of proper translation. For instance, regarding ST I, Q. 60, Art. 2, John A. Oesterle will refer to "interior affections, which are called passions of the soul." Thomas Aquinas, *Treatise on the Virtues*, trans. John A. Oesterle (Notre Dame, IN: University of Notre Dame Press, 1966), 100. However, the Dominican Fathers translation of the same text will say "interior emotions which are called the passions of the soul," ST I-II, 842.

8. ST I-II, Q. 22, Art. 3, 693; cf. Q. 26, Art. 1.

9. ST I, Q. 82, Art. 5, 417; cf. Cates, *Aquinas on the Emotions*, 66.

10. Ibid., Q. 59, Art. 4, 296.

11. Cates, *Aquinas on the Emotions*, 67.

12. ST I-II, Q. 26, Art. 1, 704.

13. Ibid., Art. 2, 705.

14. Ibid., Art. 1, 704; ibid., Art. 2, 705.

15. ST I, Q. 83, Art. 5, Reply Obj. 1, emphasis added.

16. ST I-II, Q. 22, Art. 3, 693.

17. Ibid., Art. 2, Reply Obj. 3, 692, emphasis original.

18. Ibid., Art. 3, 693.

19. Ibid., Reply Obj. 3, 693, emphasis added.

20. Ibid., Q. 59, Art. 5, Reply Obj. 3, 841.

21. That construal of affections appears in ST I, Q. 59, Art. 4, Reply Obj. 2, 297; ST I-II, Q. 22, Art. 3, Reply Obj. 3, 693; ST I-II, Q. 24, Art. 2, 698. See Cates, *Aquinas on the Emotions*, 95.

22. "Love and joy, in so far as they are passions, are in the concupisicible appetite, but in so far as they express a simple act of the will, they are in the intellectual part," ST I, Q. 59, Art. 4, Reply Obj. 2, 297.

23. ST I-II, Q. 24, Art. 3, Reply Obj. 1, 699; cf. ibid., Q. 31, Art. 3 and 4 on joy and delight.

24. Ibid., Q. 59, Art. 5, 841.

25. Cates, *Aquinas on the Emotions*, 202.

26. Ibid., 194.

27. ST I-II, Q. 24, Art. 3, 699.

28. Jonathan Edwards, "A Treatise concerning Religious Affections, in Three Parts," in *Religious Affections*, ed. John E. Smith, vol. 2 of *The Works of Jonathan Edwards* (New Haven, CT: Yale University Press, 1959), 96. Hereafter cited as RA.

29. RA, 97.

30. On the will and intellect as both constituting "perceptual" understanding in Edwards, see Ki Joo Choi, "The Role of Perception in Jonathan Edwards's Moral Thought: The Nature of True Virtue Reconsidered," *Journal of Religious Ethics* 38, no. 2 (June 2010): 269–96.

31. Smith, "Editor's Introduction," in RA, 14.

32. RA, 101.

33. See Jonathan Edwards, "A Divine and Supernatural Light," in *A Jonathan Edwards Reader*, ed. John E. Smith, Harry S. Stout, and Kenneth P. Minkema (New Haven, CT: Yale University Press, 1995), 111–12.

34. John E. Smith, "Religious Affections and the 'Sense of the Heart,'" in *The Princeton Companion to Jonathan Edwards*, ed. Sang Hyun Lee (Princeton, NJ: Princeton University Press, 2005), 110.

35. Smith, "Editor's Introduction," RA, 14–15.

36. RA, 113.

37. RA, 118.

38. Ibid.

39. RA, 113.

40. RA, 98.

41. Ibid.

42. RA, 113.

43. For example, RA, 96–98. Also note the very interesting insistence that if we purposely restrain the body, especially in relation to the exercise of spiritual things (by virtue of holy, religious affections), we will end up restraining those holy affections. See Jonathan Edwards, "Miscellanies 101," in *The "Miscellanies," A-500*, ed. Thomas A. Schafer, vol. 13 of *The Works of Jonathan Edwards* (New Haven, CT: Yale University Press), 269.

44. RA, 98.

45. RA, 132.

46. Cf. RA, 98.

47. RA, 97, emphasis original.

48. RA, 98.

49. RA, 132.

50. RA, 133.

51. RA, 132.

52. George Marsden, *Jonathan Edwards: A Life* (New Haven, CT: Yale University Press, 2003), 211–12.

53. Consider also Edwards's reflections on impassioned speech, which he thinks is no sure embodied sign of genuine religious affection, for one can speak with emotion and feeling from other sorts of affections: "That persons are disposed to be abundant in talking of things of religion, *may be from a good cause, and it may be from a bad one.* . . . It is very much the nature of the affections, *of whatever kind they be*, and whatever objects they are exercised

about, if they are strong, to dispose persons to be very much in speaking of that which they are affected with . . . to speak very *earnestly and fervently*. And therefore persons talking abundantly and very fervently about the things of religion, can be an evidence of no more than this, that they are very much affected with the things of religion; but this may be (as has been already shown), and there be no grace." RA, 136, emphases added.

54. RA, 132.

55. RA, 98.

56. RA, 132.

57. RA, 133–34.

58. Gustafson, *Can Ethics Be Christian?*, 44.

59. Gilman, *Fidelity of Heart*, 7.

60. Martha C. Nussbaum, *Upheavals of Thought: The Intelligence of Emotions* (Cambridge: Cambridge University Press, 2001), chap. 1.

61. Gilman, *Fidelity of Heart*, 24.

62. Barrett proposes that just as there is no distinct neural entity with respect to particular emotions, there are no normative emotive acts or patterns of the body; emotions are dependent on the situation. As such, emotional expressions do not necessarily correspond to one's particular inner feelings, perceptions, or commitments in some "natural" or biological way. The spirit of that thesis is not unlike what I am proposing as the relative nature of the emotions in Edwards. See Lisa Feldman Barrett, "Are Emotions Natural Kinds?," *Perspectives in Psychological Science* 1, no. 1 (March 2006): 28–58. Barrett's thesis is laid out in more detail in her *How Emotions Are Made: The Secret Life of the Brain* (New York: Houghton Mifflin Harcourt, 2017), chaps. 4–7.

63. Cf. Nussbaum, *Upheavals of Thought*, chap. 3. Many thanks to an anonymous referee for astutely pointing out the Stoic dimensions to Edwards's account of the affections and emotions. While Edwards would disagree with the Stoic suspicion of the emotions, Edwards and the Stoics converge in other ways, especially with respect to virtue. See Elizabeth Agnew Cochran, *Receptive Human Virtues: A New Reading of Jonathan Edwards's Ethics* (University Park: Pennsylvania State University Press, 2011).

64. ST I-II, Q. 46, Art. 7, 783.

65. But can being angry at something like a crashing app be reflective of a particular conception of justice/injustice? I think this is debatable and ultimately dubious, underscoring the challenges of conceiving of emotions as universally grounded.

66. "Black women are expected to use our anger only in service of other people's salvation or learning. But that time is over. My anger has meant pain to me but it has also meant survival, and before I give it up I'm going to be sure that there is something at least as powerful to replace it on the road to clarity." Audre Lorde, "The Uses of Anger: Women Responding to Racism," in *Sister Outsider: Essays and Speeches* (Freedom, CA: Crossing Press, 1984), 132.

Toward a Christian Virtue Account of Moral Luck

Kate Ward

Structural evil impacts persons' experiences differently, a reality that feminist philosophers Claudia Card and Lisa Tessman have termed "moral luck." As Christian ethicists grapple with privilege and oppression, we lack a satisfactory framework to describe how particular life circumstances impact moral lives. This essay develops a Christian virtue account of moral luck, drawing on Thomas Aquinas and womanist theologians including Melanie L. Harris and Rosita deAnn Mathews. Moral luck helps Christian ethicists attend to the impact of difference on the moral life as well as to the common experience of contingency harming virtue, requiring dependence on God's grace.

WITH ATTENTION TO PARTICULARITY AND DIFFERENCE VERY much on the rise in Christian theology, ethicists lack a framework to describe the impact of particular life circumstances on a person's pursuit of virtue. Morally significant life circumstances—including, among others, gender, ethnic or racial identity, sexual identity, and wealth and poverty—affect moral development as they influence one's self-image, treatment by others, and opportunities for action within society. Christian ethicists acknowledge this, tacitly or explicitly, in work on privilege and oppression but have yet to explore how privilege and oppression are linked in their impacts on the virtuous life. Philosophers refer to this reality as moral luck.

I begin with an account of moral luck as described by philosophers. In the second section, I show that Thomas Aquinas acknowledged the reality of moral luck as today's feminist philosophers describe it. In the third section, I show that contemporary womanist theologians also engage moral luck, bringing unique attention to how persons shaped by moral luck should respond. I argue for a Christian theological account of moral luck and show that, indeed, one is already embedded in Christian tradition.

Kate Ward, PhD, is an assistant professor of theology at Marquette University, PO Box 1881, Milwaukee, WI 53201-1881; katharine.ward@marquette.edu.

Journal of the Society of Christian Ethics, 38, 1 (2018): 131–145

Moral luck in a Christian virtue context shares with the secular account an attempt to realistically confront and understand the way life circumstances, including privilege or lack thereof, can affect persons' pursuit of virtue. All persons share the common experience of being thwarted in our pursuit of virtue by moral luck and depending on God to grow in the virtuous life. Still, it is crucial to understand the particular and different ways life circumstances can affect the pursuit of virtue. My Christian account of moral luck addresses those suffering under structures of oppression as well as those who benefit from inequalities, emphasizes both dependence on God and persons' moral agency, and roots firmly in Christian tradition.

Moral Luck in Philosophy

Claudia Card defines moral luck as "luck that impacts either on character development or on one's ability to do morally good or right things in particular contexts."[1] "Luck" in this context does not necessarily mean good or bad luck; it draws our attention to the presence of factors beyond the subject's control. As Martha Nussbaum points out, circumstances can prevent us from virtuous activity by depriving our activity of a key means or resource, or by removing the intended object of the activity (as when the death of a friend removes the activity of friendship).[2] Philosophers distinguish between incident moral luck—circumstances beyond our control that affect the moral implications of particular actions or situations—and constitutive moral luck, in which circumstances beyond our control affect who we are able to become.[3]

Card and Lisa Tessman demonstrate that systemic privilege and oppression function as constitutive moral luck, influencing the pursuit of virtue. For Card, moral luck has to do with "politically disadvantageous starting points or early positionings in life. . . . Different combinations of circumstances in fact provide opportunities for, stimulate, nurture, or discourage the development of different virtues and vices, strengths and weaknesses of character."[4] For Card, moral luck is best understood not simply as circumstances external to us but as circumstances that are "contingent to our moral agency" and that may also be internal to selves.[5] Significant relationships, such as those with partners or family members, are obvious sources of constitutive moral luck, as are relationships within social, economic, or educational structures.[6] Moral luck is not a matter of simplistically assigning or reserving praise or blame but of understanding moral agents as interlinked and shaped by circumstances, particularly privilege and oppression.[7]

Card believes the primary way oppression can damage moral agents is by making it more difficult to function as an integrated self: "Oppression splinters us (both within ourselves, as individuals, and from each other, within a group) by putting us constantly into double binds."[8] The self must be integrated in order to fully take responsibility for one's desires and actions, which is complicated by the splintering effect of oppression: "Responsible agency [dissolves when] internal connections are broken or inadequately developed."[9]

Card's analysis of gender as moral luck demonstrates how such a significant component of identity and social location can affect virtue formation. She suggests that the moral luck of gender can predispose persons to different vices, such as domination and aggression for men and passivity and trickery for women.[10] She writes, "Feminist thinkers are understandably reluctant to address publicly women's reputation for lying, cunning, deceit, and manipulation. But, are these vices, one may ask, if they are needed for self-defense? They are surely not virtues . . . [even if] needed for survival under oppressive conditions. Human good may be unrealizable under such conditions."[11] Card sees the gender differences that occasion moral luck as socialized, not innate, but it's worth noting that a physicalist understanding of gender could also acknowledge a gender component to moral luck, perhaps viewing vices like aggression or virtues like caring as physically caused but also gender-linked.

Card explains more generally how societal structures of privilege and oppression function as moral luck for those privileged and oppressed within them: "The privileged are liable to arrogance with its blindness to others' perspectives. The oppressed are liable to low self-esteem, ingratiation . . . as well as to a tendency to dissemble, fear of being conspicuous, and chameleonism. . . . It may also be our moral luck to develop special insights and sensitivities, even under oppressive institutions."[12]

At times, those who are oppressed may have no course of action to take that does not involve a "moral remainder," a negative consequence that could not be avoided. A moral remainder can indicate that harm was done to someone who did not deserve it and can also describe a negative impact on the moral formation of the agent.[13] This is one reason why, in Card's words, "human good may be unrealizable" under particular conditions of oppression.[14]

Racial identity, too, is an example of moral luck, as Card explains: "By profiting in various ways, willingly or not, from ethnic privilege, I may now have acquired moral responsibilities."[15] Thus we see that moral luck, in addition to hindering our pursuit of virtue, can impose positive duties on us. Card says: "Uncovering particular histories, such as those underlying our racial and ethnic social identities, can help us to appreciate who it is our moral luck to have become, to determine what responsibilities we now have, how we are related to one another, . . . and what kinds of choices we now have."[16] We should not assume that our identities, their meaning and the duties they do or do not impose on us are "transparent" but should interrogate our social location and its contingent duties.[17]

Building on Card's work, Lisa Tessman provides the most sustained investigation into how experiences of privilege and oppression can serve as moral luck.[18] Tessman pays particular attention to the impossibility of flourishing under oppression when she notes that both resisting and failing to resist oppression can result in moral damage, failure to develop the virtues as fully as one might otherwise have done.[19] For oppressed people, evidence of moral damage might include identifying with one's oppressors or failing to appreciate one's own human dignity. Such traits can help oppressed persons survive oppression but do not contribute to the person's overall full flourishing.[20] Tessman warns that attempting to resist oppression can also occasion moral damage. Developing virtue as an oppressed person carries a burden in that unequal societies are not set up to help oppressed persons flourish. That is, Tessman says, "resistance, while politically necessary, does not automatically release the self from the burdens or the damages that oppressive conditions evoke."[21] Being oppressed in a way that seems to demand resistance is a particular type of systemic moral luck that imperils one's development of virtue.[22]

For example, displaying courage and self-sacrifice in resisting oppression may invite danger for the activist or her loved ones. Resistors may develop insensitivity to any type of danger or vulnerability, which might compromise flourishing as persons in relationship.[23] Some resistance movements may demand members to cultivate traits that oppose the self's flourishing, such as anger or extreme self-sacrifice, or may punish members who criticize the group's actions.[24] Oppressed communities in resistance, for Tessman, are not reliable sites to develop virtue.[25]

Tessman follows Card in noting that systems of oppression damage the virtues of those with privilege as well as of oppressed persons. The privileged who are morally affected by their social position risk developing what Tessman calls "the ordinary vices of domination." She calls these vices "ordinary" to distinguish them from the types of vices that lead to acts of extreme hatred but that are almost never believed to contribute to the agent's flourishing.[26] While investigating the vices that oppressed people may exhibit can feel like victim-blaming, understanding the vices of those who benefit from oppression is all the more important because they are not usually understood as vices.[27] Tessman believes the majority of those occupying dominant roles in oppressive societies will come to exhibit the vices of domination.[28] She writes: "Those enjoying economic advantage are popularly believed to be living the good life, regardless of the moral flaws that lead them to accept, develop, or maintain their unjust position. . . . Thus many groups of people thought to be living well clearly exhibit moral vices (such as callousness, greed, self-centeredness, dishonesty, cowardice, in addition to injustice) or at least the absence of certain specific moral virtues (perhaps compassion, generosity, cooperativeness, openness to appreciating others)."[29]

Tessman acknowledges the possibility that members of privileged groups who actively resist structures of domination may be able to change their characters and resist the "ordinary vices of domination," but she reminds us that the point of moral luck is that moral development is not entirely subject to our own will.[30] She complains that too many virtue theorists speak as if the average reader were assumed to be virtuous. Instead, emphasizing the "ordinary vices of domination" invites readers who occupy places of privilege to explore the impact of their privileges on their own moral development.[31] I agree.

Tessman concludes that analyzing the burdened virtues helps us develop a realistic ethics of flourishing in an imperfect world. Oppressed persons may be called on by their circumstances to develop traits that do not contribute to their flourishing, that may actively harm their own flourishing or that of others, or that may simply enable them to survive for the time being. To acknowledge this is not to reject all hope for a world where flourishing is possible for everyone but simply to recognize that the burdens placed on oppressed people by systemic inequalities include moral burdens.[32] Oppression harms oppressed people by denying them the external conditions for flourishing and by harming their ability to flourish morally. Significantly, though, systems of oppression also morally harm those *advantaged* by oppression, predisposing them to acquire particular vices. Thus, Tessman shows, systems of oppression affect advantaged and disadvantaged similarly in just this way: by imposing moral luck.[33]

By now it is clear that moral luck helps describe broad and pervasive realities related to moral life. Yet moral luck is not the final determination of a person's moral agency. Moral luck simply acknowledges that life circumstances, including gender, race, and socioeconomic status, present us with a certain set of arenas for action. It does not deny that our own choices affect how we acquire or fail to acquire virtue within those arenas; despite the pervasive reality of moral luck, moral agency always remains present. Since virtue is linked to flourishing, moral luck helps us ask who is being helped and who denied the opportunity to flourish. It has the potential to change how we evaluate the virtue of others, including whether we regard their virtues as morally heroic. Perhaps most importantly, understanding moral luck helps persons gain a more accurate picture of what the pursuit of virtue will require of us in each of our particular lives.

While Card and Tessman draw our attention to the difficulty of flourishing through virtue under oppression, both would agree that in most circumstances moral agency still exists, and persons can pursue virtue even in situations of incredibly tragic moral luck.[34] However, it seems fair to say that these philosophers tend to emphasize the negative impact of moral luck rather than the persistence of agency; recall Tessman's judgment that the average reader is too often assumed to be virtuous. Their emphasis on moral luck is a needed corrective to optimistic approaches that seem to confine the acquisition of virtue to individual effort. As we will see, while Christian ethicists join feminist philosophers in identifying the harm of moral luck and the duties it can impose, they promote the moral agency of persons despite moral luck, maintain that communities can help form virtue, and reserve a prominent role for God's action in the moral life.

Moral Luck in Thomas Aquinas

Christian virtue ethics has given little attention to moral luck, but there is some precedent for inquiry into the impact of life circumstances on virtue.[35] Daniel Daly's structures of virtue and vice connect unjust social structures to the virtue or vice of individual persons, while theological research on moral injury shows how participating in acts the agent views as unjust can harm virtue.[36] Stephen Pope notes that the pursuit of virtue depends on the ability to reason, which is complexly affected by our social, mental, and physical development.[37] Without developing accounts of moral luck or something like it, these contemporary theologians point to the need for a Christian ethical account of the impact of life circumstances on virtue.

Thomas Aquinas and contemporary womanist theologians provide ample grounding for a Christian account of moral luck. The Christian virtue account of moral luck they help me develop retains feminist philosophers' attention to the prevalent moral impact of unjust social structures and the difficulty of pursuing the virtuous life. Uniquely, though, it retains Christian hope for moral improvement, urges dependence on God, and promotes moral agency in community.

Without using the term, Thomas Aquinas gives accounts of both incident and constitutive moral luck. A contemporary example of incident moral luck is that two people may recklessly drive drunk, but since a pedestrian is present in only one case, only one drunk driver kills a pedestrian and becomes culpable for the death of an innocent person. Thomas considers this type of situation in his discussion of whether circumstances increase the gravity of a sin. The example of the drunk driver fits Thomas's discussion of harm following directly from a sinful act, though neither foreseen nor intended by the agent. Thomas says such harm increases the consequences of a sin and in fact is directly related to such a sin in its species.[38] Even an action that is good according to its species can become bad according to its circumstances (e.g., helping another for the sake of public praise).[39]

Circumstances can aggravate sin even when connected with the sin only accidentally. Suppose someone steals a car that has a medical inhaler inside it, and the asthmatic who needed the inhaler dies. Stealing is a sin, but causing the asthmatic's death is related only by accident. Still, in this case Thomas finds the sinner culpable for having failed to consider the harm they caused.[40] Other more obvious examples of harm caused through sin include harm that is foreseen and intended in doing the sin and harm that is foreseen but not intended, which the agent in a sense writes off as the cost of sinning. For both these types of harm, Thomas says, the agent is culpable. This is Thomas's clear and detailed treatment of incident moral luck.

More aligned with Card and Tessman is Thomas's account of constitutive moral luck, luck that shapes the kind of persons we are. One example is his discussion of "whether the excellence of the person sinning aggravates the sin."[41] Thomas believes sin is more strongly "imputed" to three groups of people: those who have enjoyed many blessings and should have more reason to be grateful to God; those who violate a specific charge, like the duty of a prince to defend justice; and those who are much looked up to and cause scandal by their sin.[42] In Thomas's view, each of these privileged life circumstances can exacerbate the gravity of a sin. Thomas specifically mentions that one life circumstance that can increase the seriousness of sin is "any excellence, even in temporal goods." Sin is imputed more strongly to us if we sin despite personal talents or wealth. Our abuse of the blessing, not the blessing itself, causes the disadvantage.[43]

Thomas's understanding of vincible and invincible ignorance contributes to our Christian account of moral luck in important ways. In general, ignorance does not excuse us from sin if we are ignorant about something we should have known, whether that means basic human goods or part of our specific duty. Ignorance does excuse us from sin if we are incapable of knowing, and therefore doing, better.[44] Two types of voluntary (or vincible) ignorance do not excuse us from sin. The first is direct voluntary ignorance, wherein we intentionally prolong our ignorance in order to "sin the more freely." Voluntary ignorance is often cited today describing privileged persons who choose to remain ignorant of the effect of their privilege on others though they could easily know better.[45]

The second type of voluntary ignorance may be harder for us to accept. Thomas says that even ignorance caused by "stress of work or other occupations," which keeps us from knowing what we should have known, does not excuse us from sin.[46] There is something pitiable about the person so consumed with work and stress that she neglects her moral duty, and we may wish to avoid blaming such a person. But Thomas, probably thinking of the impact on those such a person wounds through her ignorance, charges her with "negligence." Such ignorance is "itself voluntary and sinful, provided it be about matters one is bound and able to know."[47] Finally, "natural disposition" can enable certain persons to develop virtue more perfectly than others, another example of constitutive moral luck.[48]

Thus far Thomas has identified threats to virtue in experiences of privilege and oppression. Excellence in temporal goods exacerbates sin, and the stress of a difficult life can lead to blameworthy moral ignorance. Attempting to explain how Aquinas can on one hand acknowledge that temporal goods often play a role in virtue formation and on the other assert that God gives everyone the temporal goods they need to pursue virtue, John Bowlin theorizes that "Aquinas considers the relation between external goods and virtuous action thoroughly ambiguous."[49] Any external good, such as wealth, may be used either virtuously or viciously, as may the absence of an external good.[50]

Even grace can explain why persons develop virtue to different degrees—a difficult idea to accept, perhaps, but a reminder that for Thomas, no one can form even the acquired virtues without God's help.[51] Bowlin finds that, for Aquinas, God's charity "effectively eliminat[es] fortune's authority over virtuous habits and actions," affording the possibility of perfect virtue to those struggling with no matter what life circumstances.[52] Even those who have acquired virtue need God's grace in order to persevere.[53] As Jean Porter points out, Thomas was much more comfortable acknowledging limitations on human freedom than modern thinkers tend to be, and God's predestination is a preeminent example of grace functioning as a limitation on human freedom.[54]

Thomas Aquinas clearly gives accounts of incident and constitutive moral luck. He acknowledges that privilege can be a source of moral luck, affecting our ability to acquire the virtues. In this he shares the concerns of contemporary feminist philosophers whose work raises up historically marginalized perspectives. Other examples of moral luck for Thomas include personal inclination, greater opportunity to practice a virtue, and even God's will. For Thomas, moral luck reminds us about the difficulty of pursuing virtue in this life and of our total dependence on God for all we are able to become.

Womanist Theologians and Moral Luck

To complete a Christian account of moral luck, I turn to womanist theology. Womanist theologians, who work out of the dual contexts of "the oppressed Black community's concerns and struggles and the context of women's struggle for liberation and well-being," as Delores Williams says, have done some of the most sustained and incisive work on how inhabiting oppressed identities shapes moral selves.[55] Feminist philosophers, as I showed earlier, tend to emphasize the damage moral luck does to the moral subject. Womanist theologians acknowledge this reality, too, but distinct from feminist philosophers, womanist theologians' accounts of moral luck move beyond caution or lament to emphasize the moral agency of persons subject to moral luck, an emphasis redolent of Christian hope. Distinct from feminist philosophers' focus on communities as sites of harmful moral luck, womanist theologians identify communities as places of moral agency and virtue pursuit.

Womanist theologians acknowledge the way racist social structures function as moral luck but frequently urge a broader focus on the positive moral agency of those oppressed by race, gender, and other divisive social forces. For example, womanist theologians promote the agency of the subject formed by moral luck when they hold out hope for active, embodied self-love. M. Shawn Copeland affirms James Baldwin's insight that white supremacist societies teach black people to despise themselves.[56] She recounts how, under slavery, black women's bodies were made sites of violence, with sexist and racist hatred forcibly visited on them. To heal and grow toward self-love, black women had to learn to love their own bodies—the "enfleshing freedom" of her book's title.[57] Cheryl Townsend Gilkes reinforces the importance of loving one's own despised body with her meditation on body size and its intersection with racist and sexist erasures of black women's bodies. In her own fond recounting of her experience as a larger-bodied African American woman, Gilkes models love of one's own body despite oppression and offers hope for developing self-love despite damaging moral luck.[58]

With a similar arc, Emilie Townes takes up the urgency of self-love for African Americans amid the history of slavery and lynching and the present-day realities of economic and environmental racism. The pervasiveness of these oppressive structures mean for Townes that African Americans "have learned to hate ourselves without even realizing the level of our self-contempt."[59] The urgency of self-love belies dualistic attempts to self-define as either victim or success story, so Townes urges an "ontology of wholeness," prioritizing the relationship between self and other, one that insists no one can fully flourish while many in her community remain in pain.[60] While Townes offers an insight Tessman would share, that "resistance is not synonymous with self-actualization," her focus on the urgency of self-love provides an important corrective to the moral pessimism of Card and Tessman.[61] "To dance with twisted hip" is Townes's image of flourishing despite moral luck, in relationship with community, history, self, and God.[62]

For these womanist theologians, naming and lamenting moral luck moves toward insistence on the necessity and power of personal moral agency.[63] Others, like Melanie L. Harris, move from evaluating moral luck to urging moral agency in community. Harris formulates a womanist virtue ethic drawn from Alice Walker's nonfiction writings. Resonant with Card's insistence that moral luck fragments persons and communities, Harris first shows how Walker's work recognizes the ways white supremacy and racism splinter selves.[64] Walker calls attention to the sin of dehumanization and the imperative of self-love to combat it.[65] Harris gleans seven virtues for a womanist virtue ethic from Walker's work: generosity, graciousness, compassion, spiritual wisdom, audacious courage, justice, and good community.[66]

Harris's description of the virtue of "good community" challenges Tessman's moral reservations about the burdened virtue of group loyalty for justice activists. For Harris, a virtuous community does not hold members accountable to the community at the cost of the broader world. Rather, the local community holds members accountable for their own individual good, the good of the community and the good of the world at large. Harris writes: "Being accountable means taking responsibility for one's failings, as well as one's contributions to mutual relationality. . . . For communities, being accountable means holding one another and ourselves responsible to the interdependent web of life that holds us and connects us all together."[67]

Like many of her womanist colleagues, and unlike Tessman, Harris focuses on the potential for moral improvement in community rather than on the potential moral dangers. She shares Walker's conviction that women can overcome the moral luck of oppression by racism and sexism to pursue virtue in community, and that a community for social change and virtue pursuit need not be at odds with the broader world.

An essay by Rosita deAnn Mathews provides another strikingly apt Christian response to Tessman's work. Mathews finds hope in the possibility of resisting evil by "using power from the periphery," neither completely standing outside of a system nor adopting its preexisting methods and values. Using power from the periphery means "using one's power to resist a threat by maintaining or establishing ethical principles and moral standards, and refusing to employ the aggressor's methods . . . avoiding the use of practices utilized by those in power."[68] This practice, which Mathews recommends especially to African American women who must operate within hierarchical, patriarchal, and racist systems, holds out the hope of allowing agents to "maintain our soul," to retain personal ethical standards while working against oppression.[69]

Mathews acknowledges many of the same obstacles to exercising power from the periphery that Tessman adduces in her description of the burdened virtues for social justice activists. For Mathews, those who exercise power from the periphery must maintain personal integrity and Christian commitment, resist any desire for power and status, remain accountable to and strengthened by community, and endure through heavy opposition.[70] For Tessman, personal integrity is threatened by the fragmenting effect of oppression; resisting "the ordinary vices of domination" is not fully under the control of agents; community loyalty can erode the agent's capacity to criticize injustice within the community; and endurance can require developing anger to a degree that damages the self.[71]

Both Mathews and Tessman stake out valuable positions, and it is not simply the case that one is more optimistic and one more pessimistic about the possibility of maintaining virtue as an activist against oppression. Mathews's Christian standpoint clearly contributes to the hopeful nature of her diagnosis and solutions, but more significant are their different primary audiences. Tessman addresses two groups of people who might be surprised at the very idea of the burdened virtues of resistance. By naming the "ordinary vices of domination," she cautions those who wield power in oppressive systems that their willed ignorance of inequity may harm them morally. And her warning of the burdened virtues addresses activists whose focus on social change might lead them to ignore the impact of activism on their own moral integrity. Tessman's position is particularly valuable for those in positions of power in unjust systems, including white people and those with economic privilege.[72]

Mathews addresses African American women, who, she states clearly, know all too well the burdens of struggling for justice within systems that are designed not to hear them. Her primary audience needs no reminder of the personal moral burdens of working for justice, so instead, Mathews offers clear prescriptions for how to do this and a word of hope that moral self-preservation is possible for those who struggle to maintain their own moral integrity despite occupying oppressed social locations. For Christians, Mathews teaches that we can act effectively to retain moral integrity despite moral luck only after we have fully understood moral luck's power to fragment us. Christians who occupy positions of power in systems of oppression can thus proceed from Tessman to Mathews. For those prone to the ordinary vices of domination, "maintaining our soul" may demand deliberate moves to the periphery, rejecting not only the values of oppressive systems that grant us unjust power but, as much as possible, the very power they grant us.

While the burdens of moral luck fragment selves and communities, womanist theology insists that such fragmentation need not be the last word. Womanist theologians add a rich interplay between personal integrity and reliance on community to their searing lament of the personal and community fragmentation that can indeed result from moral luck. Moving from lament of moral luck to action in response, womanist theologians propose practicing self-love, working for justice with others, naming oppressive structures, drawing on Christian theology, and remaining accountable to the Christian community.[73] A Christian account of moral luck can integrate the strong caution about the moral luck of oppression and privilege advanced by feminist philosophers and the insistence on the moral agency of oppressed persons expressed by womanist theologians. Christian virtue ethicists need the tool of moral luck to address both those whom unequal structures privilege and those whom they oppress. A Christian virtue account of moral luck demonstrates how, even as structures of privilege and oppression distribute temporal goods (wealth, education, status, safety) unequally, they harm access to the moral good of virtue for all persons implicated in such systems. We are linked by the harms of moral luck and by our need for God's grace. Understanding this common experience of moral luck can inspire all Christians to work toward wholeness for community and for self.

Conclusion: Toward an Account of Moral Luck in Christian Virtue Ethics

I have shown that a Christian virtue account of moral luck already exists in the writings of Thomas Aquinas and womanist theologians. Like the feminist philosophers who name moral luck, these theologians acknowledge the impact of life circumstances on the pursuit of virtue, find that social structures of privilege and oppression are important sources of moral luck that both inhibit the pursuit of virtue and place duties on us, and use their awareness of moral luck to remind moral agents that pursuing virtue is a difficult task.

However, it should also be clear from the work of these scholars that a Christian account of moral luck does not, and cannot, share Card's and Tessman's moral pessimism. For Thomas Aquinas, warning of the potential harm of moral luck to the subject is not to invite moral pessimism or nihilism but to remind Christians of their dependence on God in the pursuit of virtue. Womanist theologians engage in lament as they bring to light the real moral damage done by structures of oppression, particularly racism and sexism. They assert that, while moral luck can and does fragment selves, pursuing self-love and taking action in community can help restore moral agents to wholeness.

Structures of injustice, including racism, sexism, and economic inequality, fragment selves and communities. As Tessman has shown, privilege and oppression affect moral selves quite differently, but both privileged and oppressed persons experience the moral luck of life circumstances harming the pursuit of virtue. Rosita deAnn Mathews reminds us that agents and communities must first understand the power of moral luck's harms to successfully oppose it. Christian ethicists should proclaim an account of moral luck at work in both privileged and oppressed lives while insisting that moral luck is never the final word; privileged and oppressed persons alike exercise moral agency by working toward Townes's ontology of wholeness for selves and communities. A Christian account of moral luck reminds us how the pursuit of virtue depends on God's grace in ways both particular and universal.

Notes

1. Claudia Card, *The Unnatural Lottery: Character and Moral Luck* (Philadelphia: Temple University Press, 1996), ix.

2. Martha Craven Nussbaum, *The Fragility of Goodness: Luck and Ethics in Greek Tragedy and Philosophy* (New York: Cambridge University Press, 2001), 327.

3. For a variety of perspectives, see Daniel Statman, ed., *Moral Luck* (Albany: State University of New York Press, 1993).

4. Card, *Unnatural Lottery*, ix.

5. Ibid., 31.

6. Ibid., 40–41.

7. Ibid., 40.

8. Ibid., 42.

9. Ibid., 48.

10. Claudia Card, "Gender and Moral Luck," in *Justice and Care: Essential Readings in Feminist Ethics*, ed. Virginia Held (Boulder, CO: Westview Press, 1995), 79.

11. Card, *Unnatural Lottery*, 53.

12. Ibid., 53–54. Card uses "our" here from her standpoint as one oppressed by sexism.

13. Ibid., 87.

14. Ibid., 26.

15. Ibid., 175.

16. Ibid., 181–82.

17. Ibid., 182.

18. Lisa Tessman, *Burdened Virtues: Virtue Ethics for Liberatory Struggles* (New York: Oxford University Press, 2005).

19. Ibid., 17.

20. Ibid., 19.

21. Ibid., 108.

22. Ibid., 112.

23. Ibid., 125–27.

24. Ibid., 115–16, and chap. 6.

25. Ibid., 157.

26. Ibid., 54.

27. Philosopher Margaret Urban Walker suggests that moral luck helps us evaluate persons' moral integrity; we would censure someone who shrugged off blame she earned because of moral luck. Margaret Urban Walker, "Moral Luck and the Virtues of Impure Agency," in *Moral Contexts* (Lanham, MD: Rowman & Littlefield, 2003), 21–34. Tessman's treatment of the ordinary vices of domination challenges this idea: unearned privilege harms others due to moral luck, and beneficiaries of privilege rarely accept, or even incur, blame for it.

28. Ibid., 57–59.

29. Ibid., 54.

30. Ibid., 55.

31. Ibid., 57–58.

32. Tessman, *Burdened Virtues*, conclusion.

33. Ibid., 57.

34. Tessman does envision the potential loss of moral agency as among the horrors faced by Holocaust victims. Lisa Tessman, *Moral Failure: On the Impossible Demands of Morality* (New York: Oxford University Press, 2015).

35. Although see Joseph J. Kotva, *The Christian Case for Virtue Ethics* (Washington, DC: Georgetown University Press, 1996), 29–30.

36. Daniel J. Daly, "Structures of Virtue and Vice," *New Blackfriars* 92 (2011): 341–57; and Mark A. Wilson, "Moral Grief and Reflective Virtue," in *Virtue and the Moral Life:*

Theological and Philosophical Perspectives, ed. William Werpehowski and Kathryn Getek Soltis (Lanham, MD: Lexington Books, 2014), 57–73.

37. Stephen J. Pope, "Virtue in Theology," in *Virtues and Their Vices*, ed. Kevin Timpe and Craig A. Boyd (Oxford: Oxford University Press, 2014), 402.

38. Thomas Aquinas, *The Summa Theologica of St. Thomas Aquinas*, trans. Dominican Fathers of the English Province (London: Burns Oates & Washbourne, 1921), I-II 73.8.

39. John R. Bowlin, *Contingency and Fortune in Aquinas's Ethics* (New York: Cambridge University Press, 1999), 62–63.

40. Aquinas, *ST* I-II 73.8.

41. Ibid., I-II 73.10.

42. Ibid.

43. Ibid.

44. Ibid., I-II 73.3.

45. Maureen H. O'Connell, "Viability of Virtue Ethics for Racial Justice," in *Journal of Moral Theology*, ed. David M. Cloutier and William C. Mattison (Eugene, OR: Wipf & Stock, 2014), 3:83–104; and Colleen McCluskey, *Thomas Aquinas on Moral Wrongdoing* (New York: Cambridge University Press, 2016), 175–78.

46. Aquinas, *ST* I-II 73.3.

47. Ibid.

48. Thomas Aquinas, *Disputed Questions on the Virtues*, trans. Ralph McInerny (South Bend, IN: St. Augustine's Press, 1999), http://dhspriory.org/thomas/english/QDdeVirtutibus.htm, 5.3.

49. Bowlin, *Contingency and Fortune*, 178–80.

50. Ibid., 183–84. I agree with Bowlin that Aquinas acknowledges the impact of fortune on the moral life, but ultimately we are discussing different questions. Bowlin takes Aquinas to be asking whether "the virtues can succeed against fortune" (215) and to conclude that, with God's help, they can. While I think Bowlin answers his question convincingly, his framing of it strikes me as susceptible to Tessman's critique that too many accounts of virtue assume the average agent to be virtuous. As is clear throughout this essay, the question of how fortune may impede with our development of virtue appears to me far more urgent.

51. Aquinas, *Disputed Questions*, 5.3; and Aquinas, *ST* I-II 109.2.

52. Bowlin, *Contingency and Fortune*, 216.

53. Aquinas, *ST* I-II 109.10.

54. Ibid., I-II 109.6.

55. Delores S. Williams, "A Womanist Perspective on Sin," in *Womanist Theological Ethics: A Reader*, ed. Katie Geneva Cannon, Emilie M. Townes, and Angela D. Sims, 130–47 (Louisville, KY: Westminster John Knox Press, 2011).

56. M. Shawn Copeland, *Enfleshing Freedom: Body, Race, and Being* (Minneapolis, MN: Fortress Press, 2010), 17.

57. Ibid., 50–51.

58. Cheryl Townsend Gilkes, "The 'Loves' and 'Troubles' of African-American Women's Bodies," in *Womanist Theological Ethics: A Reader*, ed. Katie Geneva Cannon, Emilie M. Townes, and Angela D. Sims, 81–97 (Louisville, KY: Westminster John Knox Press, 2011).

59. Emilie M. Townes, "To Be Called Beloved: Womanist Ontology in Postmodern Refraction," in *Womanist Theological Ethics: A Reader*, ed. Katie Cannon, Emilie Maureen

Townes, and Angela D. Sims, 183–202 (Louisville, KY: Westminster John Knox Press, 2011), 198.

60. Ibid., 201–2.

61. Ibid., 201.

62. Ibid., 202.

63. On "lament," see M. Shawn Copeland, "Presidential Address: Political Theology as Inter-ruptive," *Proceedings of the Catholic Theological Society of America* 59 (2004): 71–82; and Bryan N. Massingale, *Racial Justice and the Catholic Church* (Maryknoll, NY: Orbis, 2010).

64. Melanie L. Harris, *Gifts of Virtue, Alice Walker, and Womanist Ethics* (Basingstoke, UK: Palgrave Macmillan, 2010), 61–67.

65. Ibid., 71–72.

66. Ibid., chap. 5.

67. Ibid., 122.

68. Rosita deAnn Mathews, "Using Power from the Periphery," in *A Troubling in My Soul: Womanist Perspectives on Evil and Suffering*, ed. Emilie Maureen Townes (Maryknoll, NY: Orbis, 1993), 93.

69. Ibid., 102.

70. Ibid., 103–5.

71. Tessman, *Burdened Virtues*, 18, 55, 115, 133–57.

72. Card and Tessman's shared emphasis on the negative impact of privilege on virtue is no doubt linked to the fact that both identify as white and explicitly address white supremacy as moral luck. Tessman also discusses her experience as a lesbian activist in communities of resistance to heterosexist society.

73. While Christian communities can be sites of resistance and repair following moral luck, they are also sites of moral luck. Racism, sexism, and the demonization or erasure of LGBTQ persons fragment Christian communities historically and today.

Personal Responsibility in the Face of Social Evils: Transcendentalist Debates Revisited

Emily J. Dumler-Winckler

American transcendentalists were eager to oppose structural evils such as slavery and poverty. The 1840s were characterized by experiments and debates about whether and how such evils could be opposed. Orestes Brownson, Ralph Waldo Emerson, and Henry David Thoreau, following Thomas Carlyle and William Ellery Channing, set the terms of this debate. In the end, despite their different anthropologies, ecclesiologies, and prescriptions for opposing evil, they agree that spiritual reform is integral to sociopolitical reform. This transcendentalist debate illuminates the role of personal responsibility and reform in efforts to oppose structural evil in our own time.

WHEN MARTIN VAN BUREN LOST THE 1840 PRESIDENTIAL election to William Henry Harrison, he is said to have blamed Orestes Brownson.[1] Van Buren had become widely unpopular during his presidency due to the financial panic of 1837, which resulted in the worst economic depression in the young nation's history. Harrison ran as a war hero and man of the people—the "log cabin and hard cider" candidate of change from the Wild West. Never mind that he came from a family of wealthy planters in Virginia while Van Buren's father was a tavern keeper. The Whigs managed to depict Van Buren as a political elite living a life of luxury at the public's expense. Harrison's basic campaign strategy was to avoid discussion of difficult national issues such as slavery, poverty, or the national bank and instead to exploit the public's general dissatisfaction with the Van Buren administration. And it worked. The Whig party was able to create a broad coalition with few common ideals. They say history repeats itself.

Despite this, Brownson proved an easy scapegoat. A known supporter of Van Buren, he published an article, "The Laboring Classes," in the *Boston Quarterly Review* in July of the election year.[2] The article, which prefigures Karl

Emily Dumler-Winckler, PhD, is an associate professor of Christian ethics at Saint Louis University, Adjoran Hall, 3800 Lindell Blvd. 346, St. Louis, MO 63108; emily .dumlerwinckler@slu.edu.

Journal of the Society of Christian Ethics, 38, 1 (2018): 147–165

Marx's and Friedrich Engels's *Manifesto of the Communist Party* (1848), bitterly opposed Harrison's mercantile-class-supported party. Regardless of whether Brownson's article sealed Van Buren's fate, it was a lightning rod for his fellow transcendentalists, who shared his interest in sociopolitical reform.

American transcendentalists were eager to oppose social evils such as slavery, poverty, and eventually the inequality of women.[3] The 1840s especially was a period of experiments and debates about whether and how such evils could be remedied. Brownson, Ralph Waldo Emerson, and Henry David Thoreau, in particular, carried the debate forward. Each rejects the Fourierist solutions explored in the utopian communities of their fellow transcendentalists. Their debate is about the role of individuals, governments, associations, and institutions in effecting social change, and specifically about personal responsibility and virtue in the face of social evils. The transcendentalists differ in temperament and approach as much as in their views of human nature and of the role of the institutional church in these reforms.

Nonetheless, in the end, these luminaries agree that spiritual reform is integral to sociopolitical reform. Indeed, their views might be seen as a precursor to the slogan of second-wave feminism: "the personal is political." While this mantra has meant a number of different things, the transcendentalists' emphasis is decidedly Aristotelian in tone.[4] Because human beings simply are political animals, spiritual and moral formation through the cultivation of virtue is inherently political and is a condition of systemic sociopolitical change.

Brownson: The Limits of Individual Reform

Brownson's "The Laboring Classes" is written as a review of Thomas Carlyle's 1839 book *Chartism*.[5] In his book, Carlyle took up what he called "the Condition of England question," a theme that brought the questions of poverty, the laboring class, and the Industrial Revolution to the forefront of national and transatlantic debates.[6] Brownson grants Carlyle's brilliance for naming the social evils facing the laboring classes but finds his solutions lacking: "He is good as a demolisher, but pitiable enough as a builder. . . . Hopeless himself, he makes [his readers] hopeless."[7] Carlyle commends as remedies education and emigration. Neither, for Brownson, are sufficient to the task.

In America, migration is no solution: laborers are literally or de facto enslaved.[8] Two systems of labor obtain—slave and free. But Brownson is intent to somewhat confound the distinction. At points, he writes as though slavery was already a relic, so inevitable was its demise in his mind. With the abolition of slavery in England and the Haitian revolution as recent history, he sensed that it was only a matter of time before slavery would be abolished in America. But the system of labor at wages, which he knew would take its place, is no improvement. With the most ardent abolitionists, Brownson wants the slaves freed, but not to a new form of slavery under the auspices of wage labor. Employers hasten to draw a stark contrast between the two systems, but neither is just or tolerable.

As for education, Brownson has little faith in its power to elevate those compelled to labor the better part of most days while lacking basic necessities. If an education can dispense only false hope, we should rather offer laborers opiates and diversions that they may "see the less clearly the monstrous injustice which is done them."[9] Those who call for the elevation of the laboring class, apart from just working conditions, would, he fears, ignite an intellectual spark while smothering the fire of social reform.

William Ellery Channing, a prominent Unitarian minister, is every bit as much Brownson's target here as Carlyle. In 1838 he delivered a lecture entitled "Self-Culture" to an audience of manual laborers. "Self-culture," which would become an axiom in nineteenth-century America, uses an agricultural metaphor to graft the German tradition of *Bildung* into the fertile soil of New England.[10] Those who associate the term with dandyism—an egotistic cult of self—forget its roots among these manual laborers. To *them* Channing concludes, "Awake! Resolve earnestly on Self-culture."[11] Laborers, he insists, should cultivate their holistic—moral, spiritual, and intellectual—growth. Indeed, the fact that members of the laboring class would gather after a day's work to hear lectures on science, history, and ethics is "proof of a social revolution . . . from which too much cannot be hoped"—a revolution born of self-culture.[12]

In February of 1840 Channing published two lectures entitled "On the Elevation of the Laboring Classes," which he had delivered to a group of mechanic apprentices. By elevation, Channing does *not* mean to lift the laboring classes above the need for labor. The ascent is not from labor to luxury. The goal is not to make of life one extended holiday, for Channing has great faith in hard work. Far from the postlapsarian curse of painful toil, labor is the seedbed of moral, intellectual, and spiritual perfection. That we live and grow by the labor of our hands is evidence not of a fall but of God's wisdom. An Eden that anticipated our every desire, placing its fruits at our idle fingertips, could produce only "contemptable beings." This wedding of the ideal and material, of moral formation and work, would become a refrain among transcendentalists.[13] In *just* proportions, labor is a great good: in *excess*, a great harm. It is the unjust excess that Channing aims to prevent.

Aware that the division of labor condemns most workers to "a monotonous, stupefying round of unthinking toil," which makes self-culture nearly impossible, Channing hoped that "Christian brotherhood" might create a more equal distribution of labor and the means of improvement.[14] The means are crucial. Without spiritual elevation, any quest for political power would only reproduce class warfare. Absent love, the oppressed become oppressors.[15]

Brownson admits the importance of self-culture and Christianity as means of moral or spiritual improvement, but he has no faith in them as remedies for the evils of the social state. For the evil at hand is not merely individual but social and systemic. His principle is this: "What is purely individual in its nature, efforts of individuals to perfect themselves, may remove. But the evil we speak of is inherent in all our social arrangements, and cannot be cured without a radical change of those arrangements."[16] Continue the present systems—of production, trade, banking, or slavery—and all the present evils remain, whether managed by the best or worst members of society. Make the slave master the most beneficent of men and you have done nothing to abolish slavery.

If not emigration, education, or self-culture, what method of social reform does Brownson propose? Anticipating Marx and John Brown, he predicts that the social evil of unjust labor will not be overcome without bloodshed—"the war of the poor against the rich."[17] But several social reforms are necessary to prepare the poor for this struggle.

The first remedy is the destruction of the priesthood. The article is thoroughly anticlerical. Whence the social evils of the laboring classes? Brownson faults those corporations of priests that depend for their livelihood on the upper classes, that lull people comfortably to sleep in the deception that they can serve God and mammon. He does not deny the power of Christianity. Rather, Christianity "is the sublimest protest against the priesthood ever uttered, and a protest uttered by both God and man; for he who uttered it was God-Man."[18] No priest can mediate the relation between God and human beings except he who died on a cross. Lest Protestants think they are off the hook, Brownson includes all manner of clergy in the priesthood. In practice, all clergy seek to reconcile us with God without making us godlike. This, mind you, from a former clergyman.

Having distinguished between the Christianity of the Church and that of Christ, and having condemned the former, Brownson, as his second tonic, commends the latter. In his lengthy defense of the article (1841), he emphasizes that "Jesus was a social reformer" with an earthly as well as heavenly mission.[19] His interest now, as later, is in the power of Christ to "[direct] all minds to the great social reform needed, and [quicken] in all souls the moral power to live for it or to die for it." Here he agrees with Channing. A true conversion of *all* would, indeed, cure all social evils. Again, spiritual reform simply is sociopolitical reform. Unfortunately, this solution is as impractical as true. One may as well, he thinks, try to "dip the ocean dry with a clamshell" as to cure the evils of the social state by this method.

For Brownson, the true antidote is found in the government and legislative reforms. Indeed, the state is to take the place of the institutional church, politicians that of priests. Following Channing, in what would become a transcendentalist chorus, he contends that there has been "quite too much government, as well as government of the wrong kind."[20] The government should first restrain its own powers by loosening the grip of the banks, which always represent the interests of masters over and against slaves or laborers. Next, it remains for America to abolish hereditary property as it abolished the monarchy and nobility.[21] Barbara Packer aptly depicts this curious vision by likening it to a strange casino of the state, where the management collects each night's winnings and redistributes them the next morning for another day of gaming: not exactly the New Testament vision of the kingdom of God.[22] Nonetheless, Brownson's concern that virtue alone does not remedy social evils such as slavery would hone the transcendentalist debate about reform.

Emerson: Reforming Reformers

Emerson's response would come in stages. His entire literary career can be seen as an effort to grapple with the question of personal responsibility in the face of social evil. Though renowned for his emphasis on self-reliance and self-culture, the subtheme of savagery in nature and humanity haunts his work, beginning to end.[23] His most explicit treatment of the question of reform is found in lectures and essays during the 1840s, but the theme permeates his corpus and would reach its highest pitch in the years leading up to the Civil War.[24] In January 1841 he delivers the first lecture, "Man the Reformer," to an association of mechanic apprentices. Three years later (March 1844) he delivers "New England Reformers." The first can be seen as an effort to describe human beings *as* reformable reformers; the second, to actually reform his fellow reformers.

Following Channing's "Self-Culture," "Man the Reformer" displays Emerson's indefatigable faith in human beings *as* reformers of both self and society, *semper reformanda*. We most desire neither flattery nor amusement but growth and reform to become real people rather than mere specters and phantoms, even if this requires that we be awakened from our slumber—convicted, exposed, even shamed out of all kinds of our own nonsense.[25] The very history of humanity is one of reform, built as it is into the fiber of our being. In general, the better our grasp of history, the better our reforms. Still, Emerson insists, "Reform had never such scope, as at the present hour. Lutherans, Jesuits, Monks, Quakers . . . all respected something—church or state, literature or history, domestic usages. . . . But now all these and all things else hear the trumpet, and must rush to judgment—. . . not a kingdom, town, statute, rite, calling, man, or woman, but is threatened by the new spirit."[26] A new Pentecost is afoot, a judgment day of sorts.

Emerson agrees with Channing's, Carlyle's, and Brownson's diagnoses of the social evils such as slavery facing the nineteenth century. Even the system of trade has grown selfish to the point of theft, supple to the point of fraud. But who is the thief? He refuses to lay blame squarely on the shoulders of any one group, class, or person. Whereas Channing, at points, faults laborers for their intemperance, sloth, and lack of will, Brownson wags his finger at the selfishness of the priest, merchant, and manufacturer. Emerson maintains that the system of commerce is so vitiated by abuse, the evil so thoroughly social, no one is blameless. All are complicit: "We eat and drink and wear perjury and fraud in a hundred commodities."[27] Alas, the sins of trade, slavery, and property belong to no one class or individual. "One plucks, one distributes, one eats. Everybody partakes, everybody confesses." The danger lies in a cathartic confession without repentance. Naming our complicity is pointless if it induces a sense of powerlessness rather than responsibility.

Our responsibility, Emerson suggests, is that we learn the true meaning of economy—that is, prudence and simplicity of taste. When practiced for a grand aim, economy is a sacrament whereby spiritual ideals may be tested by material practice. Indeed, the spiritual faculties are perfected through our action in the world. As Channing puts it, "the poor creature who has not learned to work . . . does not know himself."[28] Both men grasp that the contemplative life is the fruit of the active life. Human being as reformable reformer simply is contemplative actor.

Emerson finds both contemplation and action lacking not in the mechanics but among the motley crew of reformers he addresses three years later in his lecture "New England Reformers." This association of reformers designed the lecture series, which featured William Lloyd Garrison and Wendell Phillips, to replace traditional church services with addresses about radical social action.[29] From Emerson, they got more than they bargained for—more reproof than rallying cry. Trusting that provocation is dearer than placation, Emerson is bent on provoking the provocateurs, on reforming the reformers, on holding up a mirror and insisting they begin by renovating themselves. Reflecting on reform efforts of the previous decades, he concludes, "The criticism and attack on institutions, which we have witnessed, has made one thing plain, that society gains nothing whilst a man, not himself renovated, attempts to renovate things around him."[30]

He had already honed this principle, by which he would abide, in refusing to join the utopian communities of his fellow transcendentalists. In a letter to his cousin George Ripley, the founder of Brook Farm, he explained, "It seems to me a circuitous and operose way of relieving myself to put upon your community the emancipation which I ought to take on myself. I must assume my own vows."[31] In the lecture he repeats the point with no small dose of sarcasm, "Our housekeeping is not satisfactory to us, but perhaps a phalanx, a community, might be."[32]

To Emerson, what is most remarkable about the manifold reform movements is the discontent of the "movers" or reformers: "They defied each other like a congress of kings."[33] No aspect of society is immune from the disposition of dissent. The benefits are numerous: a sharper scrutiny of institutions, sincere protest against evils, and changes of habits and employment guided by conscience. But these "kingdoms of me" are not without peril. Kantian self-legislation is not exactly the form of self-reliance Emerson commends.

One danger, Emerson warns, is that many a reformer "perishes in his removal of the rubbish" because they do not embody or exemplify their own ideals.[34] When our zeal to eradicate one evil blinds us to others, including our own, we sabotage our own efforts at reform. Take, for instance, the "angry bigot" Emerson describes in "Self-Reliance" who adopts the cause of abolition: "hypocrisy and vanity [is] . . . the disgusting result."[35] Malice and conceit are most repulsive when they masquerade in the coat of philanthropy. How convenient to champion a cause in Barbados! The rude truth, if Emerson could bring himself to say it (which he nearly does in the lecture), is "Your love afar is spite at home."[36] In Emerson's "Experience," as Jeffery Stout puts the point, "Abolitionist oratory is moralistic idealism. While much of what it says is true, it is marred by cant and hypocrisy."[37] Because it is merely rhetorical and thereby ridiculous, what Emerson calls a "manipular attempt" at reform, it cannot succeed. Like Brownson's virtuous masters, vicious abolitionists loosen no chains.

This tendency to reform abroad before reforming oneself is one reason for Emerson's distrust of associations, for his own reticence to associate with abolitionists despite his abiding sympathy with their cause. Fearing the powerlessness of individuals in the face of social evils, reformers depend on numbers to fight numbers. "Against concert they relied on new concert. [But] what use," he asks, "is the concert of the false and the disunited?"[38] An association is only as good as its members. The term "concert" is multivalent—a symphony; harmony; concord, consent, and unity. Too many reformers lack unity; they are divided and alienated against themselves. One musical instrument out of tune will ruin a trio. Reversing Abraham's bargain with God for the city of Sodom, Emerson contends that only when there is justice in one can there be concert in numbers (Gen 18:16–33). His maxim is not moral purity before activism. He knows that the perfect can be the enemy of the good. Indeed, *because* of his perfectionism, he knows that even imperfect embodiments of an ideal—namely, exemplars—have transformative power. The point, rather, is that self-reform is a condition of any association worth keeping. Such natural associations, born of mutual reform, sacrifice, and love, he is prone to call friendship.

The reliance on association is related to yet another defect among reformers—namely, a lack of faith and hope in common people. The related temptations include skepticism, presumption, and despair. "Americans have many virtues," Emerson remarked in his earlier lecture, "but they have not Faith and Hope."[39] Specifically, they lack faith in the worth and reformability of their fellow citizens, in their ability to live by principles rather than expedients. In other words, they lack Emerson's faith in human beings as reformers. Convinced that society is "a hospital of incurables," we renounce all high aims.[40] Out of despair, we swap education for entertainment and abet the tyrant. But there are not two classes of people: curables and incurables.

Emerson recalls a story of a woman who begged King Philip of Macedon to grant her justice. When he refused, she appealed. "And to whom do you appeal?" inquired the astonished king, as if to remind her there's no higher court. "From Philip drunk to Philip sober" came the reply. We all have two modes: drunk and sober. One day at the polls, observing the anger of a particularly bitter political contest etched in the faces of voters, Emerson's neighbor, Edmund Hosmer, remarked, "I am satisfied that the largest part of these men, on either side, mean to vote right."[41] This is not to say that they *are* right. Perhaps, half on each side are angry drunk, the other half angry sober. But they all mean to vote right because drunk or sober, asleep or awake, all seek some aspect of the good. The doctrine of depravity, for Emerson, is sacrilege: "There is no skepticism, no atheism but that."[42] His unflagging faith is that all people are better than they appear. Those who would reform society must at least believe its members are reformable.

I have yet to mention one of the most striking features of this lecture on reform, on the virtues and vices of protest, indeed, on Protestantism—that is, Emerson's admonition to reform the church from the inside out. Part of the genius of the age, he concedes, is a certain leveling of authority. If a church censured and threatened to excommunicate one of its members for an abolitionist stance, the individual returned the favor, anathematizing the church. Any casual observer of New England in the early nineteenth century would note that "the Church or religious party, is falling from the Church nominal, and is appearing in temperance and non-resistance societies; in movements of abolitionists and of socialists" among others.[43] When no longer hospitable, the nominal church became the target of the very reform movements it birthed.

Nonetheless, six years after leaving the formal ministry, this erstwhile preacher insists "it is handsomer to remain in the establishment better than the establishment."[44] The point appears to be twofold: that it is better to remain in some flawed established institution, to reform from within rather than resist from without, and that a person can do so only as long as she remains better than the establishment. In case some doubt whether the establishment includes the church, he clarifies: "If I should go out of church whenever I hear a false sentiment I could never stay there five minutes. But why come out? the street is as false as the church, and when I get to my house, or to my manners, or to my speech, I have not got away from the lie."[45] If only reform were a matter of finding the nearest exit. Alas, we have already seen that there is no escape, no morally pure hide out. Rather, "In the midst of abuses . . . in the aisles of false churches . . . wherever, namely, a just and heroic soul finds itself, there it will do what is next at hand."[46] If one just person was to walk our streets, doing whatever the moment called for, he wagers, a series of events would conspire for social reforms. His advice to stay in the church better than the church echoes the sentiment of his address to the graduating class of Harvard Divinity school three years prior. The address is meant to inspire the spiritual ascent of these "newborn bards of the Holy Ghost."[47] Emerson is not opposed to Brownson's mantra that social evils demand social remedies. But he insists that spiritual reform is the substance and condition of social reform.

Brownson: No Church, No Reform

One month after Emerson delivered "New England Reformers," Brownson published another article in the *Boston Quarterly Review*. Its title, "No Church, No Reform," confirmed the rumors of his recent conversion to Catholicism.[48] To call the conversion radical is an understatement. With no less force than he vowed to abolish the Church and the priesthood, he now swears that until the Catholic Church is "rehabilitated in its authority and glory, no scheme of practical reform, individual or social, political or industrial, can be successfully attempted." Political reform is no longer his primary aim. Personal transformation, the Christian life itself, is the end, sociopolitical reform, the happy effect.

But the same question haunts him now as before: How to produce this transformation? Here he abandons the intellectualism and eudaemonism of the transcendentalist club he helped found. They rightly encourage Christians to live the life of Christ, but they do not, to his satisfaction, reveal the means. The "corrupt and selfish" need "not be told their duty, but . . . made to do it." According to his new theological anthropology, apart from divine assistance, human beings are depraved. Even Christ and the sinner are opposed and require mediation. Justification and sanctification come not by faith but by Christ himself, who can be received only through "some divinely instituted medium"— namely, the institution of the church, which embodies the Holy Ghost. "All that reformers have to do," he concludes "is, to cease to be 'Come-outers,' . . . return to its bosom, and receive its orders." The faith he had once placed in the state was irrevocably transferred to the living institution of the church.

Emerson would not return to the bosom of the Roman Catholic Church. In their theological anthropologies and ecclesiologies, he and Brownson part ways. Indeed, Emerson presses the Reformation slogan *semper reformanda* to its theological limit. Because Brownson has a lower estimate of human nature and a higher estimate of the institutional church than Emerson, the latter, for Brownson, is a necessary medium for sobering, awakening, and transforming our loves. For Emerson, the "indwelling Supreme Spirit" can awaken us through the appeal of a woman, in the aisles of false churches, or, as we will see, through a night in prison.[49] To be sure, these are substantive theological differences. For our purposes, the point is that *despite* these differences, these two reformers came to share profound agreement about the nature of spiritual and sociopolitical reform.

Ultimately, they concur that personal reform, understood as growth in friendship with God and Christlikeness, is the end.[50] So too, they agree that personal reform is integral to social reform, both because we are relational creatures (such that spiritual reform simply is sociopolitical reform) and because personal transformation is crucial for sustaining the movements, institutions, and organizations that effect systemic sociopolitical change (like the formal abolition of chattel slavery). In the face of structural evil, we are each responsible for discerning what it is we must do given our own talents and temperaments, genius and obligations, roles and relations. At the same time, they seem to agree that God is the source of individual transformation, conversion a matter of graced reception. Indeed, Emerson is every bit as interested as Brownson in a true conversion to a true Christ, what he describes in the 1838 divinity address as the "reception of beautiful sentiments."[51] A fellow transcendentalist, likewise persuaded that the personal is political, would become convinced through his own experiments in personal reform of the responsibility to resist social evil, even to the point of civil disobedience.

Thoreau: The Power of a Majority of One

In July of 1845 Henry David Thoreau took to Walden Pond to forge his own acetic matrimony of intellectual and manual labor. One year later Sam Staples, the former Concord tax collector, arrested Thoreau for his refusal to pay the $1.50 annual poll tax. After only one night in prison, an infuriated Thoreau was released. His fury was directed not at Sam but at the anonymous woman, likely his aunt, who bailed him out. His release threatened to make a ridiculous spectacle rather than a principled protest of his quite deliberate action. Sure enough, the whole episode left a "bad taste" in Emerson's mouth.[52] It resembled the vulgar, self-advertising egotism of Garrison and the other anti-slavery "martyrs" who marketed themselves as exemplary sufferers.[53] In the refining fire of Emerson's censure, Thoreau wrote an apologia, first read as a lecture in the Concord Lyceum, later published in Elizabeth Peabody's periodical *Aesthetic Papers* as "Resistance to Civil Government" and republished by the popular title "Civil Disobedience."[54]

As the title suggests, "Resistance to Civil Government" was written in direct opposition to William Paley's chapter entitled "Duty of Submission to Civil Government." Here Paley contends that submission to government and to God are of a piece. He admits of just resistance, but only according to utilitarian calculus, only when the potential benefits outweigh the costs. Thoreau objects. Paley never imagines cases not reducible to expediency, cases in which a people "must do justice, cost what it may."[55] Somehow the theologian forgot the biblical lessons: she that would save her life will lose it; "greater love" is not subject to cost–benefit analysis.[56] Thoreau's hardly subtle suggestion is that submission to God may *require* resistance to government. He throws down the gauntlet: "This people must cease to hold slaves, and to make war on Mexico, though it cost them their existence as a people."[57] For those awaiting a divine imperative, this is it.[58]

Part of Thoreau's genius in this piece is to sing the old revolutionary melody— unjust governance makes for just resistance—in a reformation key. Reform, not anarchy, revolution, or resistance *in se*, is the aim. He too embraces the motto of the *Democratic Review*, touted by Channing, Brownson, and Emerson: "That government is best which governs least" or, by his addendum, "not at all."[59] Michel Foucault has joined this chorus in our own time. But for Foucault, and many moderns, the motto has been nearly evacuated of its moral import—a matter of quantity, not quality—"of not being governed quite so much."[60] But for the transcendentalists the motto is inherently moral. Recall, Brownson weds his complaint that there is "quite too much government" to the claim that it is a "government of the wrong kind." So too, Thoreau asks "not at once for no government, but at once a better government."[61] By better he means more just.

Following the American founders, Thoreau insists that under certain conditions—namely, that of unjust laws and governments—citizens have not only a right but a *responsibility* to resist.[62] To challenge Emerson's conventional taste, Thoreau asks: "How does it become a man to behave toward this American government today? He cannot without disgrace be associated with it," comes the reply. It would be a disgrace to recognize the slave's government as one's own. Given *this* government, *this* institution, resistance defines good taste. Of course, civil disobedience is a double entendre. It delineates both the manner and the sphere of action—namely, just and at a minimum decent defiance of citizens in a political community. Virtuous disobedience makes all the difference.

Thoreau anticipates a common objection. Resistance is fine under a tyrannical government, but such is not ours, not yet. Recounting the present evils, he insists that "it is not too soon for honest men to rebel and revolutionize."[63] Stalling can be a sign of self-deception. Next, he anticipates an Emersonian objection. Why resist afar when our own housekeeping is mendicant? But, like Emerson, his quarrel is "not with far-off foes, but with those who, near at home . . . do the bidding of those far away."[64] More than mere spectacle, the night in prison had convinced Thoreau of the responsibilities of the citizens of Concord, given their complicity in national vices.

Following Emerson, his call is to action in the midst of pervasive complicity.[65] "Action from principle," by which Thoreau means "the perception and the performance of right . . . is essentially revolutionary."[66] It changes persons, yes, but also societies. Thousands are in principle opposed to slavery and the war but take no action against them. Not knowing what to do, they do nothing. "They wait, well disposed, for others to remedy the evil, that they may no longer have to regret it."[67] Perhaps, at best, they offer a "cheap vote," scarcely a political act. Thoreau exhorts us to cast our "whole vote" the whole weight of our influence and not merely a "strip of paper."[68] Emerson's farmer friend may be right that most voters *mean* to do right. But such well-intentioned constituents function as well-oiled cogs in the unjust machine of the state. They afford no resistance.

The questions that consume Thoreau are how a conscientious minority can exert irresistible power, how a majority of one can bring an unjust machine to a grinding halt. Following Emerson's allusion, and Abraham's faith, he makes a similar wager: "If one thousand, if one hundred, if ten men whom I could name—if ten honest men only—ay, if one HONEST man, in this State of Massachusetts, ceasing to hold slaves, were actually to withdraw from this copartnership, and be locked up in the county jail therefor, it would be the abolition of slavery in America."[69]

He and Emerson know that virtue is rare.[70] Thoreau shares his friend's faith in everyday saints but suggests that they reside where we least look for them: "Under a government which imprisons any unjustly, the true place for a just man is also a prison."[71] Can one just woman in a county jail singlehandedly abolish slavery?

Perhaps not singlehandedly, but Thoreau's short stint in prison led him to imagine how the resistance of exemplary individuals might facilitate an organized collective resistance, which in turn might lead to large-scale sociopolitical reform. Of course, this imagination would inspire Mahatma Gandhi and Martin Luther King Jr., among others. Democracy depends on accountability exercised in a million interpersonal relationships. As for Thoreau's relation to the state, he meets its representative "face to face" in his "civil neighbor" the tax collector.[72] Staples had already proven his willingness to imprison a fellow transcendentalist, Amos Bronson Alcott, for not paying the poll tax. Following Alcott, Thoreau holds this representative accountable, obliging him to consider whether he will unjustly imprison a just man, imprison a friend of the slave as an enemy of the state, incarcerate the true civil servant as a "maniac and disturber of the peace."[73] Thoreau's civil disobedience forces Staples to determine whether he will serve as a cog or a clog in the machine of an unjust state.

One Honest Man

Thoreau and Emerson recognize immediately the man who would most effectively pose this question to white antebellum America. On October 16, 1859, the zealous life-long abolitionist John Brown attempted to seize the US Arsenal at Harpers Ferry in the hope of freeing and arming enough slaves to collapse the institution.[74] Sentenced to death for murder, conspiring with slave rebellion, and treason, he was hanged December 2, 1859. The justice and civility of his disobedience were immediately called into question.[75]

Because Emerson and Thoreau had come to admire Brown during his visits to New England, they were quick to sanctify this treasonous "hero of harper ferry."[76] Upon his conviction, Emerson recalled that Brown's guiding principles were the Golden Rule, the Declaration of Independence, and the New Testament exhortation to "remember them that are in bonds, as bound with them."[77] There is another reason for Emerson's quick endorsement. If one night in prison was all it took to thoroughly sober Thoreau, the Fugitive Slave Law of 1850 prompted Emerson's conversion. Long a principled abolitionist, he became an activist.[78] He would sooner go to prison for hiding fugitive slaves than bear an unbearable law. He reached this boiling point nearly a decade before Brown's ascent to the gallows.

In his lecture "Courage," delivered a week after Brown's conviction, Emerson's aesthetic political taste appears closer to that of Thoreau. Where are the exemplars of courage to be found? "Look nearer at the ungathered relics of those who have gone to languish in prison or to die in rescuing others or rescuing themselves from chains in Slave States, or," he suggests, "look at that new saint, than whom none purer or more brave ever was led by love of men into conflict and death, the new saint awaiting his martyrdom, and who, if he shall suffer, will make the gallows glorious like the cross."[79] Aware of the danger in likening a white man to Christ in antebellum America, Emerson draws our gaze to the unsung heroes before turning it to this newly canonized saint.[80]

This is the judgment day, the event that would appeal from the masses drunk to the masses sober. All have eyes to see except "the old doting nigh-dead politicians, whose heart the trumpet of resurrection could not wake."[81] Never mind that drunken vice unites false churches and the nigh-dead politicians. Never mind that the governor of Virginia would hang a man he publicly identifies as a hero. Emerson knows that when the gallows are made glorious like the cross, a movement—at once spiritual, social, and political—is at hand. Political reform—indeed, the abolition of slavery, perhaps even the seedlings of civil rights—is bound to follow. In this particularly dark season on account of white America, John Brown was for Emerson a piercing ray of light. Indeed, Emerson would end his literary career, his final lectures at Harvard in 1871, by recalling that "when we had to praise our own martyr, John Brown" (like having to praise the sun for shining), a multitude of arguments, illustrations, and verses of old poetry appeared to have been written for the occasion.[82] As Frederick Douglass put it, "If John Brown did not end the war that ended slavery, he did, at least begin the war that ended slavery."[83]

The point is not only that courageous exemplars are contagious, though this is true. The analogy between Brown and Christ points to the complex but steady relation between religious exemplars, especially martyrs, and the associations, movements, institutions, and organizations that birth systemic sociopolitical change. After decades of abolitionist organizing, Brown's execution was a catalyst that inspired the spiritual and political will the North would need to sustain the Civil War. Union soldiers marched to "John Brown's Body," which Julia Ward Howe would remake into the "Battle Hymn of the Republic." It is no coincidence that on January 1, 1863, in one of the most symbolic acts of the Civil War, George Stearns held a grand celebration (which several transcendentalists attended) called the "John Brown Party."[84] That afternoon, President Lincoln issued the Emancipation Proclamation. Hardly the end of social evils in America, it was no less a significant reform in the right direction.

Semper Reformanda

We began with the much-hyped election of 1840. But it was a diversion. Indeed, Harrison died only a month after his inauguration. A similar diversion threatens us today. The temptation is to be distracted by the spectacle of the 2016 election and the endless train of infamous contumelies, of capital vices that have followed in its wake. Of course, we must pay attention; for Donald Trump and his advisers have their own reform agenda, one more likely to abet than to remedy social evils, one that will demand various forms of resistance. But the temptation is to be so distracted by the symptoms that we do not treat the causes of our own national malaise, what Cornel West has called "an undeniable spiritual blackout of grand proportions."[85] That Trump rose to power despite (if not because of) his xenophobic, racist, misogynist, heterosexist, and anti-Muslim platform signals not only the vices of the Trump campaign and administration but the "relative collapse of integrity, honesty, and decency . . . [as well as] the cupidity and mendacity" of the elites and respective vices of the American people.[86]

As West notes, Plato foresaw this scenario in *The Republic*, perhaps the most profound criticism of democracy in the history of Western philosophy. Plato argues that democracies produce unruly and ignorant citizens, easily manipulated by greedy elites and politicians: the perfect recipe for tyranny. In his *Politics*, Aristotle presents a more nuanced view of the possibilities and perils of democracy. Only the fifth form of democracy that he outlines gives rise to demagoguery, which resembles some of the dangers of the current situation.[87]

Despite their differences, both philosophers agree that the downfall of democratic regimes follows close on the heels of the spiritual and moral demise of its citizens. West claims that John Dewey, a protégé of the transcendentalists, offers the best response to Plato's critique of democracy. Aware of the fragility of democratic experiments, Dewey emphasizes the transcendentalist themes of personal responsibility, public accountability, courageous exemplars, the protection of rights and liberties through just laws, and especially what West calls "democratic soul craft (integrity, empathy, and a mature sense of history)."[88] For those tempted to despair in the face of Trump's authoritarian regime, revisiting the transcendentalist debates abets a mature sense of history. Of course, those on the underside of a history of horrors already know that this is just another dreadful moment in the history of our nation that "calls forth the best of who we are and what we can do."[89]

Continuing the legacy of Plato and Aristotle, the transcendentalists, despite their theological differences, agree that personal spiritual reform is tantamount to sociopolitical reform, and the condition of systemic change. The early Brownson insists that social evil cannot be opposed without a radical change in sociopolitical arrangements—that virtue alone will not suffice—while postconversion he acknowledges that the spiritual transformation of individuals is both the end of the Christian life and the only means to sociopolitical reform in the face of evil. If Brownson's motto becomes "no church, no reform," Emerson's remains "no spiritual ascent, no reform" and Thoreau adds "no resistance, no reform." In spite of theological differences, Christians today might also agree that the work of spiritual reform is vital if our nation is to be resuscitated on the brink of spiritual death.

Notes

I am grateful to Gary Slater, the anonymous reviewers, and the editors of this journal for their helpful feedback on an early draft of this article.

1. Robert Kugelmann, *Psychology and Catholicism: Contested Boundaries* (Cambridge: Cambridge University Press, 2011), 134.

2. Orestes Augustus Brownson, *The Laboring Classes: An Article from the Boston Quarterly Review* (Boston: B. H. Greene, 1840).

3. Cynthia D. Moe-Lobeda, *Resisting Structural Evil: Love as Ecological-Economic Vocation* (Minneapolis, MN: Fortress Press, 2013), 3. I take it that by "social evil," the transcendentalists mean something similar to what current ethicists such as Cynthia Moe-Lobeda mean by "structural evil" or "systemic evil" (which she uses interchangeably). For her, structural evil does not refer to metaphysical forces but rather to evils manifest as social injustices that remain beyond the power of individuals alone to counter. Nonetheless, because they are the cumulative effects of human actions, they can be dismantled or resisted by collective action. I use these terms interchangeably. Margaret Fuller, Elizabeth Peabody, Louisa May Alcott, and Lydia Emerson were among the earliest transcendentalists to advocate for equal rights and education for women. After the Civil War, Caroline Healey Dall would carry this cause forward. Here, I focus on the related issues of labor, slavery, and poverty.

4. Aristotle, *The Basic Works of Aristotle*, ed. Richard McKeon (New York: Modern Library, 2001), 1253n2. See Paula Rust for a summary of various ways that the phrase "the person is political" has been used within feminist movements. Paula C. Rust, *Bisexuality and the*

Challenge to Lesbian Politics: Sex, Loyalty and Revolution (New York: New York University Press, 1995), 329n21.

5. All citations in this section are from his article "The Laboring Classes" unless otherwise noted.

6. Thomas Carlyle, "Chartism," in *Emancipation* (Boston: Charles C. Little and James Brown, 1840), Hathi Trust Digital Library, https://catalog.hathitrust.org/Record/001023369.

7. Brownson, "Laboring Classes."

8. By laborers Brownson means those who do not own the means of production and depend solely on the work of their hands.

9. Brownson, "Laboring Classes," 9.

10. Two prominent works of the same title would follow: John Stuart Blackie's *On Self-Culture* (1874) and Frederick Clark's *Self-Culture: A Lecture to Young Men* (1864).

11. William Ellery Channing, "Self-Culture: An Address Introductory to the Franklin Lectures," September 1838, http://www.americanunitarian.org/selfculture.htm.

12. Ibid.

13. For more on Channing's notion of self-culture as spiritual formation and the imitation of Christ, see Emily Dumler-Winckler, "The Virtue of Emerson's Imitation of Christ: From William Ellery Channing to John Brown," *Journal of Religious Ethics* 45, no. 3 (2017): 510–38.

14. Channing, "Self-Culture."

15. Ibid.

16. Brownson, "Laboring Classes," 14.

17. Ibid., 9.

18. Ibid., 19.

19. Ibid.

20. Ibid., 23.

21. In his defense of the article a year later, his admission that he had not considered the effects of this policy on the likes of widows and children did not bring him to renounce it so much as to champion property rights for women.

22. Barbara Packer, *The Transcendentalists* (Athens: University of Georgia Press, 2007), 110.

23. Robert D. Richardson, *Emerson: The Mind on Fire* (Berkeley: University of California Press, 1996), 273.

24. Jeffrey Stout, "The Transformation of Genius into Practical Power: A Reading of Emerson's 'Experience,'" *American Journal of Theology and Philosophy* 35, no. 1 (2014): 3–24. Emerson's essay "Experience" is one of his most profound reflections on the theme of personal and social reform. As Jeffrey Stout provides an excellent reflection on these themes, I focus on Emerson's lectures of the same period.

25. Ralph Waldo Emerson, *The Complete Works of Ralph Waldo Emerson*, vol. 3, *Essays*, 2nd series (Ann Arbor: University of Michigan Library, 2006), 271–73, http://name.umdl.umich.edu/4957107.0003.001. Emerson knew, especially after the death of his five-year-old son, that we "crave a sense of reality, though it comes in strokes of pain."

26. Ralph Waldo Emerson, *The Complete Works of Ralph Waldo Emerson*, vol. 1, *Nature Addresses and Lectures* (Ann Arbor: University of Michigan Library), 229, http://name.umdl.umich.edu/4957107.0001.001.

27. Ibid., 1:232.

28. William Emery Channing, "On the Elevation of the Laboring Classes: Lecture I.1909-14," in *Essays: English and American*. The Harvard Classics, vol. 28 (New York: P. F. Collier & Son, 1840), Bartleby.com, April 11, 2001, http://www.bartleby.com/28/132.html.

29. Ralph Waldo Emerson, *Emerson's Prose and Poetry*, ed. Saundra Morris and Joel Porte (New York: W. W. Norton, 2001), 221.

30. Emerson, *Complete Works*, 3:261.

31. Ralph Waldo Emerson, *The American Transcendentalists: Essential Writings*, ed. Lawrence Buell (New York: Modern Library, 2006), 206.

32. Emerson, *Complete Works*, 3:265.

33. Ibid., 3:251.

34. Ibid., 3:261.

35. Ibid.

36. Emerson, *Emerson's Prose and Poetry*, 123.

37. Stout, "Transformation of Genius into Practical Power," 10.

38. Emerson, *Emerson's Prose and Poetry*, 226.

39. Emerson, *Complete Works*, 1:249.

40. Emerson, *Emerson's Prose and Poetry*, 227.

41. Emerson, *Complete Works*, 3:279.

42. Ibid., 3:278.

43. Ibid., 3:251.

44. Ibid., 3:261.

45. Ibid., 3:262–63.

46. Ibid., 3:263.

47. Emerson, *Complete Works*, 79.

48. Orestes Augustus Brownson, "No Church, No Reform," *Brownson's Quarterly Review (1844–1875)* 1, no. 2 (1844): 175. Quotes in this section are from the online version unless otherwise indicated: http://www.orestesbrownson.org/309.html.

49. Emerson, *Complete Works*, 1:127. Emerson, a former Unitarian, does not seem to believe in a Holy Spirit in the triune sense. Nonetheless, he writes of the "indwelling Supreme Spirit" as the divine spirit that reforms human beings.

50. For more on Emerson's view of self-culture as Christlikeness, see Dumler-Winckler, "Virtue of Emerson's Imitation of Christ."

51. Emerson, *Emerson's Prose and Poetry*.

52. Packer, *The Transcendentalists*, 188. As Packer notes, Emerson reportedly characterized Thoreau's behavior as "mean and skulking and in bad taste."

53. Ibid.

54. Henry D. Thoreau, *Walden, Civil Disobedience, and Other Writings*, ed. William Rossi, 3rd ed. (New York: W. W. Norton, 2008).

55. Ibid., 230.

56. Ibid.

57. Ibid., 231.

58. Although Thoreau's arguments are not explicitly theological, they depend on allusions to the Christian Scriptures and imagination at every turn.

59. Thoreau, *Walden*, 227.

60. Michel Foucault, *The Essential Foucault: Selections from the Essential Works of Foucault, 1954–1984*, ed. Paul Rabinow and Nikolas Rose (New York: New Press, 2003), 263.

61. Thoreau, *Walden*, 228.

62. Alexander Hamilton, James Jay, and James Madison, *The Federalist: A Commentary on the Constitution of the United States*, ed. Robert Scigliano (New York: Modern Library, 2001), 568. The Declaration of Independence famously states that "it is their Right, it is their Duty to throw off such [unjust] Government."

63. Thoreau, *Walden*, 230.

64. Ibid., 231.

65. For Thoreau, this duty of resistance does not oblige every person to devote herself to the eradication of all or even one social evil, but only to wash her hands of social evil—if she will not oppose it, refuse to lend it her support. Given Thoreau's and Emerson's insights about complicity, we might wonder what this hand-washing amounts to.

66. Emerson, *American Transcendentalists*, 233.

67. Thoreau, *Walden*, 231.

68. Ibid., 236.

69. Ibid., 235.

70. Ibid., 231.

71. Ibid., 236.

72. Ibid., 235.

73. Ibid., 335.

74. Ralph Waldo Emerson, "Courage," in *The Complete Works of Ralph Waldo Emerson, with a Biographical Introduction and Notes by Edward Waldo Emerson*, 12 vols. (New York: Houghton, Mifflin, 1904), Bartleby.com, 2013, n1, http://www.bartleby.com/br/90.html.

75. Orestes Augustus Brownson and Henry F. Brownson, *The Works of Orestes A. Brownson* (Detroit: T. Nourse, 1882), 17:106, 112, 116, 191, Hathi Trust Digital Library, https://catalog.hathitrust.org/Record/001915178. Brownson opposed Brown's raid as an unlawful and thereby unjust means to justice.

76. Ralph Waldo Emerson, *The Complete Works of Ralph Waldo Emerson*, vol. 11, *Miscellanies* (Ann Arbor: University of Michigan Library, 2006), 267, http://name.umdl.umich.edu/4957107.0011.001.

77. Ibid., 11:269; and David S. Reynolds, *John Brown, Abolitionist: The Man Who Killed Slavery, Sparked the Civil War, and Seeded Civil Rights* (New York: Knopf, 2005), 354.

78. Richardson, *Emerson*, 499. Emerson's response to the fugitive slave law and the Thomas Sims affair, Richardson notes, had the "depth of a conversion experience. The change was permanent."

79. Ralph Waldo Emerson, *The Complete Works of Ralph Waldo Emerson*, vol. 7, *Society and Solitude* (Ann Arbor: University of Michigan Library, 2006), 19, http://name.umdl.umich.edu/4957107.0007.001; and Reynolds, *John Brown*, 366. Emerson borrowed this line from Mattie Griffith.

80. Richardson argues that Emerson's later "forceful confrontational politics of emancipation have been underestimated since his death for three reasons." See Richardson, *Emerson*, 497–98.

81. Emerson, *Complete Works*, 7:272.

82. Ralph Waldo Emerson, *Natural History of the Intellect: The Last Lectures of Ralph Waldo Emerson* (Wrightwood Press, 2008). Emerson did not publish these lectures himself. Rick Spaulding and Maurice York published this version, having plumbed Emerson's lecture notes, outlines, and student notes.

83. Reynolds, *John Brown*, 1.

84. Ibid., 34.

85. Cornel West, "Spiritual Blackout in America: Election 2016," *Boston Globe*, November 3, 2016.

86. Ibid.

87. Aristotle, *Basic Works*, 1292n12.

88. West, "Spiritual Blackout."

89. Cornel West, "Goodbye, American Neoliberalism. A New Era Is Here," *Guardian*, November 17, 2016.

Moral Injury, Feminist and Womanist Ethics, and Tainted Legacies

Karen V. Guth

The prevalence of tainted legacies within Christian ethics, across the academy, and in contemporary public debate raises difficult questions about handling legacies implicated in traumatic pasts. This essay uses the concept of moral injury to illuminate the moral complexities of tainted religious legacies (e.g., John Howard Yoder's) and employs feminist and womanist ethics to provide strategies for moral repair in the wake of these and other such legacies (e.g., Georgetown University's participation in slavery). It first argues that, despite significant limitations, moral injury provides purchase on the experience of encountering tainted religious legacies by naming the type of agency involved, describing the moral harm tainted legacies cause, and highlighting the social and institutional context of that harm. It then argues that feminist and womanist responses to morally injurious forms of Christianity—particularly explorations of redemptive suffering—not only resonate with responses to Yoder's case and other tainted legacies current in public debate but also provide criteria for assessing those responses.

IN JANUARY 2015 THE MENNONITE CHURCH USA OFFICIALLY documented widespread sexual abuse perpetrated for years by its best-known theologian, John Howard Yoder, a leading theorist of pacifism.[1] Yoder's violence against women ignited vigorous debate about the status of his theological legacy. Yoder scholars condemned his behavior but often insisted on the enduring value of his theology. The women he violated, however, identified a different problem: the harm Yoder caused lives on through the continuing acclaim of his theology. For them, the issue is not how to reconcile a pacifist's theory with his violent actions but how to prevent past trauma from being carried into the present.

Far from being an isolated Mennonite or religious ethics issue, Yoder's case replicates countless others that span human history, all raising difficult

Karen V. Guth, PhD, is an assistant professor of religious studies at College of the Holy Cross, 1 College St., Worcester, MA 01610; kguth@holycross.edu.

questions about how to handle legacies implicated in traumatic pasts. Is it ethical to use knowledge derived from Nazi medical experiments? What about the
intellectual contributions by renowned phenomenologist—and Nazi—Martin
Heidegger? Are monuments, flags, and other highly contested public symbols
from South Africa to South Carolina of any value given their racist history?
These profound questions refuse to be relegated to the past. They linger on,
haunting us here and now. In the words of Jorge Luis Borges: "Into this present
the Past intrudes."[2]

Nor are these questions merely academic. Citing the predominance of such
issues in public debate, *New York Times* columnist David Brooks has called
2015 the "year of unearthed memories." As he puts it, "Many of the issues we
have been dealing with in 2015 revolve around unhealed cultural memories:
how to acknowledge past wrongs and move forward into the light."[3] He identifies race relations as the most obvious case, listing discussions about the Confederate flag, Woodrow Wilson's status at Princeton, and unmarked lynching
grounds as examples. But other cases abound, such as the widespread discussion
about sexual trauma that arose after allegations of sexual assault against Donald
Trump, then the 2016 Republican nominee for president.

All these examples indicate the pressing nature of questions about legacies implicated in past evils. This essay argues that the construct of moral injury—native to the psychological literature on war-related trauma—provides
purchase on the experience of encountering tainted religious legacies, and that
the field of Christian ethics—particularly feminist and womanist thought—not
only provides responses to such legacies but also contributes to public discussion of other comparable legacies. First, I will use Yoder's case to argue that
the construct of moral injury illuminates the moral experience of encountering tainted legacies. Despite significant limitations, moral injury nevertheless
names the type of agency involved, describes the moral harm tainted legacies
cause, and highlights the social and institutional context of the harm. Most
importantly, moral injury points to the need for moral repair.

Second, I argue that feminist and womanist ethics is particularly well suited
to provide strategies for moral repair in the wake of tainted legacies. The
interest of feminist theologians in moral injury is telling. It connects their
work structurally to those assisting the morally injured in other fields but,
more importantly, reveals a central aspect of the feminist theological task: to
provide responses to wounds caused by tainted forms of the Christian tradition. In other words, feminist interest in moral injury provides a new way of
understanding the very nature and purpose of feminist theologies. I show that
feminist and womanist responses to morally injurious forms of Christianity—
particularly explorations of redemptive suffering—not only resonate with responses to Yoder's case and other tainted legacies but also provide criteria for
assessing those responses.

What Is Moral Injury?

In recent decades, psychologists working with war veterans have identified moral injury as "an alternative (but also complementary) model" for addressing wounds of war not well captured by a diagnosis of posttraumatic stress disorder (PTSD).[4] While a PTSD diagnosis identifies some of the mental, psychological, and behavioral injuries veterans sustain, it fails to name or enable care for soldiers' emotional and spiritual wounds. Consequently, psychologists now identify moral injury as a clinical diagnosis distinct from PTSD. Brett T. Litz and coauthors argue that moral injury results from "perpetrating, failing to prevent, or bearing witness to acts that transgress deeply held moral beliefs and expectations."[5] Others, like service member Tyler Boudreau, focus on the moral and social nature of such injuries. For Boudreau, moral injuries are not about "treatment or medications" but "our society and our moral values"; they "must be healed communally, not medically."[6] For still others, like psychiatrist Jonathan Shay, attention shifts from those who perpetrate acts to those who experience "(1) . . . a betrayal of what's right (2) by someone who holds legitimate authority (3) in a high-stakes situation."[7]

Each understanding provides some purchase on the experience of encountering tainted legacies. Litz's definition—particularly the component of bearing witness to moral transgressions—names the type of agency involved in encountering tainted legacies but also identifies significant limitations in applying moral injury to tainted legacies. His medical descriptions of the severe emotional and physical suffering of those who sustain moral injuries in war make clear the (mostly) formal nature of the analogy I pursue between war and exposure to tainted religious legacies.[8] Boudreau's conception, with its emphasis on the communal aspect of moral injury, draws attention to the wider context of the harms, pointing to both the high stakes involved and the need for institutional forms of repair. And Shay's focus on "leadership malpractice" describes the specific moral transgression involved, proving particularly helpful in analyzing Yoder's case, with his status as an authority in peace church theology.[9]

Indeed, both Shay's and Boudreau's descriptions not only afford insight into why Yoder's violations register as particularly egregious but also reveal the connection between Yoder's case and other tainted legacies. In addition to the potential extension of such traumas into the future, each case—Yoder's violations of pacifism, Georgetown's participation in slavery, medical professionals' engagement in Nazi experiments—shares another central feature: they all involve venerated authorities, whether individual leaders or institutions, whose harmful actions betray the very moral values they claim to uphold. The abhorrent nature of these violations, committed by individuals or institutions dedicated to human flourishing, makes them high-stakes cases. If violations were less egregious in each case, or if Yoder were a mathematician rather than a Mennonite and pacifist theorist, if Georgetown were a corporation rather than a Jesuit institution of higher education, and if the Nazis were not also medical doctors under Hippocratic oaths—the moral harm and outrage their violations produce would be lessened and the stakes lower. As such, Shay's description of moral injury as "a betrayal of what's right . . . by someone who holds legitimate authority . . . in a high-stakes situation" aptly describes these violations, connecting seemingly disparate cases. Moreover, Boudreau's emphasis on the communal context alerts us to the nature of the high stakes. Both human well-being and the moral credibility of religious traditions and public institutions are at risk.

Limitations of Applying Moral Injury to Tainted Religious Legacies

Just as moral injury enables psychologists to deliver better treatment for soldiers, so, too, does the construct provide needed purchase on the experience of encountering tainted religious legacies. Because the analogy is primarily formal in nature, I must acknowledge the significant limitations involved. War is clearly a different context from most in which one encounters tainted religious legacies: the kinds of actions, high-stakes situations, and injuries sustained (and, indeed, whether such injuries constitute clinical moral injury or fit Shay's formal definition of moral injury) will differ drastically from those of war.

First, differences between relevant actions must be considered. War often requires combatants to perpetrate or experience harmful acts such as "accidental or intentional killing of noncombatants, torture or sadistic killing, indiscriminate aggressive behavior or killing . . . , mutilation of corpses, sexual assault, failure (real or perceived) to prevent death of comrades, and failure (real or perceived) to prevent death of or atrocity to civilians."[10] If moral injury results from such acts, it seems wildly inappropriate to apply it to contexts where one might encounter Yoder's work—an ethics classroom, a scholarly project, a church setting—and the acts required in these settings: assigning, reading, and discussing texts. For some, like the women violated by Yoder, being required to perform these actions may indeed be morally injurious. But for most students, scholars, or others exposed to Yoder's legacy, the actions required of them are hardly equivalent to those expected of soldiers. Unlike warriors, those in a classroom do not ordinarily bear witness to violence or killing, or perpetrate acts of violence or fail to prevent them. When comparing such acts to assigning, reading, and discussing texts, it is clear that war zones and settings where one might encounter Yoder's theology are fundamentally different contexts that admit fundamentally different forms of action.

Second, the high-stakes nature of each situation differs. War is high stakes in part because the kinds of acts performed often run counter to the strict moral codes service members possess. As Litz notes, "because of their traits and lifestyles, warriors may be . . . more vulnerable to the deleterious effects of violations of moral codes or the loss of cherished attachments than others who are less devoted to moral values and guiding ideals."[11] This discrepancy between soldiers' commitment to the moral values of the military and the acts they might perpetrate in war are difficult to reconcile. Consequently, service members can suffer an especially acute sense of moral transgression. I argue that teaching Yoder within the context of academic disciplines (ethics) and institutions (academy and church) explicitly dedicated to human flourishing constitutes a similar type of high-stakes situation. But war is also high stakes for reasons not applicable to encountering tainted legacies. The kinds of acts being perpetrated and the potentially lethal consequences render war high stakes in a way unlike most experiences of encountering tainted religious legacies.

A third limitation involves the kinds of injuries suffered. The moral injury that results from war often "entails severe social withdrawal, anhedonia/dysphoria, and disinterest in previously pleasurable activities . . . [and can lead to] anomie, pervasive shame and guilt, reductions in trust in self and others in terms of moral behavior (a *broken moral compass*), poor self-care, self-harming, and selfhandicapping behaviors, loss of faith in God (if applicable), and, in the case of betrayal-based experiences, externalizing, blaming, and aggressive acting-out behavior."[12] When the women Yoder violated are asked to engage Yoder's theology or see others upholding Yoder as the authority on pacifism, clinical moral injury may apply. It may also be the case that others who have suffered sexual assault—and perhaps those who have suffered other violations—may also experience a triggering of past trauma. Moreover, students of Yoder or others with deep ties to him who were not sexually violated but who learn of his violence may feel the betrayal of moral injury. But most encountering tainted religious legacies like Yoder's are unlikely to experience comparable effects. As Litz notes, war trauma has a "unique phenomenology."[13] When applying moral injury to contexts outside war, it is important to avoid what Litz calls "a false, tacit assumption of the equipotentiality of widely varying types of traumas and traumatic contexts."[14]

How Moral Injury Illuminates Tainted Legacies

Despite these significant limitations, the construct of moral injury—while developed to meet the needs of those suffering the harms of war—has tremendous power to illuminate the experience of encountering tainted legacies. Although the contexts differ, the formal features of moral injury nevertheless capture the moral complexities tainted legacies produce. In other words, while the experience of encountering tainted religious legacies will usually fall short of the standards for a clinical diagnosis of moral injury, the construct itself provides a powerful explanatory tool for making sense of the complex moral reactions these legacies often cause. Taking a classroom context as my example, I show how moral injury names the particular types of agency and moral harm involved and points to the larger social and institutional context of such harm and the need for moral repair.

First, Litz's definition of moral injury as "bearing witness to, or learning about acts that transgress deeply held moral beliefs and expectations" names the agency exercised by professors and students and the nature of the potential transgression.[15] Like service members, most professors and students who engage Yoder's legacy are "neither victims nor executioners."[16] Although they are not, in most cases, survivors of or eyewitnesses to Yoder's violence, they are witnesses to his violence in a figurative sense. They bear "witness to the aftermath of violence," and they certainly "learn about" his acts.[17]

Second, Shay's definition of moral injury names the particular kind of transgression involved (a moral one) and the reason it results (the betrayal, by an authority, of deeply held moral convictions or expectations when stakes are high). While students are unlikely to suffer clinical moral injury as a result of engaging tainted legacies, they certainly may experience a transgression of moral commitments that "creates dissonance and conflict because it violates assumptions and beliefs about right and wrong and personal goodness."[18] This violation occurs on multiple levels. In learning that Yoder—an authority in peace church theology and the wider field of Christian ethics—violated the very convictions espoused in his work, students are exposed to the kind of betrayal and "leadership malpractice" that Shay identifies as producing moral injury.[19] This transgression is often heightened by the context of the ethics classroom. Students expect thinkers in ethics, theology, and other disciplines that reflect on human flourishing to practice what they preach. Apart from their other moral commitments, this idea itself constitutes a "belief" many students possess. Not unlike the soldiers whose high moral standards make it especially difficult to abide moral transgressions in war, students experience a violation of both moral ideals and their specific moral expectations for the authors they read.

That this learning occurs in an institutional setting (academic or ecclesial) also devoted to the common good exacerbates the high-stakes nature of the situation. Rita Brock and Gabriella Lettini note the "paradox of war": "Few major social institutions teach moral integrity, courage, personal discipline, humility, a sense of purpose and responsibility, and commitment to the lives of others better than the armed services. And none works so thoroughly to compromise, deny, dismantle, and destroy the very values it teaches."[20] The same might be said of ecclesial and academic institutions committed to the common good that abide unethical practices or fail to hold their members accountable for abusive behavior. Because "meaning making" is just as much "an explicit function" of ethics classrooms as it is "of military cultures," students can find themselves in high-stakes situations when the religious professionals they study commit egregiously unethical acts.[21] Indeed, it is striking that Litz compares service members with religious professionals as those who "explicitly dedicate themselves to live by moral codes" and are therefore susceptible to a stronger sense of violation and moral outrage when committing or learning about atrocious acts.[22] The result is the same: "It *destroys the capacity for social trust* in the mental and social worlds" of the betrayed.[23] For both groups, their "confidence in moral authority and moral structures is shaken."[24] Both are challenged to "understand how the betrayal has affected [their] ability to trust others, believe in institutions, and value ideals such as right and wrong."[25] In short, nothing less than the moral credibility of religious and educational institutions and believers' faith in the Christian tradition itself is at stake. These are not the lethal consequences one might experience in war, but they are incredibly high stakes nonetheless.

Finally, the construct highlights the "irreducibly social and contextual phenomenon" of moral injury and the need for institutional forms of moral repair.[26] The literature on moral injury in war rightly points beyond the soldier to the cultural attitudes and practices that create the contexts where moral injury occurs. Similarly, applying the concept to Yoder's work reveals the structural, cultural, and institutional scope of the problem, drawing attention to a culture that allows for violence against women and highlighting the widespread relevance of the problem. This approach spotlights the academic and ecclesial institutions that fail to hold the powerful accountable when they prey on the vulnerable. In Yoder's case, it invites analysis of how Mennonite institutions both failed initially to hold Yoder accountable and later sought institutional forms of moral repair.

Once again, these similarities are often formal. The differences between war and encounters with Yoder's theology—and therefore between the types of acts, high-stakes situations, and nature of the injuries—clarify the limitations in applying moral injury to encounters with tainted legacies of thought. While engaging legacies like Yoder's will not ordinarily produce clinical moral injury, the formal features of the construct nevertheless capture the moral complexities experienced when dealing with such legacies, illustrating the promise of moral injury beyond its original war-related context—and particularly for reflecting on tainted religious legacies like Yoder's. In fact, Litz's and others' clinical treatment strategies for war-related moral injury are also helpful in thinking about potential pedagogical strategies for handling tainted legacies—strategies that equip students with tools to navigate their moral experience, that enable more robust understandings of ethics as a discipline, and that encourage students to claim their moral agency in seeking moral repair.

And, as others note, this potentially mutually enriching relationship between moral injury and theological ethics runs both ways, with theological traditions providing resources moral injury seems to demand yet psychology cannot provide.[27] For example, Warren Kinghorn argues that "faith communities, unlike the clinical disciplines, are able to embrace thick and particular conceptions of human flourishing and human failing and are, thereby, equipped much more robustly than the clinical disciplines to facilitate the healing of morally injured veterans."[28] What about other fields and public institutions? Might theological resources be equally beneficial for addressing the moral complexity of tainted legacies outside the field of religious ethics? Recent reliance on religious resources in various truth and reconciliation commissions and other restorative justice movements certainly illustrate the contributions religious traditions can make to public life when traditional legal and political responses fall short. The next section explores the ways theological ethics—particularly feminist and womanist reflection—both provide responses to cases like Yoder's and suggest strategies for moral repair of harm caused by some of the tainted legacies that feature prominently in public life.

Feminist Theologies and Moral Injury

Many of the theologians and ethicists who have turned to moral injury in recent work are feminists, suggesting resonances between these fields. Feminist receptivity to moral injury reflects the sustained efforts of feminist theologians and ethicists to address various forms of moral harm and trauma, but it also signals their recognition that the Christian tradition is itself a morally injurious, tainted legacy. Not unlike those in the military, Christians must operate within an institution and tradition that often betrays its own moral values. The connection between moral injury and feminist theology becomes even clearer in light of feminist conceptions of theologies as responses to wounds. As Mary McClintock Fulkerson notes, "like a wound, theological thinking is generated by a sometimes inchoate sense that something *must* be addressed."[29] And as Serene Jones puts it, "the balmlike work of theology and of religion is to uncover and mend such wounds."[30] In this sense, feminist theologians share with those who work with the morally injured a concern to heal the wounds sustained when powerful institutions, traditions, and leaders violate their professed values.

As such, feminist theologies are especially helpful for addressing both Yoder's case and other instances of tainted legacies. Indeed, the strategies of those who have reflected on how to approach Yoder's theology map onto feminist strategies for handling tainted forms of the Christian tradition. Moreover, such feminist responses often map onto predominant responses to other tainted legacies. At the least, these resonances clarify the nature and task of feminist theologies as responses to a morally injurious tradition. At best, they recommend feminist theological resources as potentially powerful resources for healing moral injury inflicted by other tainted legacies. I argue that feminist and womanist reflection demands special consideration because these theologians engage one of the most powerful and authoritative tainted legacies in human history—the Christian tradition—as well as various evils that impact it, such as sexism and the legacies of slavery. This work equips these thinkers with particular insight to the nature, gravity, and scope of problems tainted legacies present. Furthermore, their sustained reflections on the nature of suffering and its redemptive possibilities—or lack thereof—provide principles of criticism for assessing efforts at moral repair in public cases of tainted legacies.

Feminists and womanists are particularly well positioned to contribute to public discussion because their theological projects respond to a tainted legacy that not only has the potential to inflict moral injury but does so by appealing to ultimate authority. Like service members who suffer moral injury by experiencing betrayal of what's right by a legitimate authority in a high-stakes situation, Christians who suffer due to distorted expressions of their religious tradition experience moral transgressions of the highest order. Brock and Lettini's "paradox of war" might be extended to describe a "paradox of the church." Like the military, the church often betrays the very values it teaches. When the church abides unjust practices, covers up, or even aids abusive behavior, or when its teachings and doctrines violate human dignity, Christians become "people who sustained moral conscience within a system designed to compromise and even destroy it."[31] It is striking that of all social institutions and roles "explicitly dedicate[d] . . . to liv[ing] by moral codes," Litz identifies the priest (and, by extension, religious traditions) as most comparable to the warrior (and, by extension, the military). Litz argues that the military differs in that it also requires a commitment "to protect the social order and promote its highest development," which exacerbates the harm.[32] But religious traditions also espouse the common good, and, unlike the military's commitments, these claims—as feminists and other liberationists have noted—are reinforced by the highest, ultimate, most transcendent claims to power, thereby raising the stakes.

In addition to dealing with the gravest of morally injurious tainted legacies, feminist and womanist theologies enable robust understanding of the complexity of tainted legacies. Confronting tainted legacies is not simply a matter of dealing with past events once and for all. Moral injury and trauma are moral phenomena of peculiar kinds, given their respective elements of leadership malpractice and the return of the past. The harm caused is especially acute, involving the betrayal of values by a moral authority under high stakes, and the suffering often continues beyond the original violation. Trauma is "not simply a singular event. . . . It is an event that continues, that persists into the present. . . . It persists in symptoms that live on in communities, in the layers of past violence that constitute present ways of relating."[33] The moral authority of religious traditions heightens the impact of the harm; perhaps even more importantly, the power and longevity of the Christian tradition raises the stakes in that it increases the likelihood that past harm will be carried far into the future.

It adds another layer of complexity to recognize, as feminists and womanists often do, that Christianity is a peculiar kind of religious tradition: one with a traumatic event—the crucifixion of Christ—at its heart. As Jones puts it, "Christianity does not need to discern the relationship between trauma and grace from a blank slate; after all, it was founded on the story of the crucifixion and resurrection of Jesus. So in a very real way its central story is one of trauma and grace."[34] Similarly, Brock and Rebecca Ann Parker contend, "Christianity bears the marks of unresolved trauma."[35] Christian theologians possess resources developed over two millennia to make sense of this trauma; these resources are likely to be useful for responding to other tainted legacies. Feminists and womanists in particular pay special attention to the very doctrines most closely connected with the traumatic event of Jesus's crucifixion—namely, doctrines of atonement.

Feminist and womanist engagement with the tainted legacy of Christianity is especially attuned to the dynamics of suffering. Here again, the value to those working not only with tainted religious legacies but also with those in other fields and public institutions cannot be understated. If medical approaches to moral injury are, for example, limited by their inability "to distinguish between meaningful and nonmeaningful moral suffering," feminists and womanists provide more nuanced approaches.[36] Their theological reflection reveals a wariness to embrace suffering as inherently redemptive while also acknowledging that in certain situations, under certain conditions, suffering may have redemptive value. Feminist and womanist perspectives illuminate possible strategies for enacting moral repair of the harm that tainted legacies inflict.

Feminist and Womanist Resonances with and Contributions to Public Discussion of Tainted Legacies

Some feminists reject the idea of redemptive suffering because of the burden it places on victims, suggesting one valid response to tainted legacies: refusing attempts to redeem them. Joanne Carlson Brown and Rebecca Parker, perhaps the best-known representatives of this view, reject the idea of redemptive suffering because it "makes victims the servants of the evildoers' salvation."[37] This view is certainly present in discussions of Yoder's legacy. Because of his sexual violence, some view Yoder's work as irredeemably flawed and refuse to teach or otherwise engage his work out of concern for those he violated. Andy Alexis-Baker, for example, describes his editing of Yoder's work as "a waste of time." "I regret that I spent all those hours, days, months, even years making his work accessible to more and more people," he writes. "I no longer assign or even mention his work in my classes."[38] This strategy mirrors that of feminists, like Mary Daly, who declared the Christian tradition hopelessly patriarchal and proceeded to identify themselves as post-Christian. It also resonates on a formal level with responses to other tainted legacies, ranging from those who argue Nazi medical research ought not be used to those who argue that the names of slaveholders and other morally compromised figures should be removed from public buildings, roads, and other landmarks. When asked, for example, whether the medical data from Nazi medical experiments should continue to be used despite the suffering it caused, Holocaust survivor Eva Mozes Kor said:

> I know that it will always hurt to remember that we were reduced to the lowest form of existence. We were treated like animals—we were his guinea pigs. But it hurts 10 times more today to realize that some American scientists and doctors want to use this data regardless of the unethical manner in which it was obtained; regardless of the pain and suffering paid by the victims. The advocates for the use of the data claim they want to save human lives. It is obnoxious to me that some of the advocates are so magnanimous with other peoples' lives and suffering.[39]

Kor's response explicitly rejects the idea of redeeming this knowledge by using it to save lives, and she does so by drawing attention to how such a response offers up the suffering of victims for others' benefit. Those who advocate for the removal of morally compromised figures' names from buildings and other landmarks often make similar arguments. Ozioma Obi-Onuoha, a member of the Black Justice League, a student group advocating the removal of Woodrow Wilson's name from Princeton's public policy school, describes Wilson's presence on campus as "a haunting." The *New York Times* reports that many students "said they had often felt excluded and continually if subtly called on to justify their presence" and that "Wilson's name and image around campus feel like constant reminders that they are not entirely welcome."[40] Although clearly different in important respects from the case of Nazi medical data, these calls for the removal of Wilson's name cite the ongoing suffering and burden that the descendants of Wilson's victims continue to bear. For them, for Kor, and for those who refuse to engage Yoder's work, the only appropriate response—the one that does not require victims to bear further burdens—is to refuse to repair or redeem tainted legacies. While often the minority perspective, this stance witnesses to that which is "unwitnessable" and cautions against a too-easy embrace of "the rhetoric of 're'—rebuilding, restoring, recovering."[41]

Other feminist theologies follow this "re" path of repurposing tainted doctrines and practices. In their critique of patriarchal, racist, and classist formulations of Christian doctrines and practices, these theologians engage tainted aspects of Christian tradition to revive and redirect them to redemptive purpose. Kathryn Tanner makes a compelling argument for this approach. Drawing on a politics of culture that views the production of meaning as a constant cultural struggle, she notes, "the past use of cultural elements does

not determine present or future interpretations or articulations of those elements."[42] She advocates that feminists engage in a "realignment of cultural
items—their disarticulation from service to patriarchy and their rearticulation
for feminist purpose."[43] In contrast to the first approach, which focuses on the
irredeemable harm that tainted legacies cause, this response emphasizes their
status as contingent cultural articulations. This is not to deny their destructive
power, but it is to refuse the idea that their problematic articulations are fixed.
"The continuous nature of human practices over time and the inevitability
with which human memory drags the happenings of the past into the present
and future" indicates the power that tainted legacies wield but underscores that
this power is not absolute.[44] Tainted legacies can also be rearticulated. In fact,
the most effective response to tainted legacies on this view is not to refuse to
engage or to bypass them through the creation of "new" ones but to repurpose
explicitly tainted organizations and articulations of Christian tradition for new
political purpose. This strategy acknowledges the power of tainted forms of
organization or articulations, but it also reveals their vulnerability. It shows
the availability of those same cultural items for rearticulations that counter
their tainted forms. Commitment to this reproduction of meaning therefore
becomes the most effective strategy for dislodging the power of tainted legacies.

A good example of this approach appears regarding both Yoder's case and
instances of tainted public symbols. Some continue to engage Yoder's work but
reconfigure this engagement to redemptive ends. Gerald Schlabach's approach
provides an example here. "I can understand the calls from younger Mennonite
scholars to do peace theology without relying on Yoder," he writes. "And if a
middle course is at least to apply a hermeneutic of suspicion about the ways his
patriarchy and worse might have shaped his theology, I've been doing this in
my own way. But I just don't see how they/we can do without him."[45] Schlabach
continues to teach Yoder's work, but in applying a hermeneutic of suspicion,
he acknowledges Yoder's violence and uses this knowledge as a critical tool of
interrogation, both refusing to allow previous conceptions of Yoder's pacifist
vision to remain unchallenged and enabling the possibility for more redemptive expressions of pacifist theology. I have also argued for a version of this
approach, identifying Yoder's sexual violence as an occasion for peace church
theologians to correct their failure to address sexual violence and structural
forms of violence like sexism, racism, and classism.[46]

This approach is also visible in public cases of tainted legacies. Harvard Law
School recently voted to replace its school shield because it resembled that of a
slaveholding donor family, the Royalls. Annette Gordon-Reed, a professor of
legal history, was one of two dissenters on the twelve-person committee. She
argued that replacing the seal also erases the memory of the enslaved persons
whose labor contributed to the school: "People *should* have to think about slavery when they think of the Harvard shield; but from now on, with a narrative

that emphasizes the enslaved, not the Royall family."[47] In her view, "we owe it to the enslaved to work through those feelings and think of ways to carry their stories forward. And we should do that in a way that shows the inherently entwined nature of the good and bad of our past, using written text and symbols like the sheaves and, even, buildings like Monticello."[48] Gordon-Reed's strategy is similar to that of South Carolinians who advocated for the transfer of the Confederate flag from the state house grounds to a museum. Doing so places such symbols in "a fuller context" that "preserve[s] such memorials and recognize[s] history while not extolling the ideas they embody."[49] These examples demonstrate the kind of rearticulation Tanner advocates: through their rearticulation, the power of these symbols is acknowledged but then directed to purposes that undermine that very power.

Womanist Contributions to Moral Repair of Tainted Legacies

Feminist and womanist theological approaches do not merely map onto approaches to other tainted legacies; they also provide needed criteria for assessing responses to these cases. Womanist articulations of criteria that need to be met for suffering to be rendered meaningful are particularly helpful. JoAnne Marie Terrell's emphasis on the possibility of learning as the key condition for whether suffering might be redeemed is one such approach. She suggests "death has saving significance inasmuch as we learn continuously from the life that preceded it."[50] Her account construes those who suffer "not as victims who passively acquiesced to evil" but "empowered, *sacramental*, witnesses."[51] This emphasis on learning, on seeing how those who suffer "exercised or did not exercise their moral and creative agency," is present in responses to Yoder's case and many of the public cases already discussed, including those over Nazi data, Wilson's legacy, the Harvard Law School seal, and the Confederate flag controversy.[52] On this view, tainted legacies should be approached as occasions for learning—and particularly learning from the ways "victims" exercised their moral agency—and only in this way do they have redeeming value. As Princeton president Christopher L. Eisgruber put it, "One of the benefits of having a genuine public discussion, informed by scholarly opinion, about some of these questions is that it can help educate people about problems that go beyond the symbol in our society."[53] Malinda Berry articulates a similar strategy in her discussion of why she continues to teach Yoder's work: "I agreed to assign *Body Politics* because I would have felt academically irresponsible to exclude Yoder's voice and perspective from our course where Anabaptist perspectives on the church are central. And it is this same work that afforded me the opportunity to speak about the crisis our denomination has experienced because of Yoder's actions. . . . Collectively, we failed over and over to enact justice *and* we can learn from our mistakes."[54] Others, like historian Rachel Waltner Goossen, have drawn attention to the significant roles played by Mennonite women like Martha Smith Good, Carolyn Holderread Heggen, and Ruth Krall in their mobilization to stop Yoder's violence and to hold the relevant Mennonite institutions accountable.[55] Marvin M. Ellison argues that it is these women, rather than Yoder, who are the real experts on peace church theology: "The truly exemplary theologian-activists of Christian non-violence are the women survivors of Yoder's abuse. Against the odds, they courageously stepped forward, demanded justice, not retribution, and called both Yoder and the wider Mennonite community to account. . . . We should honor the collective power and wisdom of such communities of resistance and alternative consciousness as sources of fresh theological vision and truth telling, not only about violence/violation but also about the requirements of authentic peacemaking and relational justice."[56]

In each of these approaches, learning from and honoring the agency of those violated and their allies is key. Ellison's approach not only emphasizes the moral agency of those violated, it also suggests that one form of moral repair is to reassess who constitutes the "legitimate authority" and to move forward in ways that acknowledge that authority.

Womanist work is of particular importance because of its engagement with tainted forms of Christianity as it intersects with the morally injurious legacy of slavery. In her analysis of enslaved persons' reflection on "the distinction between a pure or true Christianity and that poisoned by slavery," M. Shawn Copeland constructs a womanist theology of suffering that "is characterized by remembering and retelling, by resisting, by redeeming."[57] Her account highlights not that suffering is redemptive but that suffering *can be made* redemptive. This emphasis on the ways black women have claimed their moral agency for the purposes of meaning making in the wake of slavery and "its living legacy" recasts victims as powerful moral agents.[58] Such an approach is prominent across a variety of womanist perspectives, calling to mind womanist conceptions of redemption as the process of "making a way out of no way," all of which emphasize the moral agency of those confronted with death-dealing situations and structures.

In this case, womanist responses not only resonate with responses to other tainted legacies, they also illuminate inadequate responses, suggesting some of the ways religious resources might be useful for moral repair of tainted legacies like Yoder's and those prominent in public debate. The recent outcry over Georgetown's response to its legacy of slavery provides an excellent case study. Among American universities to acknowledge deep institutional ties to slavery, Georgetown has offered the most robust response. To atone for its sins, Georgetown issued a public apology and announced plans to erect a public memorial to the persons it enslaved, renamed two campus buildings that previously had honored presidents involved in the sale of enslaved persons, will now award preferential status in admissions to descendants of the enslaved, and will create an institute for the study of slavery and its legacies. But when it formally announced these measures in September 2016, descendants of persons enslaved by Georgetown expressed disappointment. Some wanted the response to include scholarships for descendants. But even more offensive for others was Georgetown's failure to include them on the committee that made these recommendations and its failure to invite them to President John J. DeGioia's public announcement. Karran Harper Royal, an organizer of one group of descendants, expressed her disappointment: "It has to go much further," she said. "They're calling us family. Well, I'm from New Orleans and when we have a gathering, family's invited."59

In light of womanist insights about the importance of learning and agency as criteria for whether meaning can be made of tainted legacies, one might argue that Georgetown's response prompted the reaction it did (despite its emphasis on learning, visible in its efforts to learn from its mistakes as an institution and in its creation of the institute of slavery) because it did not properly acknowledge the agency of the descendants of persons it enslaved. Indeed, after a recent religious ceremony and renaming of two buildings—one for Isaac Hawkins, an enslaved person sold by the school in 1838, and the other for Anne Marie Becraft, a black nineteenth-century educator—a descendant of Hawkins, Mary Williams-Wagner, again expressed disappointment that descendants were not included in reparation plans: "Everybody has to have a seat at the table to talk about what it is we're going to do as we move forward," she said.60 Clearly, neither Royal nor Williams-Wagner considers Georgetown's response adequate. To use Copeland's language, neither felt that Georgetown had honored their meaning-making ability by including them as active participants in plans for moral repair.

One detects a similar problem in Mennonite responses to Yoder's harmful legacy. According to Goossen's account, various concerned women approached the relevant Mennonite institutions repeatedly to get them to put an end to Yoder's violence and to take responsibility for their complicity, but these institutions were more interested in protecting their and Yoder's reputation than in addressing the problem. It was not until Sara Wenger Shenk became president of Anabaptist Mennonite Biblical Seminary that the voices of Carolyn Holderread Heggen and others were fully heard, leading to a public apology and institutional reparations.61 Here again, one sees the need for institutional responses that honor the agency and meaning-making ability of those harmed. In this way, Terrell's emphasis on learning and agency and Copeland's emphasis on black women's power to make meaning out of senseless suffering provide principles of criticism by which other institutions might judge the adequacy of their responses to moral violations and the tainted legacies that result. Does the response acknowledge the moral agency of those affected or does it repeat the patterns of the past by continuing to deny persons their dignity, voice, and agency?

Conclusion

The first part of this essay argues that the concept of moral injury possesses the power to illuminate problems in religious ethics. While it is critical to acknowledge the significant limitations in applying moral injury to tainted legacies, doing so nevertheless clarifies the moral complexities of encountering them. It identifies the kind of moral transgression involved, it highlights the high-stakes nature of the situation, and it points to the social and institutional context of the harm. The damage that tainted legacies inflict may be substantively different from that of war, but the construct of moral injury identifies formal similarities in the experience of encountering tainted legacies, the moral harm that results, and the need for moral repair.

Other scholars have convincingly argued that clinical conceptions of moral injury have much to learn from Christian moral theology.[62] I have extended this argument, highlighting the especially significant contributions feminist and womanist theologies make in this regard. But I also argue that the value of feminist and womanist resources extends beyond the moral injury literature and the public contexts of war and psychology to other tainted legacies—all of which are connected not merely by their power to perpetuate past trauma into the present and the future but also by their status as leaders or institutions who in high-stakes situations betray the very moral commitments they purport to uphold. I have shown how feminist responses to tainted Christian traditions resonate with responses to Yoder's case and other tainted legacies. Through this comparison, I offer a construal of feminist theologies as responses to wounds sustained from morally injurious forms of Christianity. I also argue that feminist and womanist theological resources may provide needed resources in responding to tainted legacies prominent in public life. I have provided one example by showing that womanist ethics provides principles of criticism that reveal why Georgetown's response to its legacy of slavery—as robust as it was— ultimately proves inadequate. Further consideration is warranted as to whether feminist and womanist theologies provide further resources for addressing public cases of tainted legacies. One might look, for example, to their use of neglected theological genres like lament, their emphasis on neglected moments in the Christian narrative such as Holy Saturday to reconceive redemption as "remaining," or similar conceptions of salvation as "survival and quality of life."[63]

Ultimately, I hope to have shown the benefits of a cross-disciplinary engagement between moral injury and feminist and womanist religious ethics.

Such dialogue can certainly never eliminate moral injury or entirely prevent the passage of past trauma into the present. But approaching tainted religious legacies through the lens of moral injury and approaching other tainted legacies through the perspectives of feminist and womanist reflection nevertheless holds promise for professors, students, and citizens alike. At the very least, it illuminates the complexities involved. At best, it aids in discerning how to promote human flourishing when institutional resources, representatives, and practices are implicated in traumatic pasts.

Notes

I'd like to thank the SCE audience and anonymous reviewers for their helpful feedback. Special thanks to Grace Kao and Craig Danielson for extended conversation.

1. Rachel Waltner Goossen, "'Defanging the Beast': Mennonite Responses to John Howard Yoder's Sexual Abuse," *Mennonite Quarterly Review* 89, no. 1 (January 2015): 7–80.

2. Jorge Luis Borges, "Waking Up," trans. Alastair Reid, *New Yorker*, March 22, 1999, 56.

3. David Brooks, "The Year of Unearthed Memories," *New York Times*, December 15, 2015, https://www.nytimes.com/2015/12/15/opinion/the-year-of-unearthed-memories.html.

4. Brett T. Litz, Nathan Stein, Eileen Delaney, Leslie Lebowitz, William P. Nash, Caroline Silva, and Shira Maguen, "Moral Injury and Moral Repair in War Veterans: A Preliminary Model and Intervention Strategy," *Clinical Psychology Review* 29 (2009): 699.

5. Ibid., 695.

6. Tyler Boudreau, "The Morally Injured," *Massachusetts Review* (Fall/Winter 2011–12): 754.

7. Jonathan Shay, "Casualties," *Daedalus* 140 (2011): 183.

8. I say "mostly" here to recognize that whether Yoder's legacy actually causes what psychologists would diagnose as moral injury will depend on the person(s) encountering it. The women Yoder violated and perhaps others who have experienced sexual assault may sustain moral injury. Other students of Yoder who were not sexually violated but who feel betrayed by his wrongdoing may also be morally injured. For most others, the analogy functions formally, clarifying why Yoder's violations register as particularly egregious.

9. Shay, "Casualties," 184.

10. Brett T. Litz, Leslie Lebowitz, Matt J. Gray, and William P. Nash, *Adaptive Disclosure: A New Treatment for Military Trauma, Loss, and Moral Injury* (New York: Guilford, 2016), 117–18.

11. Ibid., 42.

12. Ibid., 22; italics in original.

13. Ibid., 9.

14. Ibid., 8.

15. Litz et al., "Moral Injury and Moral Repair," 700.

16. Robert Jay Lifton, *Home from the War: Vietnam Veterans: Neither Victims nor Executioners* (New York: Simon and Schuster, 1973).

17. Litz et al., "Moral Injury and Moral Repair," 700.

18. Boudreau, "Morally Injured," 748.

19. Litz and coauthors identify two major types of war-related moral injury: perpetration and betrayal-based injuries. See Litz et al., *Adaptive Disclosure*, 117. On "leadership malpractice," see Shay, "Causalities," 183.

20. Rita Nakashima Brock and Gabriella Lettini, *Soul Repair: Recovering from Moral Injury after War* (Boston: Beacon Press, 2012), 128.

21. Litz et al., *Adaptive Disclosure*, 32.

22. Ibid., 38.

23. Shay, "Casualties," 184; italics in original.

24. Litz et al., *Adaptive Disclosure*, 122.

25. Ibid.

26. Warren Kinghorn, "Combat Trauma and Moral Fragmentation: A Theological Account of Moral Injury," *Journal of the Society of Christian Ethics* 32, no. 2 (2012): 62.

27. Ibid., 67.

28. Ibid., 71.

29. Mary McClintock Fulkerson, *Places of Redemption: Theology for a Worldly Church* (New York: Oxford University Press, 2007), 13–14.

30. Serene Jones, *Trauma and Grace: Theology in a Ruptured World* (Louisville, KY: Westminster John Knox Press, 2009), 2.

31. Brock and Lettini, *Soul Repair*, 126.

32. Litz et al., *Adaptive Disclosure*, 38.

33. Shelly Rambo, *Spirit and Trauma: A Theology of Remaining* (Louisville, KY: Westminster John Knox Press, 2010), 2.

34. Jones, *Trauma and Grace*, 21.

35. Rita Nakashima Brock and Rebecca Ann Parker, *Proverbs of Ashes: Violence, Redemptive Suffering, and the Search for What Saves Us* (Boston: Beacon Press, 2001), 250.

36. Kinghorn, "Combat Trauma," 67.

37. Joanne Carlson Brown and Rebecca Parker, "For God So Loved the World?," in *Christianity, Patriarchy, and Abuse: A Feminist Critique*, ed. Joanne Carlson Brown and Carole R. Bohn (New York: Pilgrim, 1989), 20.

38. See the comments section of Grace Yia-Hei Kao's blogpost, "A Time of Reckoning: The SCE and John Howard Yoder," *Feminism and Religion*, January 13, 2017, https://feminism andreligion.com/2017/01/13/a-time-of-reckoning-the-sce-and-john-howard-yoder-by -grace-yia-hei-kao/.

39. Eva Mozes Kor, "Nazi Experiments as Viewed by a Survivor of Mengele's Experiments," in *When Medicine Went Mad: Bioethics and the Holocaust*, ed. Arthur L. Caplan (Totowa, NJ: Humana, 1992), 3–4.

40. Andy Newman, "At Princeton, Woodrow Wilson, a Heralded Alum, Is Recast as an Intolerant One," *New York Times*, November 22, 2015, https://www.nytimes.com/2015/11/23 /nyregion/at-princeton-addressing-a-racist-legacy-and-seeking-to-remove-woodrow -wilsons-name.html?_r=0.

41. Rambo, *Spirit and Trauma*, 23, 143.

42. Kathryn Tanner, "'New Social Movements' and the Practice of Feminist Theology," in *Horizons in Feminist Theology: Identity, Tradition, and Norms*, ed. Rebecca S. Chopp and Sheila Greeve Davaney (Minneapolis, MN: Fortress, 1997), 192.

43. Ibid., 188.

44. Ibid., 195.

45. Gerald W. Schlabach, "Only Those We Need Can Betray Us: My Relationship with John Howard Yoder and His Legacy" (blog), July 10, 2014, http://www.geraldschlabach .net/2014/07/10/only-those-we-need-can-betray-us-my-relationship-with-john-howard -yoder-and-his-legacy/.

46. Karen V. Guth, "Doing Justice to the Complex Legacy of John Howard Yoder: Restorative Justice Resources in Witness and Feminist Ethics," *Journal of the Society of Christian Ethics* 35, no. 2 (2015): 119–39.

47. Anemona Hartocollis, "Harvard Law to Abandon Crest Linked to Slavery," *New York Times*, March 4, 2016, https://www.nytimes.com/2016/03/05/us/harvard-law-to-abandon -crest-linked-to-slavery.html.

48. Ibid.

49. Richard Fausset, "South Carolina Faces the High Cost of Curating History's Dustbin," *New York Times*, December 26, 2015, https://www.nytimes.com/2015/12/27/us/south -carolina-faces-the-high-cost-of-curating-historys-dustbin.html.

50. JoAnne Marie Terrell, *Power in the Blood? The Cross in the African American Experience* (Eugene, OR: Wipf & Stock, 2005), 142.

51. Ibid.; italics in original.

52. Ibid., 143.

53. Newman, "Woodrow Wilson."

54. Malinda E. Berry, "Avoiding Avoidance: Why I Assigned *Body Politics* This Spring," *Mennonite Life* 68 (2014), https://ml.bethelks.edu/issue/vol-68/article/avoiding-avoidance- why-i-assigned-body-politics-th/; italics in original.

55. See Goossen, "'Defanging the Beast'"; and Rachel Waltner Goossen, "Mennonite Bodies, Sexual Ethics: Women Challenge John Howard Yoder," *Journal of Mennonite Studies* 34 (2016): 247–59.

56. Marvin M. Ellison, "Christian Sex, Christian Ethics: Marvin M. Ellison on Jung and Stevens's *Professional Sexual Ethics*," *Marginalia: A Los Angeles Review of Books*, October 27, 2015, http://marginalia.lareviewofbooks.org/christian-sex-christian-ethics-by-marvin -m-ellison/.

57. M. Shawn Copeland, "'Wading through Many Sorrows': Toward a Theology of Suffering in a Womanist Perspective," in *Womanist Theological Ethics: A Reader*, ed. Katie Geneva Cannon, Emilie M. Townes, and Angela D. Sims (Louisville, KY: Westminster John Knox Press, 2011), 148, 153.

58. Ibid., 153.

59. Rachel L. Swarns, "Georgetown University Plans Steps to Atone for Slave Past," *New York Times*, September 1, 2016, https://www.nytimes.com/2016/09/02/us/slaves-georgetown -university.html.

60. Ian Simpson, "Georgetown University Renames Buildings to Atone for Slavery Ties," Reuters, April 18, 2017, https://www.reuters.com/article/us-washingtondc-georgetown-slavery/ georgetown-university-renames-buildings-to-atone-for-slavery-ties-idUSKBN17K2AR.

61. Goossen, "Mennonite Bodies, Sexual Ethics."

62. Kinghorn, "Combat Trauma," 67.

63. On "lament," see, for example, Emilie M. Townes's use of lament in *Breaking the Fine Rain of Death: African American Health Issues and a Womanist Ethic of Care* (Eugene, OR: Wipf & Stock, 2006). Similarly, Serene Jones highlights the power of lament to express the suffering of trauma, connecting Calvin's use of the psalms of lament with trauma theorist Judith L. Herman's second stage of recovery: remembrance and mourning. See Jones, *Trauma and Grace*, 59. On "remaining," see Rambo, *Spirit and Trauma*, 16–17, 26, 34. On "salvation as 'survival and quality of life,'" see, for example, Delores S. Williams, *Sisters in the Wilderness: The Challenge of Womanist God-Talk* (Maryknoll, NY: Orbis, 1993).

Book Reviews

REVIEW OF

Egalitarian Liberalism Revisited: On the Meaning and Justification of Social Justice

Per Sundman

UPPSALA, SWEDEN: UPPSALA UNIVERSITET, 2016. 242 PP. $72.50

Across a range of contemporary disciplines, discussions about justice abound. Despite the prevalence of these discussions, however, there is little consensus about what justice is and whether (and, if so, how) appeals to it should be made. Moreover, if the interconnectedness and pluralism that obtain in our rapidly globalizing world are taken seriously, concerns about the content, meaning, and use of justice are amplified. Against this backdrop, Per Sundman aims to explicate and evaluate one particular form of justice: egalitarian liberalism. On his definition, egalitarian liberalism is "best understood as a triune conjunction of equality of opportunity, desert and self-ownership" (10). Over the course of eight substantive chapters, Sundman labors to show how these criteria both reinforce and don't contradict each other, aiming to clarify the meaning of social justice while considering known alternatives.

To develop this argument, Sundman covers a truly impressive range of topics in contemporary debates about justice, including consequentialism and deontology, equality of opportunity and equality of resources, capabilities and rights, corrective and distributive policies, the natural and social lotteries, status in moral and political communities, and the politics of recognition and misrecognition. On the whole, covering such a range of topics proves to be a strength. Sundman introduces the reader to a number of important topics and how several important thinkers have treated those topics, and his discussion of these topics and thinkers is evenhanded and insightful. If you're familiar with (and interested in) one or more of these debates, you will be delighted to find a theological ethicist engaging in them. There's also a further reason for delight: Sundman enters and engages in these debates without bringing the all-too-frequent (and oftentimes empty) charge that liberalism is "impoverished"—a point to which I'll return. But depending on your level of familiarity with recent debates in moral and political philosophy, you may be left unsatisfied with some aspects of Sundman's discussion. Specifically, some of these topics and thinkers deserve further attention and scrutiny than Sundman provides, especially important given Sundman's stated desire to navigate alternative understandings.

I do want to draw the reader's attention to the penultimate chapter of Sund-man's book, "Save Us from Liberalism." But first I want to make a larger point. I mentioned what I think is an all-too-frequent charge made in theological ethics: namely, that liberalism is impoverished. Sometimes, this charge is entirely warranted. But oftentimes, at least in my experience, it is empty: the person bringing the charge neither distinguishes among the diversity that obtains within liberalism nor charitably reads and represents the thinker with whom they are trying to engage. Given this disciplinary shortcoming, Sundman is to be commended for turning to Christian critiques of liberalism only after he's carefully worked (and guided the reader) through the myriad topics and thinkers that constitute egalitarian liberalism writ large.

So what about this chapter in particular? Focusing on Christian communitarians—for example, Stanley Hauerwas and John Milbank—Sundman explores whether *authentic* Christian ethics contradicts and is superior to egalitarian liberalism. In the first half of the chapter, he examines the different ways in which Christian communitarians understand obedience to God's commands and have criticized the putative liberal obsession with "autonomy." Following an important discussion where he contrasts Christian and liberal understandings of the circumstances of justice, the second half of Sundman's chapter argues briefly but persuasively against Christian exclusivity (e.g., the recently popular Benedict Option) and for Christians to act out *of* love, *for* justice, and *in* the world.

There is much to recommend about this book. Both substantively and structurally, it is admirable and instructive.

Bharat Ranganathan
University of Notre Dame

REVIEW OF

Why People Matter: A Christian Engagement with Rival Views of Human Significance
Edited by John F. Kilner
GRAND RAPIDS, MI: BAKER ACADEMIC, 2017. 240 PP. $26.99

Although *Why People Matter* does not use the word, it is an apologetic for the Christian faith and ethical tradition. Its argument begins with a moral intuition that the authors take to be near universal: "people matter." If Christian theological and ethical thought can be shown to explain and shore up the notion that "people matter" better than other ethical outlooks—and the authors believe it can—then the work will have (1) established a proper moral foundation for holding and acting on the conviction that people matter and (2) provided a reasoned argument for why Christianity as a fundamental belief system is better and truer than the other ethical systems examined.

The text of *Why People Matter* is accessible and well written. The essays weave together coherently around two central ideas: each human person has inherent, inalienable dignity, and Christianity is the truest way of understanding and acting on that conviction. To demonstrate what Christianity has to offer, the book begins (after a summative introduction by Kilner) with a set of essays describing five ethical outlooks: utilitarianism, collectivism, individualism, naturalism, and transhumanism. In each, a different author lays out an ethical foundation and concept of the outlook, shows how the concept illuminates why "people matter," explains why it may seem compelling, and argues that it fails to grasp something crucial about why people matter and how to live as if they matter. As Kilner puts it, "each [outlook] recognizes and champions something important that is missing in other ways of thinking. However, each is dangerously reductionistic by making that missing element the all-encompassing focus of its approach" (190).

Next, Kilner examines the Christian conviction that every human being is made in the image of God. He argues that this conviction, rightly understood, provides the only adequate foundation for the idea that "people matter." Respect for the image of God leads to proper respect for the human rights of others. Following this, David Gushee analyzes biblical passages and themes to argue that encounters with human beings are always also encounters with God; thus, we must treat people accordingly.

Why People Matter accomplishes its purpose as an apologetic, and it seems especially likely to help committed Christians understand how their moral convictions can hold up in debates with common Western philosophical ethical outlooks. A wise friend once described C. S. Lewis (referenced several times in the work) as "a master of convincing Christians that what they already believe is true." That sort of persuasion is one of the appropriate goals of apologetic, and *Why People Matter* seems likely to achieve it.

I have two comments on areas where readers may come away unsatisfied. First, the contributors' descriptions of the ethical outlooks they discuss are necessarily brief; those who hold these outlooks would likely wish to quibble with or nuance their arguments. Second, the work addresses only Western philosophical outlooks; the authors do not engage non-Christian religious traditions. In the spirit of interreligious cooperation, this is an excellent decision: frankly, I would not want to read a work that spent several chapters explaining why Christian ethical thought is superior to the ethical thought of, say, Hinduism or Judaism. But the work does leave unanswered, and unasked, the question of whether a reader who does come to reject individualism, transhumanism, and so on might not just as well embrace Islam or Buddhism as Christianity.

That said, this is an engaging work on the title question. It traces the basic contours of certain ethical outlooks, shows their strengths and potential weaknesses, and argues for a deep understanding, based in Christian Scripture and ethical thinking, of why people matter.

Laura Alexander
University of Nebraska at Omaha

REVIEW OF

Theology as Interdisciplinary Inquiry: Learning with and from the Natural and Human Sciences

Edited by Robin W. Lovin and Joshua Mauldin

GRAND RAPIDS, MI: EERDMANS, 2017. 202 PP. $32.00

How can Christian theology engage in fruitful dialogue with fields of inquiry such as cognitive science, anthropology, and law? Might discoveries in the natural and human sciences open creative possibilities for theology, and vice versa? Can Christian theology maintain its integrity while integrating insights from other disciplines? *Theology as Interdisciplinary Inquiry* takes up these questions as its central aim. This volume of six essays emerges from a three-year Templeton Foundation initiative that brought an interdisciplinary set of scholars together at the Center for Theological Inquiry to explore how their research might collaboratively push theology in new directions. These conversations centered on three themes: evolution and human nature, religious experience and moral identity, and law and religious freedom.

In the first essay, Celia Deane-Drummond proposes an alternative approach to traditional readings of the Genesis creation account that looks to "resonances" between von Balthasar's notion of "theo-drama" and niche construction theory. Her argument allows for human agency while drawing theology into a complementary, rather than conflictual, relationship with evolutionary science. The next three essays take up the theme of religious experience and moral identity. Michael Spezio proposes that both theology and cognitive science look to moral exemplars as the phenomenological basis for more realistic and mutually informative moral theology and cognitive models of learning. Colleen Shantz draws on cognitive science to demonstrate how the material and relational are constitutive of cognitive processes, arguing that it is precisely through "development and change" that we bear the *imago Dei* (66). Andrea Hollingsworth offers a rereading of Nicholas of Cusa's *De visione Dei* to demonstrate how a medieval mystical text echoes elements of contemporary neurocognitive processes of self-transformation. The final two essays center on law and religious freedom. John Burgess examines the privileging of religious freedom for canonizing martyrs in post-Soviet Russian Orthodoxy, arguing that this provides theological grounding for the legal right to religious freedom. Mary Ellen O'Connell proposes aesthetics as a more adequate modern grounding for legal authority than science. She argues that aesthetics takes us beyond the limits of self-interest, drawing us into concern for the good of others through the contemplation of beauty.

What holds these essays together is the pursuit of "transdisciplinarity": "paying close attention to the other discipline(s) in a way that has a substantial and mutual impact, but at the same time retaining a clear sense of disciplinary integrity" (14–15). Lovin and Mauldin argue for humility and hope as virtues that enable us to navigate the tension between openness and integrity. While humility enables us to recognize the limits of disciplinary boundaries and assumptions, hope propels us forward, promising that however incomplete our knowledge remains, by the grace of God we will make advances in understanding our world and ourselves.

Just as Christian Scharen and Aana Marie Vigen's *Ethnography as Christian Theology and Ethics* argues for the value of engagement with ethnography and its related disciplines to produce theology and ethics grounded in lived reality, this volume argues for the value of engagement with the natural and human sciences to produce "theological realism" that accounts for the complexity of "human personality and community" (xviii). It is unsurprising, then, that both volumes respond to objections from the neo-Radical Reformation and Radical Orthodoxy camps. In his conclusion, Douglas Ottati argues that these camps cannot account for the ways in which theological production inevitably interacts with natural and cultural processes. He argues further that insulating Christian theology is a form of cultural accommodation because it mirrors the formation of discrete modern disciplines, the very limitation these essays seek to transcend.

This volume advances the live discussion in Christian ethics about the promise and risks of engaging natural and social sciences. It is a valuable resource on this topic, and its essays are suitable for use in seminary course discussions on transdisciplinarity in theology and ethics.

Sara A. Williams
Emory University

■

REVIEW OF

Friends and Other Strangers: Studies in Religion, Ethics, and Culture

Richard B. Miller

NEW YORK: COLUMBIA UNIVERSITY PRESS, 2016. 416 PP. $60.00

In his studies on casuistry, war and peace, pediatric ethics, and other occasional topics Richard B. Miller has for some time been a leading source of creative impulses in the field of religious ethics, so it is a welcome event to have this volume organizing past essays of his into a thematically cohesive presentation. His book sets out a vision of the character and concerns of religious ethics that helps counter critics, such as Stanley Hauerwas, who have expressed skepticism about the field.

The governing conception of *Friends and Other Strangers* is that the study of religious ethics is properly shaped by attending to how "our lives ineluctably oscillate between experiences of intimacy and otherness" (5). Accordingly, Miller seeks to guide the field beyond either a one-sided focus on matters of friendship and special relations or a preoccupation with alterity and heterology. To grasp how the dialectic of intimacy and alterity shapes the normative character of personal and public life, he recommends religious ethicists should employ "the category of culture as an organizing rubric" (6).

In the book's initial section Miller elaborates on his view of the enterprise of religious ethics and its place in the broader intellectual landscape. In a discussion drawing on Ludwig Wittgenstein, Stanley Cavell, and James Gustafson, Miller first offers his account of the characteristic concerns and history of the field. He then presents the case for a "cultural turn" in religious ethics, arguing not only that practitioners would benefit from incorporating anthropology and cultural studies into their work but that they should extend their ambit to normative questions throughout the academy. Responding to the problems of ethnocentrism and the moral authority of outsiders in criticizing cultural practices, Miller rounds out the section by proposing constructive norms for nonchauvinistic social criticism in multicultural contexts.

Among the remaining essays are several that showcase Miller's appreciation of Augustine as a principal source of ethical insight. In a chapter scrutinizing the case for replacing disembodied patterns of moral reasoning with an "ethics of empathy," he proposes that Augustine's ethics of love can sharpen our grasp of both the possibilities and pitfalls of empathy as a moral value. Writing on friendship and evil, Miller invokes the Augustinian "theocentric imaginary" as a guide to how intimacy and alterity are balanced in friendship. And taking up the ethics and social psychology of war, he presents Augustine's writings on the morality of killing as a source for just war standards that can be applied in cross-cultural normative criticism. That Augustine's seminal reflections on time and memory do not appear in a further chapter on "the moral and political burdens of memory" is a slight disappointment, no doubt attributable to the chapter's origins as a review essay.

Other topics tellingly subjected to Miller's characteristically nuanced and sharp analysis include indignation and solidarity, responsibilities to children, and democracy and public reason. A bonus chapter collects six lengthy reviews of recent books—five on topics related to Islam—touted by Miller as exemplary in their embodiment of a cultural turn in religious ethics.

Given its endorsement of a "cultural turn" in ethics, the book would have benefited from deeper reflection on discrete meanings of "culture," "cultures," and their various cognates. In addition, the individual chapters, originating in diverse settings, are not all equally well integrated into the book's governing themes. Overall, however, Miller's book amply succeeds in its Geertzian task of presenting both a *model of* and a *model for* the field of religious ethics. A fine distillation of the thought of a leading figure in the guild, it is essential reading for serious students of ethics.

Bill Barbieri
Catholic University

REVIEW OF

Hope for Common Ground: Mediating the Personal and the Political in a Divided Church

Julie Hanlon Rubio

WASHINGTON, DC: GEORGETOWN UNIVERSITY PRESS, 2016. 264 PP. $89.95 / $29.95

Julie Hanlon Rubio wrote *Hope for Common Ground* to address divisions over ethical and political issues within the Catholic Church. Rubio writes in a spirit of hope, affirming that it is possible for Catholics to find common ground by drawing on resources within their tradition and within themselves. She proposes that "the potential for seeing and developing common ground is particularly strong if we focus on what can be done in the 'local' sphere—that is, in the space between" the personal and the political (xvii). Localized focus is recommended by the Catholic principle of subsidiarity, which means working on social problems from the bottom up through the small- and medium-sized groups that matter greatly for people's well-being, such as families, churches, and neighborhoods.

Rubio's project is vital because civic spaces have become so fraught. Although this book was published early in 2016, these words are even more apt in 2017: "In both popular and academic Catholic circles, politics has become a very uncomfortable space. . . . Catholics are more divided than at any point in their history, and in this they mirror society rather than providing an alternative to it" (xiv–xv). If Catholic Christians, claiming a common life and common Lord, are as divided as society itself, they testify poorly to their values. By contrast, if they redirect some of their energies from the personal and the political to the local, then "instead of fighting each other, Catholics can participate more, agree on more, and, consequently, build up more" (229).

Part 1 of the book draws on Church tradition and ethics texts to articulate a vision of what it means to be a faithful citizen. Divisions within the Catholic community are shaped in part by interpretations of Church teaching that discourage Catholics from thinking they should cooperate with others who think differently. In recent years, the American bishops have pushed Catholic citizens to consider some political issues, such as abortion and gay marriage, as more important than others. Rubio aims to right such imbalances by showing that Catholic teaching supports pluralism, appreciates the pragmatic side of politics, and holds a nuanced account of how people can act conscientiously in an imperfect world. She offers "a social ethic for ordinary Christians" (58), equally focused on faithfulness and effectiveness.

The payoff in part 2 of the book is excellent. Rubio enters the culture-war debates over the family, poverty, abortion, and end-of-life care; elsewhere she briefly but insightfully examines white privilege, sweatshop clothing, and police violence. In each of these cases, Rubio describes the current divide, provides background analysis that cuts through misconceptions and slanted data, and suggests ways that Catholics can find common ground and build up the common good in church and society. Here is one small example of the kind of applications she makes: "A Catholic Charities center in my city included a conversation on advance directives in the agenda for a weekly meeting of mothers in a poor neighborhood. Though the instruction was quite simple, it gave the women a chance to talk about their faith, experiences, fears, and hopes in relation to death and dying. . . . These women are now better equipped than many for the tough conversations that are surely ahead" (218).

Rubio practices what she preaches, exhibiting a conversational tone and capacious vision throughout. While focused on Catholic sources and issues, *Hope for Common Ground* is by no means narrow. Not only other Christians but also all people have to face the social issues discussed here, and it matters to all citizens how religious communities are addressing them. Therefore, this book is a great launching point for honest conversations in college courses, while scholars in the field will do well to engage with Rubio's theory of local action. The book deserves a wide readership within and outside Catholic circles.

Brian Stiltner
Sacred Heart University

REVIEW OF

The Cosmic Common Good: Religious Grounds for Ecological Ethics
Daniel P. Scheid

NEW YORK: OXFORD UNIVERSITY PRESS, 2016. 264 PP. $31.95

Published shortly after the first encyclical to focus on the environment (Pope Francis's *Laudato Si'*), Daniel Scheid's first book is a significant advance in Christian ethics and religious ecology. Scheid argues that resources in Catholic social thought and other religious traditions can move one to an appreciation of a common good that includes the "more than human world" (xiv). In particular, he "aim[s] (1) to extend Catholic social thought ecologically, and (2) to extend Catholic ecological ethics comparatively" (8).

The argument begins by broadening the notion of the common good into a "Catholic cosmic common good," which "emphasizes the centrality of God, the goodness of creation, and humanity's dignified and privileged but contextualized role within the story of creation" (32). This vision is then informed by Augustine, Aquinas, and Thomas Berry. Next, Scheid widens solidarity, a virtue that (per John Paul II) involves "commit[ting] oneself to the common good" (86), into "Earth solidarity," which attends to all ecosystems and species, particularly those most impacted by environmental damage. Solidarity cannot be exercised without respecting others' rights, and Scheid contends that these include "Earth rights" of biota, abiota, and ecosystems. Finally, in order to really "test the potential for the cosmic common good as a ground for interreligious ecological ethics" (124–25), he turns to three non-Abrahamic traditions that each support, augment, and challenge elements of his vision. A Hindu dharmic ecology is theocentric and blurs the line between humans and nonhumans, Buddhist traditions are nontheistic and highlight how all are interrelated, and American Indians (specifically the Lakota) condemn individualism and demonstrate certain advantages of a more spatial (rather than simply temporal) perspective.

The Cosmic Common Good covers an impressive range of thought in under two hundred pages of main text. While the argumentation is intricate, the logical ordering of chapters, the repetition of important points, and some vivid examples assist the reader in following along. The case for Earth rights is especially bold and well argued; Scheid considers objections to them and shows that they can be intelligibly grounded (as prima facie and proportionately weighted) in self-governance and creaturely dignity. This is a very promising development in Catholic social thought, as recent key magisterial teachings do not explicitly affirm that animals have dignity (or rights) but limit themselves to the notion that harming animals is "contrary to human dignity" (see *Laudato Si'*, §§ 92, 130, quoting *Catechism of the Catholic Church*, § 2418).

While the book is generally comprehensive, there are a few surprising lacunae. First, although Scheid himself recognizes that "a properly Catholic ecological ethics would certainly not dismiss the centrality of the Bible" (198n16), there is very little reference to it. The author briefly alludes to the Psalms' portrayal of the natural world (47, 181), but more integration of the Old and New Testaments would have been illuminating. And while *The Cosmic Common Good* makes a commendable last-minute effort to incorporate insights from *Laudato Si'*, Francis's predecessor Benedict XVI (often dubbed "the Green Pope") receives too-short shrift. Benedict's ecological views are referenced only on one page, perhaps because they are somewhat more anthropocentric than the "Earth-centered or cosmos-centered" ethic developed by Scheid (24). Regardless, the former pope's frequent calls for environmental responsibility to the poor, future generations, and animals would surely lend some healthy support to the cosmic common good. But these omissions do not detract much from the merits of this book, which should be read "not as a definitive conclusion but as an invitation to generate greater interreligious dialogue and cooperation on an issue that demands extensive and immediate action" (11). Professional academics, graduate students, and others who are somewhat versed in the sophisticated issues Scheid raises would do well to take up his invitation.

John J. Fitzgerald
St. John's University (New York)

■

REVIEW OF

Ethics as a Work of Charity: Thomas Aquinas and Pagan Virtue

David Decosimo

STANFORD, CA: STANFORD UNIVERSITY PRESS, 2014. 376 PP. $65.00 / $29.95

If "*debeo distinguere*" represents the programmatic scholarly agenda for "prophetic Thomism," over against the more mystical narrative "*exitus et reditus*" itinerary of Dionysian Augustinianism, David Decosmio should be considered a virtuous practitioner of this Thomistic craft in the domain of political ethics. To put it more accurately, Decosimo provides a complex, lucid account of his reading of Thomas as one who tutors Christians and especially Christian ethicists through "fraternal correction" in what it means to provide a generous, charitable account of "pagan virtue" via the making of distinctions. For Decosimo the word "pagan" refers to non-Christian "outsiders"—that is, "all those without charity" (11). While that may seem to be a noncharitable way to put it, Decosimo means it to bespeak that form of charity that allows non-Christians to be and to speak as non-Christians, absent (or refusing) those virtues that Thomas calls "theological"—those habits infused supernaturally by God through the "redemptive grace" that orders and unites humans "in loving friendship with the God revealed in Jesus Christ" (11). Thomas's representative pagan is, of course, Aristotle. Decosimo insists that a correct reading of Thomas opposes both "hyper-Augustinian Thomism" (on which account non-Christians are incapable of true virtue) as well as a "public reason Thomism" (which avoids theological claims). At the same time, Decosimo claims that Thomas remains fully Augustinian in his theological account of charity and yet "unites and transforms Aristotle and Augustine alike to teach charity toward outsiders and their virtues" (1). To put it in terms of the formula Decosimo reiterates throughout the book, Aquinas "strives to be Aristotelian by being Augustinian and vice versa" (41, 70, 181 253, etc.). In so doing, he offers resources for a prophetic Thomism that more charitably navigates the church's relations to secular politics by welcoming the contributions of pagan virtue to its own Christian virtue.

If "charity's scholarly work is the multiplication of distinctions" (8) then Decosimo's book is a model of charity. Decosimo works as an analytic philosopher at a high level of erudition to elucidate the linguistic and syllogistic puzzles in Thomas's accounts of virtue in a close reading of a range of works to show that, for Thomas, natural human virtue oriented toward the shared human and political good (the highest good attainable without charity) is true virtue in which Christians and non-Christians, Augustinians and Aristotelians, may fully share and participate together. Indeed, the theological virtues must be devoted to the charitable interpretation of all contributions dialectically considered and ordered to the highest human good. Only by adhering to such a vision of virtue that welcomes pagan virtue will Christians practice the ethics of charity, and prophetic Thomism provides a model for how the church may engage difference in a way that honors others while being faithful to its own vision of the gift of grace.

I hope it will not be taken as uncharitable or (ugh!) "hyper-Augustinian" to suggest that Decosimo's account of prophetic Thomism is more attuned to Aristotelian logic and the dialectic of definitional distinctions than it is to Augustine's more Platonic account of pagan virtue as a Dionysian erotic dialectic in which the "logos is wild." But I am in full agreement with Decosimo's claim that ethics as a work of charity ought to be open to both (and "all") in providing resources to Christian and non-Christian ethicists alike for engaging contemporary political challenges concerning otherness and difference in the service of justice.

Travis Kroeker
McMaster University

■

REVIEW OF

Just Sustainability: Technology, Ecology, and Resource Extraction
Edited by Christiana Z. Peppard and Andrea Vicini
MARYKNOLL, NY: ORBIS, 2015. 304 PP. $42.00

Just Sustainability offers a detailed journey through various Catholic contextual understandings of what ecological sustainability means today in light of the demands of justice. In the first section of the book, called "Locations" (11–53), the contributors put concepts of sustainability into dialog with concerns of socioeconomic, gender, and racial justice from contexts as diverse as Europe, East Asia, India, Africa, and North America. The various locations share common themes, such as the importance of deep meanings of the term "sustainability," the priority of education and advocacy, the resource and energy challenges behind structures of injustice, and the primary role of economics. Yet distinctive emphases emerge from the diverse contexts as well. Examples include the need for humility instead of the ironic arrogance of nuclear energy in Japan, the widespread challenges of corruption in Africa and Mexico, and the problem of the agriculture lobby in the United States.

The second section, "Structures" (57–156), steps back from specific cultural contexts and explores various systemic approaches to the challenge of just sustainability. Using Catholic social teachings, the authors again often speak from diverse global contexts, but with reference specifically to economic and societal systems such as politics, measurements of well-being, urban planning, food and agriculture, and health care. In this section the authors speak of which structures have worked and which have failed to build just and sustainable societies. For example, in the Philippines, more accountability through transparency and regular reporting helped impact energy efficiency. In Kenya and Chad, the authors highlight the need for reliable social systems of access, communication, collaboration, and government in order to counter corruption and build sustainable programs to address HIV, hunger, employment, and food sovereignty. Several authors also describe the positive impact of more democratic and egalitarian participatory structures that involve the people most affected by ecological decisions and policies.

The last section, "Theological Stances and Sustainable Relations" (159–268), delves more deeply into Catholic theological resources to provide both a foundation as well as specific practices of just sustainability. The authors wrestle with theocentric, biocentric, and anthropocentric concepts of humanity and the *imago Dei*, the Eucharist as a potentially powerful way to connect ideas of inequity, the promise of ecofeminist theologies in elevating the wisdom of local peoples to build just sustainability practices, and virtue ethics and Catholic social teachings to foster ecological conversion and build solidarity, hope, and efficacy.

The book sets itself a challenging task, to provide a coherent picture of Catholic approaches to building just sustainability while presenting a spectrum of not only diverse cultural and geographical contexts but also diverse theologies. In the end, the book reveals the ways in which Catholic laity and leaders are creatively responding to the challenge of just sustainability across much of the globe by using a combination of ecclesial, theological, and social scientific resources. The book would have benefited from a concluding essay to tie together some of the salient themes from the numerous, somewhat disparate essays, and a chapter from South America would have strengthened the global orientation of the collection. Nonetheless, the reader is left with a more holistic understanding of the difficult task of just sustainability as well as the wealth of work toward this goal from many parts of the Earth.

Tallessyn Zawn Grenfell-Lee
Boston University School of Theology

■

REVIEW OF

Christianity, Democracy, and the Shadow of Constantine

Edited by George E. Demacopoulos and Aristotle Papanikolaou

NEW YORK: FORDHAM UNIVERSITY PRESS, 2017. 304 PP. $125.00 / $35.00

Since the collapse of Communism in Eastern Europe, one of the new rapprochements that has emerged is between the worlds of Eastern Orthodoxy and that of Protestants and Catholics. In this set of constructive essays, contributors from each of these veins of Christianity explore the relationship between Christianity and democracy from their vantage point. Drawing together political theologians, ethicists, and historical theologians, the volume creates an encounter between "East" and "West" that addresses some critical questions facing the whole of Christianity.

The first section of essays details the post-Communist situation for Orthodox churches and how they wrestle with traditions of human rights. These essays set the scene broadly for the second set of essays, which bring together Protestant and Catholic political thought together with their Orthodox counterparts. In this section, essays from Luke Bretherton on consociational democracy, Eric Gregory on Augustine and the Good Samaritan, and Nathaniel Wood on Russian visions of theosis in a liberal world make for compelling and informative contributions. The third section—a historical set of essays—explores the actual influence of Constantine's theopolitical vision in the East and West. Contributions from luminaries such as Timothy D. Barnes and J. Bryan Hehir elucidate some of the effects of a theopolitical synthesis in various historical epochs. Barnes's essay on what did and did not occur in Constantinople is of particular note here. The final section, a single essay by Stanley Hauerwas, "How (Not) to Be a Political Theologian," is a vintage essay reflecting on legacies of "Constantinian" thinking in American Christianity.

The most prominent strengths of the volume are twofold. First, it brings into focus one of the critical challenges facing Christianity globally: political representation. Presently, the globe is engulfed in any number of challenges to popular sovereignty, whether conceived of in terms of revolution or tyranny. As such, democracy—while imperfect and theologically problematic in many respects—is the de facto form of governance standing between these extremes. Christian traditions of all persuasions have reasons to be suspicious of even the best of these alternatives, making this set of essays all the more pressing. Second, it contributes in a practical way to the ecumenical labors taking place in synods and councils across the world. While the World Council of Churches has undertaken some of the common moral issues affecting various Protestant

communions, cooperation among Orthodox, Protestant, and Catholic communions remains ad hoc. Volumes such as this contribute to the practical work
of more highly publicized doctrinal discussions.

As with most edited volumes, the vast theme of the book tends to be cum-
bersome; linking together Protestant, Catholic, and Orthodox sources around
democracy and liberalism creates a wide-ranging but at times unfocused conversation. The quality of the essays themselves is quite uniformly good—a
rarity among edited volumes!—but such a wide range of topics and contributors makes for a set of essays that is more indicative of future discussions than
definitive. In short, the volume illuminates and provocatively indicates future
directions without being a definitive statement on democracy and Christianity,
opening new doors for future work.

Myles Werntz
Logsdon Seminary,
Hardin-Simmons University

REVIEW OF

The Place of Imagination: Wendell Berry and the Poetics of Community, Affection, and Identity

Joseph R. Wiebe

WACO, TX: BAYLOR UNIVERSITY PRESS, 2017. 272 PP. $49.95

The Place of Imagination is an artful narration of Wendell Berry's poetics focused
distinctively on his works of fiction. Moralists concerned about issues of land
use or racialization could commend or criticize "what" they assume Berry's
stories (re)present—nostalgia or some abstract, principial program. But Joseph
Wiebe ventures a thesis about "how" Berry's imaginary Port William community discloses the nature of good, real-world community. Understanding
how Berry's poetics reflect his real-world moral imagination clarifies *what* we
may learn from his fiction. So, in part 1, Wiebe traces Berry's journey of local
adaptation, through which he developed a moral imagination and discovered
the agonizing details of his entanglement in his place's history and his neighbors' problems.

Berry's poetics starts with imagination opening itself to the genius of a place
and the other (friend and foe alike) as a living soul. Such imagination engages
our sympathy to see others as complex subjects without controlling their stories, objectifying them to realize some idealist worldview. In sympathy, we

perceive the other as a neighbor and develop affection for them in their difference. This affection is no mere sentiment but a Humean moral sentiment that motivates behavior and, when properly nurtured, makes moral reasoning subservient to itself. Affection "disrupts habits of pity" that reduce others to mental objects and inspires a kenotic movement toward concrete neighbors (37). Problems felt at the societal level are habituated in local communities. While idealist solutions may satisfy the white, Western mind's impulse for complete knowledge, their resources prove incompetent before these problems as such. We must affectionately open ourselves to others who disrupt our mental worlds and draw us into real-world habits that change underlying communal dynamics. Relinquishing control of our storied identities (or idealist worldviews) to the others in our place, we might truly locate ourselves in those problems—and start undoing them.

In part 2, Wiebe offers glimpses of "what" Berry's poetics teach us about a placed life together through select members of a quaint Kentucky farming community: Jack Beechum, Jayber Crow, and Hannah Coulter. His imaginative attentiveness to each character exemplifies the art of discovering the virtues of place-based identity. The way through Port William offers no shortcuts. Its imaginary community does not merely stand in for some universal idea of community. Neither potential solution nor nostalgic phantasm, Port William is the setting for parables that reveal something true about good community. "If there is something to imitate, it is the underlying processes that generate the particulars of Berry's narratives rather than the characters that furnish them" (152). In Port William, one can practice relinquishing control and patiently "imagining" the contours of a place; in the real world, one can deploy that imagination to develop fidelity to their place.

Wiebe aptly follows Berry's method, yielding control over Berry's biography and work by taking a third-person narrator's perspective. He focuses on what Berry's life and writing reveal parabolically to the patient reader. The book beckons readers to hold Berry and his stories as a mirror—to engage in introspection and self-interrogation—that we might learn something about sympathy and affection needed for engaging our places non-imperialistically. Wiebe's adept style may appear to some as a flaw; the narrator gives no academic cues (e.g., "I will argue") for rapidly consuming principial content. There are only Berry's life and work and the reader, hopefully changed. *The Place of Imagination* will be of greatest interest to those who already have some affection for that "artful crank from Kentucky" (10). Beyond the agrarian crowd and its auditors, this book holds appeal for a range of explorations, from the fecundity of poetics in ethics to the disruptiveness of Christian imagination vis-à-vis whiteness.

Jacob Alan Cook
Friends University

■

REVIEW OF

Methodist Morals: Social Principles in the Public Church's Witness

Darryl W. Stephens

KNOXVILLE: UNIVERSITY OF TENNESSEE PRESS, 2016. 320 PP. $48.00

Darryl W. Stephens's *Methodist Morals* presents a historical, theological, and ethical analysis of a particular form of social witness in the United Methodist Church (UMC): the Social Principles. Stephens mainly argues that the Social Principles are not only an institutionalized "document" on contemporary social issues but also an "ongoing moral discourse" within a set of democratic, legislative, and participatory practices of the UMC as a "moral community" (6–8). This ongoing moral discourse illustrates the public church as an authentic social witness in the world and the process of moral formation of its members.

Stephens's case study of the public church proceeds in three parts. The first part (chapters 1–3) explores the historical development of the Social Principles and examines the distinctive nature and function of it. From its inception, the Social Principles were to function as "middle axioms," a level of ethical deliberation placed between "universal principles and specific policy recommendations" (22). They were intended to promote "dialogue" among different opinions and "conscientious discernment" on social issues (22). The Social Principles' commitment to the dialogue and discernment is further bolstered by representative democratic and legislative procedures in its quadrennial revision at the General Conference.

The second part (chapters 4–7) examines the texts and contents of the Social Principles. Through a comparison of the Social Principles to secular human rights documents, Stephens reveals a "deep-seated commitment to human rights" with a theological emphasis on "the universality of God's grace" in the texts of Social Principles (72). On the other hand, Stephens points out a lack of engagement with the broader Methodist social teaching tradition and the undeveloped theological foundations and languages for the commitments in the Social Principles (92–94). Specifically, Stephens calls for developing a "theology of marriage," which has been neglected in the history of Methodist teachings on marriage (140). In addition, Stephens proposes the need of theological guidance for "ecclesial disobedience" as an alternative paradigm for clergy ethics in response to the issue of homosexuality (171–73).

In the final part (chapter 8 and the conclusion), Stephens sketches "the public church ecclesiology implied by the Social Principles" (178). He points out the sectarian tendency in the ecclesiologies of Paul Ramsey and Stanley

Hauerwas and argues for a different form of public engagement: the public church is "sometimes distinct from but always part of and partner with the world" (194). In other words, the public church should embrace "the challenges of worldliness," and the Social Principles illustrates "the messiness of genuine moral engagement in life here and now" (197–99).

Stephens presents a rich and well-balanced analysis of the UMC Social Principles as a distinctive form of social witness in the public church. Eschewing a biased analysis praising his own denomination's social teaching, Stephens critically points out "the messiness of actual moral meaning-making" in the UMC (3). Chapter 5 highlights his critical evaluation of the Social Principles: the sin of "US-centrism" and the marginalization of the European, African, and Asian UMC bodies (107–9). However, Stephens's critical evaluation could be developed further. As he points out that the US-centrism is about a "perceived hegemony and uniformity of a white, US, middle-class elite," he could also critically address the dominance of a certain racial/ethnic group's perspective within the US context. Some readers might wonder why Stephens does not substantially cover the issue of racism and white privilege that lies at the heart of the US-centrism critiqued in this book.

Nevertheless, *Methodist Morals* has added rich insight into the public church's social witness and its members' moral formation. This book would be a great resource for theological educators in their courses on Christian ethics, public theology, and Methodism.

Wonchul Shin
Emory University

REVIEW OF

The Seductiveness of Virtue: Abraham Joshua Heschel and John Paul II on Morality and Personal Fulfillment

John J. Fitzgerald

NEW YORK: BLOOMSBURY T&T CLARK, 2017. 240 PP. $114

The Seductiveness of Virtue offers a close study of the twentieth-century Polish-American rabbi Abraham Joshua Heschel, and the first Polish pope, St. John Paul II, on the relationship between being good and being happy. Overall the book advances the conversation on the meaning and continued relevance of virtue in contemporary ethics, though its eagerness to build bridges across competing religious and philosophical traditions opens the argument to both methodological and substantive criticisms.

Fitzgerald divides the book into an introduction and four chapters. Chapter 1, "The Meaning of Our Question," establishes the definitions of concepts that Fitzgerald addresses throughout the rest his argument, including "happiness," "meaning," "freedom," "personal fulfillment," "good and evil," and "doing." Fitzgerald locates each term within the theologies of Heschel and John Paul II and provides his own definitions. Chapter 2, "Heschel and the 'Joys of Mitsvah,'" enters more deeply into Heschel's theology, arguing that, despite some ambiguity about whether morality will *always* lead to personal fulfillment, Heschel establishes a firm theological and practical connection between following the law (mitzvah) and being happy. Chapter 3, "John Paul II and the Good We Must Do to Have Eternal Life," engages in a similar analysis of John Paul's thought (including his writings before becoming pope) and, despite using different theological categories (chief among them "Christ"), arrives at a similar conclusion: there is a necessary connection between being good and being happy. Chapter 4, which also functions as a conclusion, places the comparison between Heschel and John Paul into a wider comparative context, examining how their respective conclusions on morality and the good relate to insights from other contemporary perspectives, including the Dalai Lama, Peter Singer, and present-day "positive psychology." Fitzgerald concludes by offering five reasons why it is important to continue, in his words, an "interworldview" and "interdisciplinary" dialogue on how virtue relates to happiness.

The book is richly sourced—containing 199 footnotes, bibliography, and detailed index—and serves as a good addition to the libraries of those working on John Paul II, Abraham Heschel, virtue theory, or comparative ethics more broadly. Yet its breadth on the comparative front also highlights its vulnerabilities, particularly on the question of what defines the relationship between virtue and happiness from a normative perspective. While providing lucid descriptive accounts of different conceptions of God and the good, for example, Fitzgerald acknowledges near the book's conclusion, "whether one finds [any] author persuasive will depend in large part on one's prior conclusions about the existence and nature of God and the afterlife" (184) and notes that this topic "cannot be resolved or even explored here" (185). However, these "prior conclusions" themselves are ultimately most meaningful for answering the book's central question.

This reticence to engage in meta-ethical questions also leads the text to a problematic epistemological and ethical equalizing of each perspective, one that allows Fitzgerald to claim, for example, "while there is much common ground between Heschel, John Paul II, and [Peter] Singer on the relationship between morality and fulfillment, there are also key differences" (174). Here Fitzgerald understates the contrast: one of the "key" differences between Singer's utilitarian materialism and John Paul II's gospel of life is that Singer's position could serve as a paradigmatic representation of the "culture of death" that John Paul spent his papacy resisting. Thus, while providing an excellent analysis of each thinker individually, the book's argument would benefit from establishing a firmer and more transparent standard for evaluating ethical claims across traditions.

Matthew R. Petrusek
Loyola Marymount University

∎

REVIEW OF

Transformed Lives: Making Sense of Atonement Today
Cynthia S. W. Crysdale
NEW YORK: SEABURY BOOKS, 2016. 192 PP. $16.00

Cynthia Crysdale aims to show how atonement can have meaning for modern and postmodern Christians who reject the idea that God wills Jesus's violent death. She starts with stories of people who were estranged from God but have been given grace to love God anew. Their subsequent lives are not perfect and involve multiple deaths of the old self and resurrections into the new. Yet there is a reconciliation not present beforehand: not a change in God, who has always loved us, but a change in us. Crysdale seeks to navigate between two undesirable positions: a penal substitutionary doctrine of the atonement, which she thinks posits a violent God, or a rejection of the idea of atonement altogether. She sees atonement as not only moral influence showing an example but a relationship that involves our whole being.

Crysdale then presents a historical overview to show that this understanding of atonement is a plausible interpretation of scripture and tradition. Biblical sacrifices were not intended to propitiate an angry deity but to expiate human sin. New Testament writers who saw Jesus's death on the cross in continuity with these sacrifices were not implying that God was punishing Jesus. Jesus's statements about giving his life as a ransom prophesied the subversion of patron–client power relations rather than predicting a transaction whereby Jesus would pay for sin. Subsequent writers who saw Jesus as gaining victory over the devil saw God and Jesus as united against the powers and Jesus as attaining justice by love. Even Anselm, sometimes blamed for the penal substitutionary view, intended to avoid the idea of the crucifixion as God's punishment of Jesus. In the honor code of the time, either satisfaction *or* punishment was required. Therefore, Jesus's act of making satisfaction is precisely *not* punishment. Crysdale sees subsequent conflations of satisfaction and punishment as distorting Anselm's original intent and implying that God requires violent punishment of sin.

Crysdale then takes readers on a tour of changes in scientific, historical, and epistemological consciousness in the modern era to ask how theology might be done today. Drawing on Bernard Lonergan, she describes multiple dimensions of conversion that are all instances of grace when they occur. She then interprets the incarnation as indicating God's offer of friendship with humanity and Jesus's death and resurrection as indicating the transformation of power and oppression. Believing that an abstract atonement over the heads of human beings does not exist, she concludes with further stories of lives transformed by an encounter with God, including Martin Luther King Jr. and Dorothy Day.

This book is suitable for educated lay adults, advanced undergraduates, or introductory seminary courses. Protestant audiences may find it typically Catholic, even though Crysdale is an Anglican, because it emphasizes changed lives rather than God's act of justification prior to any change in us. Theologically, it does not deal with every possible objection to its thesis. Those concerned with cultures of impunity, where malevolent lawlessness gets its way, may think that rejecting any sense of punishment of sin in the crucifixion throws the baby out with the bathwater. Recently, Fleming Rutledge (in *The Crucifixion*), drawing on Karl Barth, has made a point of retaining punishment as one meaning of the atonement even while emphasizing that God's wrath is always in the service of God's love. *Transformed Lives* does not have the last word on the atonement and would not claim to, since Crysdale wants to invite readers to do theology befitting their changing context. However, readers at many levels will benefit from its accessible treatment of its topic and invitation to reflection that befits a loving, reconciling, evil-opposing God.

Virginia W. Landgraf
American Theological Library Association

■

REVIEW OF

Not by Nature but by Grace: Forming Families through Adoption

Gilbert C. Meilaender

NOTRE DAME, IN: UNIVERSITY OF NOTRE DAME PRESS, 2016. 136 PP. $25.00

I was adopted as an infant through a Catholic Charities office in 1961, and just three years ago, thanks to an online DNA analysis service, I met both of my biological parents, with whom I have an ongoing, loving relationship. So my keen interest in this book and its topic is more than just theological curiosity. It includes personal and emotional dimensions, as I'm sure it will for many readers.

This book is an attempt to understand modern adoptive practices from a primarily Christian/Catholic perspective, with helpful allusions to the beliefs and practices of the other Abrahamic faiths. Overall, I believe the book succeeds in presenting a solid theological foundation for adoption in general and, more specifically, for its current mainstream manifestation in the developed world. The author doesn't shy away from the various controversies related to adoption—like assisted reproduction, LGBTQ adoption, embryo adoption—and he takes on other authors who make claims about adoption that he believes distract or obscure the central purpose of adoption, which is to provide a child a "needed place of belonging" within the network of loving relationships that is the ideal of the family (38).

My reservations about the book are two. The first has to do with the inconsistent tone of the book, which tends to swing, abruptly at times, from a theological and analytical tone to one that feels more popular and homiletic—even to the point of being maudlin. As stated earlier, I have high regard for most of the analytical sections and find the overarching thesis convincing. Generally, in these sections, the method begins with the lived experience of adoptees and their parents and works through scripture, tradition, and critical reflection to arrive at a reasonable conclusion. However, occasionally the book drifts into uncritical and merely emotive territory, and this is especially the case in the sections called "interludes," where the author presents letters to adoptees from their parents reprinted from the *Christian Century* magazine. These seem out of place and even distracting. Of even greater concern is the concluding chapter, where the author should be summarizing and highlighting the strengths of his thesis. Instead he chose to draw homiletic lessons from Anne of Green Gables (110).

My second reservation is not so much a critique of this book but of the state of contemporary Catholic sexual ethics, which forms a backdrop for the entire book. The book accurately reflects a mainstream position in Catholic sexual ethics, which abandoned a narrow focus on procreation decades ago in favor of one highlighting the unitive and relational aspects of human intimacy. This move away from a strictly deontological framework stressing the duty to procreate and toward a teleological ethic stressing the need to model human relationships after divine ones has been celebrated for good reasons, but it has not come without costs. Like all teleological ideals, this sexual ethic is attractive to purveyors of high philosophy but tends to be thoroughly abstract and almost entirely incapable of offering concrete, practical guidance. Because it is so abstract, its application to specific moral issues can seem arbitrary and at the whim of the author. Such is the case in this book, for instance, when this teleological ideal is wielded to shed doubt on LGBTQ adoption. It is particularly telling that the author neglects to consult lived experience in this section, ignoring the mountains of evidence readily available that LGBTQ families can be just as loving and nurturing as those of traditional families. Ultimately, a second Renaissance would benefit Catholic sexual ethics—one that balances deontological and teleological elements by introducing practical, consequential, and proportional methods.

Thomas O'Brien
DePaul University

■

REVIEW OF

On Secular Governance: Lutheran Perspectives on Contemporary Legal Issues

Edited by Ronald W. Duty and Marie A. Failinger

GRAND RAPIDS, MI: EERDMANS, 2016. 382 PP. $45.00

In editing this collection of essays, Ronald Duty and Marie Failinger describe their goal as seeking "to bring more Lutheran voices to the pressing legal issues" in local and global contexts (1). They point out that in discussions between the fields of religion and law to date, "Jewish, Muslim, Catholic, and Reformed perspectives have largely dominated" (1). In bringing Lutheran perspectives to questions of law and religion, this collection begins an important task of retrieving a theological perspective on law that was integral for the formation of modern legal thought but has been largely absent from contemporary discussions of law and religion.

The strength of this collection of essays lies in the breadth of contemporary legal questions addressed and in the diversity of perspectives offered. Since, as Duty and Failinger point out, recent Lutheran scholarship has been relatively silent on questions of law and religion, there is a broad field of issues to explore. This collection avoids too narrowly focusing on any one "hot-button" issue of law and religion, such as questions of religious liberty or relationship between church and state, although these questions are addressed. Rather, it benefits from a truly expansive view of contemporary legal issues and includes essays on issues as diverse as immigration reform, family law, fiduciary duties, military chaplaincy, and water rights in the American Southwest. The collection also shows geographical breadth, and looks beyond the contemporary American and European legal arena to consider how theology could affect law in Nigeria and Rwanda. The volume also benefits from a wide range of theoretical approaches, including contributions from both legal scholars and theologians. In the dialectic that results as theologians consider law and legal scholars consider theology, we see a performative example of the Lutheran concept of two kingdoms, both coexisting under God's domain.

The collection would have benefited from a broader use of theological sources to accompany this admirably broad approach to legal issues. Many, although not all, of the essays, draw only on Martin Luther's understanding of Christian engagement with legal authority. This focus on Luther's somewhat limited legal corpus can result in a slightly repetitive theological approach among the essays. However, this narrow focus on Luther indicates a potential next stage for further development of Lutheran engagement with contemporary legal issues. In the closing essay in the book, "How Should Modern Lutherans Try to Shape Secular Law?," Robert Benne references John Witte's work in tracing how Philipp Melanchthon and the Lutheran jurists developed Luther's original theory of law to "build bridges between the two kingdoms" (332). While this book provides a good starting point for bringing Lutheran perspectives to bear on contemporary legal issues, it also indicates the need for future research to excavate the perspectives of Melanchthon and jurists such as Johannes Eisermann and Johann Oldendorp, along with more modern Lutheran scholars of law and religion, such as Helmut Thielicke, who considered the legacy of Lutheran legal theory in the wake of post-Nazi Germany. Both Lutheran theological approaches to law and legal approaches to religion will undoubtedly be enriched if the editors' project continues, resulting in continued excavation of later Lutheran interpretation and reception of theories of law, which will bring Lutheran theology ever closer to the challenges of contemporary legal issues in the modern nation-state.

Elisabeth Rain Kincaid
University of Notre Dame

REVIEW OF

Just Revolution: A Christian Ethic of Political Resistance and Social Transformation

Anna Floerke Scheid

LANHAM, MD: LEXINGTON BOOKS, 2015. 208 PP. $84.00

Anna Floerke Scheid argues that the Christian just war and just peacemaking ethical traditions lack a comprehensive ethic for revolutionary nonviolent activity and warfare. She proposes to fill this lacuna through a theological exploration of what constitutes a just revolution. While Scheid maintains a consistent preference for nonviolent resistance against tyranny, she remains open to the possibility of revolutionary warfare.

The author articulates four stages of a just revolution. The first stage is *jus ante*, nonviolent resistance against a tyrannical government. Here the opposition develops a democratic and revolutionary vision of society that respects human rights, models that vision within its organizations, and resists through nonviolent acts. Second is *jus ad*, the stage where a tyrannical government eliminates all avenues for negotiation and represses peaceful resistance. This forces the revolutionary opposition to consider armed resistance as a last resort. Here Scheid grapples with two limitations of traditional just war theory. The first reserves the authority to start a war with governments. She argues that the legitimacy for a just revolution comes from a revolutionary organization's ability to envision and model a just society. Because a tyrannical government's authority is illegitimate, a revolutionary movement's just vision and practices gain for it a de facto legitimate authority. This legitimacy is reinforced by a revolutionary movement's ultimate intention to effect reconciliation with their oppressors postwar. The second limitation is the reasonable hope of success. Scheid analyzes the history of this criterion and demonstrates how it supports defensive wars despite the uncertainty of success. Oppressed persons, as the subjects of their own hope of liberation, ought to decide what constitutes the probability for success in fighting tyranny. Throughout this stage, revolutionary warfare must be practiced in tandem with continuing nonviolent resistance.

The third stage is *jus in*, the justice practiced during armed revolutionary resistance. Fighting is deemed necessary to force a tyrannical government to negotiations. Meanwhile, revolutionary military units would work to minimize violence and loss of life. The last stage is *jus post*, the reconciliation needed to prevent revolutionary warfare from spiraling into revenge. Here the exercise of restorative justice—where responsibility for past injustices is assumed by all sides and a just resolution developed for social reconciliation and the development of a new, democratic society that respects human rights—is all important. Throughout the book, Scheid uses the African National Congress's revolutionary struggle against the South African apartheid government as a successful example of her theory in practice.

Scheid's well-argued proposal deserves careful consideration by ethicists. Students will profit from her excellent summary of just war theory, where she brilliantly recovers some of its forgotten features. On the other hand, her concluding chapter considering the Arab Spring's potential for just revolution would have been stronger if she extended beyond a comparison to South Africa to incorporate similar features found in other successful revolutions. The 1986 Philippine People Power Revolution, the 1989 collapse of Eastern European Communist regimes, and the 1974 Carnation Revolution in Portugal come to mind. Moreover, important for South Africa's success was the durability of the political institutions the British left behind. These institutions provided the framework that handled the transition of power from the pro-apartheid National Party to the post-apartheid African National Congress government. This feature could have been brought to light, as many recognize this structure as contributive to the peaceful transition of power in other countries that won independence through revolution, from the United States in the eighteenth century to India and the Caribbean in the twentieth.

Ramon Luzarraga
Benedictine University at Mesa

REVIEW OF

Ethics and the Elderly: The Challenge of Long-Term Care
Sarah M. Moses
MARYKNOLL, NY: ORBIS, 2015. 206 PP. $38.00

Loving Later Life: An Ethics of Aging
Frits de Lange
GRAND RAPIDS, MI: EERDMANS, 2015. 169 PP. $19.00

Today many women and men live beyond the so-called third age of life and enter their eighties, the "fourth age," during which the toll of time and the growing incidence of life-limiting conditions wear down even the best-preserved of the human species. Debilitating disease and normal ebbing of human function become more concentrated in this demographic bubble. As people enter their eighties, their world tends to narrow both physically and mentally, creating a need for increasing care. Often the elderly are rendered passive and dependent, forced to cede both autonomy and dignity. They become objects with little voice, requiring greater care and increasing cash. Likewise, as the baby boom generation enters this group, those living in the fourth age make up an increasing percentage of the population. Additionally, modern models of care for the elderly, often based on efficiency and cost-effectiveness, tend to erode their human dignity. Together these factors demonstrate a growing moral problem.

What to do? These two books provide valuable road maps for how to proceed. They detail the reality and moral urgency of the situation. Both offer principles from philosophical and religious traditions that outline a good moral model: one of care, compassion, dignity, and community. They draw insights from Augustine and Thomas Aquinas, Karl Barth, and Dietrich Bonhoeffer, among others. Both reference the Western biblical tradition, which honors the elderly even in the face of their limitations.

Although the authors offer wise and thoughtful suggestions to address this growing moral crisis, they approach the serious moral issue very differently. Sarah Moses outlines a compelling case for a new interventional model for elderly living. While her book plays some muted chords that hint at "dissertation," the melody it conveys is strikingly forte and well worth the read.

She presents two concrete examples of what good interaction with the elderly might look like. One draws from the international intentional outreach and residential community (the Community of Sant'Egidio), the other is a brick-and-mortar model (the Green House Project). Using both biblical paradigms and church teaching over the centuries, Moses makes the case for treating all persons with dignity and promoting their involvement in decision making as much as possible. The scriptural message she highlights—both our duty to the elderly and the "disappointment and depression" (105) of growing old—is particularly compelling.

In her examples of good long-term care, community development is important. In the Sant'Egidio model, volunteers share a common life "through gathering for prayer and various outreach services to the poor" (39). There is motivation to support elderly in their own homes, but the project promotes small, family-like resident facilities when this is not possible. The physical place is less emphasized than the relationship among various age and economic groups.

The Green House Project is based in a new vision of homes for the challenged elderly. Results of the project show that not only did staff remain in their jobs longer (nursing home employment turnover is extensive) but visitation by family members increased. Even such a simple thing as a different physical model for the actual building—replacing long halls and routinization with a more home-like environment—has positive results.

Moses calls on leadership in church and community to educate, to designate funds for elder care, and to look beyond the caring and the construction of good facilities. She notes how important it is to work politically to change attitudes and actions.

She sees care for all dependent people as a responsibility of both the church community and society in general. This includes fostering awareness, encouraging ongoing participation of the elderly in life—including church life—and allocating public resources. Bottom line: she calls for smaller institutions, meaningful opportunities for the aging, and a cultivation of cross-generational friendships. Her book is a valuable contribution to the ongoing dialogue on elder care. Her models are concrete and compelling. Nevertheless, Moses spends little time discussing those who have lost cognitive function.

Frits De Lange's book does. He, too, situates the discussion within the rich philosophical and moral tradition of the past. Nonacademic readers might wish to skip this portion of the book. While it supports the author's argument abundantly and well, it might seem a parsley sprig to the rich main course. The meat comes in the next chapters, when the author outlines an ethics of love as the basis for moral choices for the elderly. Unlike Moses, he spends little time on institutional solutions. Rather, his focus is on the personal.

Aging is not easy, he notes. He argues that those of us not in the fourth age perceive those who are with fear, disgust, and hatred. Even death is viewed more favorably than living into an appalling dotage. Wrinkles embrace the body, serious illnesses and dementia take away its vigor and function. Old bodies—how they look, how they function—repel us because they forebode the ugliness we will become.

In his final compelling section, de Lange draws on the biblical demand to love neighbor as self. Self-love, particularly love of our own aging bodies, our own diminishment, must come first. We must not eschew our future selves. Rather, we must engage in what the author calls "terror management" (74). This self-love is rooted and thrives in the metanoic experience that God loves each of us personally. It flowers into our love of the aging neighbor.

In his call for embrace of the elderly, de Lange references the Van Gogh painting of the Good Samaritan. Rather than lowering ourselves to what might be viewed as a lesser human, the Samaritan lifts the body of the victim to a place of parity, placing him tenderly on his own beast. In the final portion of the book the author soars above the dusty philosophical prose of the earlier chapters to a persuasive poetry. He speaks eloquently of those who are totally dependent. "One's life story, however, does not end at the threshold of the nursing home. . . . Identity is a dynamic matter of 'continuation' but also of 'becoming'" (135).

This said, the book is not a Pollyanna treatise on the loveliness of old age. The final chapter paints a realistic picture of old age: pain, suffering, and loss of function are acutely real. Nevertheless, we are called to lament *with* and *for* those who live in that reality. As I finished the book, I found I was crying. His last paragraph describes old people cut off from others, unable to express their complaint. De Lange calls us to "sit down with them and share their cry" (138).

These books are well researched and well written. They offer compelling examples and arguments as well as extensive bibliography and footnotes. Students, particularly those in preparation for helping professions, could read them with profit. Both should be required reading for those who influence policies and funding for institutions (Moses's book especially) and those who encounter aging in themselves, their family members, or in the agora (de Lange)—that is, all of us.

Dolores L. Christie
Catholic Theological Center of America,
John Carroll University (retired)

The Journal of **Jewish Ethics**

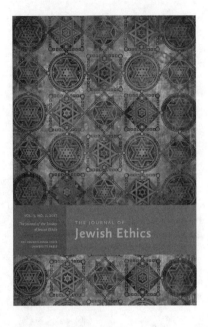

JONATHAN K. CRANE AND
EMILY FILLER, EDITORS

The Journal of Jewish Ethics publishes
outstanding scholarship in Jewish
ethics, broadly conceived. It serves
as a location for the exchange of
ideas among those interested in
understanding, articulating, and
promoting descriptive and normative
Jewish ethics. It aspires to advance
dialogue between Jewish ethicists
and ethicists working out of other
religious and secular traditions.
The journal welcomes articles that
engage contemporary moral and
ethical issues using philosophical
and theological methods, historical
and textual criticism, and other
approaches.

Individuals (2018 prices)
1 Year (2 issues): $49 (print or online)
1 Year (2 issues): $70 (print and online)

Libraries/Institutions (2018 prices)
1 Year (2 issues): $160 (print or online)
1 Year (2 issues): $233 (print and online)

ISSN 2334-1777 | E-ISSN 2334-1785
Biannual | Available in print or online

Submissions to: www.editorialmanager.com/jje

PENN STATE UNIVERSITY PRESS

www.psupress.org
journals@psu.edu

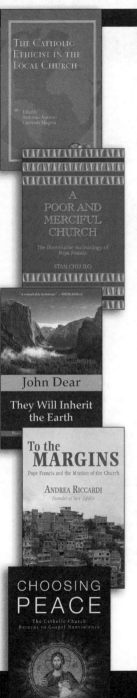

The Catholic Ethicist in the Local Church

Catholic Theological Ethics in the World Church Series

ANTONIO AUTIERO and LAURENTI MAGESA, Eds.

Twenty-five international scholars reflect on the role of Catholic ethicists in the context of their own local churches and in light of the ecclesiological shifts following Vatican II.   **978-1-62698-274-1 336pp pbk $48**

A Poor and Merciful Church

The Illuminative Ecclesiology of Pope Francis

STAN CHU ILO

Addresses key questions that face modern Catholicism, particularly in Africa. Ilo shows how two key themes of Pope Francis—the church of the poor and the church of mercy—have deep roots in biblical, patristic, and diverse ecclesial traditions.   **978-1-62698-265-9 320pp pbk $44**

They Will Inherit the Earth

Peace and Nonviolence in a Time of Climate Change

JOHN DEAR

Drawing on personal stories of his life in the desert, as a chaplain at Yosemite, his experience at Standing Rock, as well as his work with the Vatican, John Dear invites us to return to nonviolence as a way of life and a living.   **978-1-62698-264-2 176pp pbk $20**

To the Margins

Pope Francis and the Mission of the Church

ANDREA RICCARDI

Translated by DINAH LIVINGSTONE

Traces the many ways Christians have opted for the marginalized and excluded, from the early ministry of the church, the Worker Priests in France, and the witness of modern figures like Bl. Charles de Foucauld, Mother Maria Skobtsova, and the work of San'Egidio itself.   **978-1-62698-277-2 192pp pbk $25**

Choosing Peace

The Catholic Church Returns to Gospel Nonviolence

MARIE DENNIS

From an historic conference at the Vatican in 2016 here are contributions by Lisa Sowle Cahill, Terrence J. Rynne, John Dear, Ken Butigan, Rose Marie Berger, and Maria J. Stephan, among others.

978-1-62698-270-3 272pp pbk $25

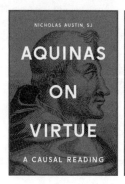

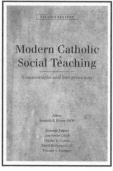
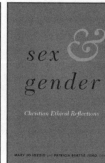

GEORGETOWN

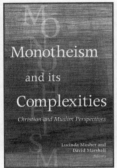 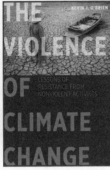  

AVAILABLE JUNE 2018!

Monotheism and Its Complexities

Christian and Muslim Perspectives

Lucinda Mosher and David Marshall, Editors

paperback, $29.95, 978-1-62616-584-7
hardcover, $89.95, 978-1-62616-583-0
ebook, $29.95, 978-1-62616-585-4

The Violence of Climate Change

Lessons of Resistance from Nonviolent Activists

Kevin J. O'Brien

paperback, $24.95, 978-1-62616-435-2
hardcover, $49.95, 978-1-62616-434-5
ebook, $24.95, 978-1-62616-436-9

AVAILABLE MARCH 2018!

A Concise History of Sunnis and Shi'is

John McHugo

paperback, $29.95, 978-1-62616-587-8
hardcover, $89.95, 978-1-62616-586-1
ebook, $29.95, 978-1-62616-588-5
Available: Only for sale in the United States and it dependencies, Canada, Mexico, and the Philippines

The War against al-Qaeda

Religion, Policy, and Counter-narratives

Nahed Artoul Zehr

paperback, $32.95, 978-1-62616-428-4
hardcover, $64.95, 978-1-62616-427-7
ebook, $32.95, 978-1-62616-429-1